Hard Cop, Soft Cop

Hard Cop, Soft Cop
Dilemmas and debates in contemporary policing

Edited by

Roger Hopkins Burke

WILLAN
PUBLISHING

Published by

Willan Publishing
Culmcott House
Mill Street, Uffculme
Cullompton, Devon
EX15 3AT, UK
Tel: +44(0)1884 840337
Fax: +44(0)1884 840251
e-mail: info@willanpublishing.co.uk
website: www.willanpublishing.co.uk

Published simultaneously in the USA and Canada by

Willan Publishing
c/o ISBS, 920 NE 58th Ave, Suite 300
Portland, Oregon 97213-3786, USA
Tel: +001(0)503 287 3093
Fax: +001(0)503 280 8832
website: www.isbs.com

First published 2004

ISBN 1-84392-047-6 (paperback)
ISBN 1-84392-048-4 (hardback)

British Library Cataloguing-in-Publication Data
A catalogue record for this book is available from the British Library

Project management by Deer Park Productions, Tavistock, Devon
Typeset by GCS, Leighton Buzzard, Beds.
Printed and bound by T.J. International, Padstow, Cornwall

Contents

List of contributors

Mark Button is Senior Lecturer at the Institute of Criminal Justice Studies at the University of Portsmouth. He is author of *Private Policing* (Willan Publishing, 2002).

Chris Crowther is Principal Lecturer in Criminology and Community Justice at Sheffield Hallam University. His research interests include policing and criminal justice policy-making. He is author of *Policing Urban Poverty* (Palgrave, 2000).

Roger Hopkins Burke is Senior Lecturer in Criminology at Nottingham Trent University. He is author of *Zero Tolerance Policing* (Perpetuity Press, 1998) and *An Introduction to Criminological Theory* (Willan Publishing, 2001).

Andrew Karmen earned a PhD in sociology from Columbia University in 1977 and since the following year has been a member of the Sociology Department at John Jay College of Criminal Justice, City University, New York City. He author of *Crime Victims: An Introduction To Victimology* (Wadsworth, 2004), now in its fifth edition, and *New York Murder Mystery: The True Story Behind the Crime Crash of the 1990s* (New York University Press, 2000).

Kavita Modi completed her masters in Human Rights Law at University College London in 2002. In 2002–3, she worked at Liberty, the human rights and civil liberties organisation, as a researcher. She currently works in the Human Rights Department at Leigh, Day & Co. Solicitors.

Ruth Morrill completed her postgraduate studies in criminological research at Cambridge University in 2003. She now works for the London Probation Service delivery accredited treatment programmes (to offenders).

Mandy Shaw is Senior Lecturer at the Nottingham Trent University. Her doctoral research was completed at the University of Manchester on the relative effect of gender and repeat victimisation of fear of crime. She has been a researcher in the Applied Criminology Group at the University of Huddersfield, where she was involved in the evaluation of the Home Office's Burglary Reduction Programme. Some areas of recent research include domestic violence, burglary reduction and the impact of crime on victims.

Graham Smith is Senior Lecturer in Criminology at the Nottingham Trent University. He has published widely in the area of policing and the law, in particular police accountability and the police complaints process.

Basia Spalek is a Lecturer in Criminology within the Institute of Applied Social Studies at Birmingham University. Her research interests include victimisation, white-collar crime and religious identity, having recently edited *Islam, Crime and Criminal Justice* (Willan Publishing, 2003).

Paul Sparrow is Head of the Division of Criminology at the Nottingham Trent University. He was previously a probation officer and has published widely in the area of the probation service.

Mike Sutton is Reader in Criminology at Nottingham Trent University, Director of the Nottingham Centre for Study and Reduction of Hate Crimes, Prejudice and Bias, and is General Editor of the Internet *Journal of Criminology*. Mike conducted research into stolen goods markets while working as Senior Research Officer in the Home Office and went on to design and develop the Market Reduction Approach to illicit markets. Mike is currently actively involved in researching and publishing in the fields of general crime reduction, hi-tech crimes and hate crimes.

Nick Tilley is Director of the Policy Oriented Social Sciences research group at Nottingham Trent University, where he is Professor of Sociology. He is also a visiting professor in the Jill Dando Institute of

Crime Science at University College London. He has published very widely in the areas of crime prevention, policing and social science methodology.

John Wadham is currently Deputy Director of the Independent Police Complaints Commission. He was previously Director of Liberty, the UK's human rights and civil liberties organisation, for eight years. He has acted for a large numbers of applicants in cases before the Commission and Court of Human Rights. He is the co-editor of *Your Rights: The Liberty Guide*, the civil liberties section of the *Penguin Guide to the Law* and the case law reports for the *European Human Rights Law Review*, and is co-author of *Blackstone's Guide to the Human Rights Act 1998* and *Blackstone's Guide to the Freedom of Information Act 2000*. He is also editor of the Blackstone's Human Rights Series.

David Webb is Senior Dean and Dean of the Faculty of Economics and Social Sciences at Nottingham Trent University. He has previously worked at the School of Social Work at Leicester University, as a school teacher and as an adviser for the validating body for social work education and training. He has published in the fields of sociology of social work, social work theory, juvenile justice, mentally disordered offenders, the sociology of health and illness and penology.

Colin Webster is Senior Lecturer in Criminology at the University of Teesside. He has published in the areas of youth crime, victimisation, racial harassment, the construction of British 'Asian' criminality, and violence and disorder in Northern England.

Lorna White Sansom is Lecturer in Criminology at Nottingham Trent University. She is currently completing her PhD on 'stalking'.

Alick Whyte spent nearly thirty years as a provost officer in the Royal Air Force. He was the security officer for the Supreme Headquarters Allied Powers Europe (SHAPE) in Belgium and retired in 1993 as a wing commander to take up a Civil Service appointment as a police adviser to the British Forces in Germany. He has had extensive contact with police forces throughout the world including the Middle East, Singapore, the USA and Europe. In 2002 he finally retired, returning to Newark in Nottinghamshire where he lives with his family.

Chapter 1

Introduction: policing contemporary society

Roger Hopkins Burke

Introduction

This book is about the policing of contemporary society in both the more specific public police service and a more generic sense. Its origins are in a visit to New York City in June 1995, where within a few hours of arrival, I came close to being the pedestrian victim of a driving mis-demeanour. The lesson learned from that experience was to be more alert and, indeed, vigilance brought swift reward. Walking around the streets I observed not just all manner of minor criminal activity, but also the presence of many police officers, invariably standing around in often fairly sizeable groups and apparently oblivious to – or at least not taking any interest in – these activities.

A senior officer encountered at a policing social function was subsequently confronted with these observations. I suggested that intervention in such cases might send out an unambiguous message to the public about a realignment of acceptable moral boundaries and consequently lead to a reduction in these minor offices. The officer was unimpressed. New York, he explained, was a large volatile and dangerous city, police officers were poorly paid, and they wanted to 'get in their twenty years' and retire physically unscathed with a pension. They did not want to put that all at risk by stopping some potentially 'crazy guy' who probably had a gun and might be quite happy to use it.

Now while sympathetic to the safety issues, I was somewhat less impressed with the overall argument. Both the senior officer and I had spent the previous two days at an international conference on police corruption. I pondered whether the failure of NYPD police officers to do what ostensibly appeared to be their duty was in fact some form of corruption. I was to discover that two significant persons in New York City shared my viewpoint, Mayor Giuliani and Commissioner Bratton.

Meanwhile, two further incidents focusing on the NYPD caught my attention. First, a group of officers attending a conference in Washington, DC, got drunk and 'trashed' their hotel; in the second, a smaller group had visited a coastal resort in New Jersey, became involved in an altercation with some locals in a bar and beat them up. Immediately, television reporters were pressing both Commissioner Bratton and Mayor Giuliani for action. Indeed, the former moved quickly and announced the dismissal of all personnel involved in both incidents. There were to be no extended inquiries, no suspension on full pay and retirement on the grounds of ill health with full pension rights intact before disciplinary proceedings could be convened. I became immersed in the media coverage of these and similar events until my return to the UK some weeks later. It was, however, only then that I first consciously heard the term 'zero tolerance policing' used.

Both my initial observations and subsequent documentary research supported the supposition that the term 'zero tolerance' might usefully and accurately be used to describe the Bratton/Giuliani offensive against police incompetency and ineffectiveness. Central to this agenda had been the replacement of two-thirds of precinct commanders and the introduction of a computerised managerial system known as 'CompStat' (Kelling and Coles, 1996). The latter is a crime management tool which uses weekly crime statistics, computer mapping and intensive strategy sessions to direct the implementation of crime fighting strategies and has been used most noticeably to target 'quality of life' crimes – the so-called 'zero tolerance' policing strategy – as a means of recovering the streets of New York City for the law-abiding citizen (Silverman, 1998).

Zero tolerance policing and 'broken windows' theory

The New York City zero tolerance policing strategy – and variants introduced elsewhere (see Dennis, 1997; Hopkins Burke, 1998a) – are informed by the 'broken windows' thesis. This proposes that just as an unrepaired broken window is a sign that nobody cares and leads to more damage, minor incivilities – such as begging, public drunkenness, vandalism and graffiti – if unchecked and uncontrolled, produce an atmosphere in a community in which more serious crime will flourish

(Wilson and Kelling, 1982). Over time, individuals may feel that they can get away with minor offences and this encourages – or at least does not discourage – them to commit more serious offences.

Proponents of such policing strategies, such as Bratton in New York City (see Bratton, 1997) and Ray Mallon of the Cleveland Constabulary in the UK (see Dennis and Mallon, 1997; Romeanes, 1998) consciously adapted the 'broken windows' thesis and argued that a positive police presence targeting petty offenders on the streets can produce substantial reductions in the level of crime. They point to the success of experiments in their own jurisdictions – where there were large reductions in the number of recorded criminal offences during the mid-to-late 1990s – to support those assertions (Dennis, 1997; Hopkins Burke, 1998b).

Opposition to zero tolerance-style policing has predominantly focused on two closely linked arguments. First, such strategies are considered reminiscent of the failed military-style 'hard' policing measures introduced by metropolitan forces in inner-city neighbourhoods in the UK during the 1970s and early 1980s, with 'Swamp 81' and the subsequent disorders in Brixton, South West London, considered to be the defining events. Observing the inequity of primarily targeting the poor, the socially excluded and the large numbers of ethnic minority members over-represented within those groups, and the simultaneous potential to incite serious disorder in the streets, opponents of 'hard' policing styles demand a return to community-style 'soft' policing strategies introduced following the Scarman Report into the Brixton disorders (1982) (see Morgan, 1997; Read, 1997; Pollard, 1997; Currie, 1997; Bowling, 1998; Crowther, 1998; Wadham, 1998).

Second, there is no clearly identified evidence supporting a direct causal link between 'hard' policing styles and the decline in the recorded crime figures. Substantial reductions in recorded offences have been noted in all major cities in the USA regardless of whether or not any specific policing initiatives – of either the 'hard' or 'soft' variety – have been introduced. Demographic factors, a substantial decline in crack use and a general disinclination towards criminal behaviour among certain young people have all been proposed as the real reasons for this decline (see Blumstein and Wallman, 2000).[1] The 7,000 extra police officers recruited during the Bratton/Giuliani strategic policing offensive in New York City are not widely considered to have made an impact (see Hopkins Burke, 1999a).

Two significant observations were made in that earlier zero tolerance policing text (Hopkins Burke, 1998a). First, there is a widespread general consumer demand in society for a highly visible police presence on the streets and basically this requirement exists across all ethnic and interest group divisions. Eli Silverman (1998) noted a considerable demand among black communities in the poorer neighbourhoods of New York City for the same levels of policing as in the affluent white areas, while George Kelling and Caroline Coles (1996) had previously clearly implied in their seminal text – forensically examining the ambiguities and contradictions between the rights of individuals and those of communities in the policing of incivilities – that widespread public support for recently implemented 'hard' policing styles in various locations in the USA had come from a wide-range of victimised and fearful citizens in all social classes and ethnic groups.

Recognition of the ambiguous nature of 'hard' policing strategies – and acknowledgement of legitimate widespread popular support – has subsequently come from an at first sight surprising source, two eminent liberal criminologists in the UK, Jock Young and Kevin Stenson. Young (1999) has noted that liberal criticisms of the targeting of street incivilities and the protection of actual and potential victims from this conduct seem incongruous considering the demand from similar groups for zero tolerance of such behaviours as domestic violence. In a similar vein, we might note a virtually unquestionable extensive enthusiasm for zealously seeking out and eradicating school bullying, child abuse and paedophilia. Stenson (2002) has noted that the targeting of illegal economies and bullies in some run-down working-class housing estates often on the periphery of towns and cities is very much in the interest – and has the support – of the wider community.

A key theme to emerge from that first observation – and by implication present in the work of Stenson and Young – is the notion of (moral) ambiguity. Controlling and policing diverse fragmented societies, where there are a multitude of interest groups with their own often incompatible but legitimate viewpoints on a whole range of activities, where moral ambiguity and multiple truths prevail over moral certainty, consensus and absolute truth, provides a not inconsequential challenge both to politicians needing to build often complex electoral coalitions and to the police service who invariably need to adjudicate between those different interest groups. Crime control is nonetheless an issue with very widespread public support even among those oppressed groups whom the authorities apparently overly target. Thus zero tolerance policing styles have been widely popular in the localities in which they have been introduced but less so with most liberal criminologists and commentators. There is, therefore, considerable moral uncertainty – indeed ambiguity – around issues of crime control, due process, civil liberties and human rights.[2]

Thus there may well be a widespread populist enthusiasm for a proactive confident visible police service on the streets but this is dependent on a service perceived to be acting professionally and intervening as a neutral arbiter in societal problems. 'Hard' policing strategies need to be sensitive to the policing requirements of the particular community in order to gain – and significantly retain – widespread support and legitimacy. Indeed, as noted above, there are crucial difficulties in sustaining widespread political support over an extended period essentially because pressure to reduce crime has coincided in some constituencies with an escalation in levels of unprofessional behaviour and in some cases instances of outrageous brutality committed against members of those very ethnic minority communities seeking quality policing. The outcome has been a spiral of decline in police–community relationships that has dealt an almost terminal blow for the legitimacy of robust interventions (Hopkins Burke, 2002).

The second significant observation made in the earlier zero tolerance policing text was that of an extremely convenient convergence between two influential policing discourses. On the one hand, there was a liberal/libertarian criminal justice perspective widely supported by academic orthodoxy that proposed the police should withdraw from whole areas of the social world in order not to further criminalise groups of dispossessed unfortunates; on the other hand, there were the material concerns of senior police management with the problem of managing inadequate resources. Taken together, there appears to have been a most convenient justification for doing very little (Hopkins Burke, 1998b) and for some years this considered withdrawal from the streets, dressed up in liberal guise, was de facto policing policy in both the USA and the UK (see Bratton, 1997; Dennis and Mallon, 1997).

Police (in)effectiveness

The contemporary police service has long been criticised for its ineffectiveness. The level of recorded crime in England and Wales, for example, has been rising at an average of 5.1 per cent per annum ever since 1916 and over the last two decades of the twentieth century the rise had been particularly sharp (although the figures have fallen back a little during the past five years). In 1979 there were around 2.4 million offences recorded but by 1992 the figure had reached over 5.4 million with offences against property constituting three-quarters of the total (Wilson et al., 2002: 47). Moreover, the British Crime Survey has consistently shown that these official crime figures considerably underestimate the real incidence of crime for reasons that need not detain us here.

The police clear-up rate for England and Wales has meanwhile fallen from 40 per cent in 1980 to 23.5 per cent by 2003 (Home Office, 2003), mean averages that conceal considerable local variations. The Audit Commission (1999) revealed that the police fail to solve as many as 92 per cent of burglaries and less than half of street robberies, although detection rates for more serious crimes are far better and have remained consistently high. Nevertheless, while crime rates have risen and clear-up rates fallen, governments have not kept the police short of resources, regardless of what they may try to tell you. Between 1979 and the early 1990s budgets rose in real terms by almost 90 per cent and by 1998 total expenditure on the police stood at £7.21 billion.

There is, however, little doubt that the extent and nature of 'police business' has increased considerably since the formation of the 'new police' during the early nineteenth century and discussion regarding that expansion is linked to the academic debate about motivation for the establishment and continuation of the public police service. In short, exactly what is the purpose of the police and exactly in whose interests do they pursue that purpose?

The purpose of the police: competing perspectives

The orthodox social progress perspective on the development of the public police service observes the emergence, expansion and consolidation of a bureaucratic service as part of a progressive humanitarian development of institutions necessary to respond to crime and disorder (Reith, 1956). At the other end of the spectrum, the revisionist Marxist-inspired view proposes that the police were 'domestic missionaries' with an emphasis on the surveillance, discipline and control of the rough and dangerous working-class elements in society in the interests of the capitalist class (Storch, 1975). From this perspective contemporary 'hard' policing strategies targeted at socially excluded groups in society are simply a continuation of that tradition (see Crowther, 1998). The reality nevertheless appears to lie somewhere in the middle of these two polar opposite viewpoints as the following left-realist perspective suggests.

While revisionists consider definitions of crime and criminality to be class-based with the public police service agents of a capitalist society targeting the activities of the socially excluded and at the same time ignoring the far more damaging behaviour of corporate capitalism (see Scraton and Chadwick, 1996, originally 1992); left realists consider the situation more ambiguous, crucially recognising that crime is a real problem for ordinary people and that it is therefore appropriate that the criminal justice system – of which the police service is a key institution – should seek to defend the weak and oppressed (see Lea and Young, 1984; Matthews and Young, 1986; Young, 1997; Hopkins Burke, 2001).

Observed from a left-realist perspective it is apparent that from soon after the introduction of the new police in the mid-nineteenth century there was a widespread – and admittedly at times tacit and fairly grudging – acceptance and support for this body. The police may well have targeted criminal elements within the working class and they might on occasion have taken the side of capital in trade disputes but at the same time their moralising mission on the streets coincided conveniently with the increasing enthusiasm for self-betterment among the great majority that has been described from differing sociological perspectives as 'embourgeoisement' (Goldthorpe, 1968–9) and 'the civilising process' (Elias, 1978, 1982).

This left-realist perspective nonetheless dismisses neither the orthodox or revisionist accounts but produces a synthesis of the two. For it seems self-evident that the police – in some form or another and we will return to this point shortly – are essential to deal with conflicts, disorders and problems of coordination necessarily generated by any complex and materially advanced society (Reiner, 2000) and that there is a widespread demand for policing throughout society. Recent studies have shown that while during the nineteenth century prosecutions for property crime emanated overwhelmingly from the more affluent groups, poorer sections of society also resorted extensively to the law as victims (see Storch, 1989; Philips and Storch, 1999; Emsley, 1996; Taylor, 1997; Miller, 1999). Indeed, at crucial times these poorer groups had considerable interest in the maintenance of the status quo. For example, with the end of the Crimean War and the prospect of a footloose army of unemployed soldiers returning – at the very time that transportation to the colonies had ended – meant that 'an organised race of criminals' would be roaming the countryside looking for criminal opportunities and from whom all would need protection (Steedman, 1994; Hopkins Burke, 1998c, 1999b). Thus, while working-class antagonism may have been exacerbated by police intervention in recreational activities and labour disputes, a close reading of the issues suggests a more complex situation than previously supposed (Hart,

1978). There certainly seems to be little doubt that the police were closely linked with the general increase in orderliness on the streets of Victorian society (Gatrell, 1980; Taylor, 1997) and this was again widely welcomed. Indeed, it has been argued that the crucial way in which the police affect law enforcement is not by the apprehension of criminals – for that depends on many factors beyond their control – but by symbolising the existence of a functioning legal order, by a having a visible presence on the street and being seen to be doing something (Gatrell, 1980). It is a discourse that coincides neatly with a consistent widespread contemporary public demand for police on the streets frequently expressed in contemporary crime surveys and regardless of the academic policing orthodoxy that has repeatedly stated the service on its own can have little effect on the crime rate (see Morgan and Newburn, 1997).

The establishment of the police was thus inevitable but the question remains as to whether the service had to take the form that it did. In short, some form of policing is socially necessary but state-sponsored policing is not necessarily so. The emergence of a police bureaucracy in Britain was not inevitable but dependent on the vision of the political elite as to what an orderly disciplined society should be like. In many parts of the UK this vision of social order and authority was contested and from the outset each new policing service had to struggle to establish the legitimacy to exist, while a wide range of other individuals and groups – the old parish constables, gamekeepers and private watchmen, the docks and railway police, and the increasingly expanding private security industry – continued to operate (Emsley, 2001).

Thus, from their inception, the new public police service was never the only organisation undertaking police work in British society; new forms were negotiated with different audiences and multiple versions were produced, 'each with particular symbolic and instrumental meanings for specific groups' (McLaughlin, 2001: 75). What differentiated the new police from their predecessors and competitors was that they were an instrument of government. Political opposition obliged the nineteenth-century policing reformers to drop all hopes of creating a national service on the continental model and consequently an assortment of forces gradually took to the streets alongside those other individuals and groups performing policing functions. A progressive rationalisation and de facto nationalisation nonetheless took place throughout the twentieth century and to the present day as the local response to the increasing threats posed by public order and crime appeared inadequate to the task. Nevertheless, the extensive expansion in demands placed on the public police service has increasingly stretched their resources however much these may have expanded.[3]

The great expansion in police business

A considerable decrease in police effectiveness as measured by crime clear-up rates during the past half century was noted above, at the same time as there has been a huge increase in public expectations and demands for the wide range of services they provide. Five broad and closely interlinked developments can be detected that have accelerated the growth in these expectations on which the police cannot realistically deliver.

The first broad development has been the *increase in criminal opportunities* that has occurred as a result of the increasing affluence in British society since the end of war-time rationing and the beginning of the consumer society circa 1955. Two interlocking aspects of that development are explained by Felson (1998)[4] and his notion of 'opportunity theory' where he observes that a huge increase in the number of high-value portable domestic products attractive to criminals has occurred at the very same time as there has been a considerable *decrease* in informal capable guardians – such as ourselves – with the great expansion in dual income households that invariably leave homes unoccupied for long periods.

The second development has been the *increase in motivated offenders* notably ignored in earlier variants of contemporary opportunity theories. Mike Sutton (1995, 1998, and see this volume) argues persuasively that it is the existence of stolen goods markets that provides the crucial stimulus for theft, much of the motivation for seeking out those markets invariably provided by the large increase in drug addiction in recent years. Bennett, Holloway and Williams (2001), in a study conducted for the Home Office, detected a considerable correlation between heroin and crack cocaine use and offending behaviour, finding that that those who used both drugs regularly spent on average £290 a week or £15,000 a year, were rarely employed and invariably needed to steal to fund their habit.[5]

The third development is the increasing embourgeoisement or *civilising process* – noted previously – whereby standards of acceptable behaviour change over time. Elias (1978, 1982) – in what constitutes a sociological history of manners – observes a progressive moderation and discipline of personal behaviour that centres on a restraint in emotions and the possibilities for embarrassment and shame. Although this linear social progress model has been criticised for ignoring the class-based nature of social manners (see Slaughter, 2003) it has become increasingly persuasive in view of the expansion of white-collar employment and the often enforced accompanying changes in acceptable behaviour, particularly those – popularly termed 'political correctness' – endemic in the burgeoning state sector. Adopting that thesis for our present purposes we might note that whereas a fight among drunken men outside a public house in a working-class area might well have passed with little comment and certainly minimal intervention on the part of the authorities fifty years ago, this is not the case today, where such young men in particular flock to city-centre alcohol vending establishments and where their movements are resource-intensively policed pending outbreaks of the rather inevitable violence.

The fourth development has been the increasing *social construction of crime* and the *criminalisation* of a whole range of new offences, many associated with technological innovations. For example, consider the number of criminal offences associated with the motor car and there are many more than the simple theft of the vehicle. Computer crime was unknown until fairly recently but now provides widespread and very varied criminal opportunities. There are offences where computers are the *objects of crime*, for example they can be damaged or stolen; they provide a *criminal environment* for the unauthorised copying of pro- grammes or, increasingly, music and films; and they can be the *instrument of the criminal act* in the case of downloading pornography.

Other recently defined offences are closely linked with the notion of the civilising process and include domestic violence, stalking and date rape. Lorna White Sansom in this volume cites the then Metropolitan Police Commissioner Kenneth Newman twenty years ago dismissing domestic violence as 'rubbish work' akin to dealing with stray dogs and not worthy of police time. Following a concerted campaign by feminists to put the issue firmly at the top of the policing agenda it is now almost universally taken seriously by the service, although Martin (2003) observes that it has become a popular offence with detectives under considerable pressure to obtain convictions because of the relative ease in detecting the offender.[6]

The fifth development is the *increasing complexity of society*. The public police service is very much a product of modern mass societies characterised by moral certainty and confidence in the capacity of grand social and political theories (see Hopkins Burke, 2001). Such societies have sought to develop social and economic programmes that satisfy the different and often antagonistic class interests in society and have been in the recent past relatively successful, not least in the twenty-five years following the Second World War. The role of the church, education system, and mass media have all been cited at various times as helping to develop and maintain an invariably conservative social consensus (see, Althusser, 1969; Anderson, 1968). Others have – as we have seen above – noted the disciplinary role of the public police service in the pursuit of those goals (see, for example, Bunyan, 1976; Cohen, 1979; Scraton, 1985; Storch, 1975). Essential to that disciplinary and missionary project has long been the nature and – often unintended – outcomes of recruitment policies.

Sir Robert Peel had decided from the outset of the Metropolitan Police in 1829 that his officers should come from the unskilled and semi-skilled working class and this policy became the orthodoxy with the other 'new police' forces. Emsley (2001) notes that many of the early recruits had joined as a temporary measure to alleviate a period of unemployment and had little idea what the job would entail. He observes that many loathed the rigorous discipline, the night work and the exhausting and physically dangerous nature of the job, a hard physical existence that contributed significantly to the development of a tough, masculine culture that came to dominate the service.[7] Indeed, these were essential behavioural traits for dealing with the authentic police business of the time, the rougher elements of their own social class.

This tough working-class police culture – 'canteen culture' as it has been subsequently termed (see Holdaway, 1983; Fielding, 1988; Reiner, 2000) – as transmitted and adapted to changing circumstances across the generations was undoubtedly *relatively* non-problematic during the relatively consensual modern era. The disciplinary missionary intervention against the rougher elements of the working class had undoubted support from most elements of society, including essentially the socially aspiring respectable elements of that class who lived cheek-by-jowl with the roughs and sought protection from them.

It was with the fragmentation of modernity that accelerated particularly during the final quarter of the twentieth century – a situation that some have come to term the postmodern condition (see Lyotard, 1984) – that this macho-police occupational culture was to become increasingly problematic in a society made up of myriad interest groups as diverse as major industrialists and financiers, small business proprietors, the unemployed and dispossessed, wide-ranging gender and sexual preference interests, environmentalists, the homeless and the socially excluded. In this complex social formation, the objective reality – or competing objective realities – of modernity has been replaced with the multiple realities or moral ambiguities of the postmodern condition and it has become increasingly the role of the contemporary police service to intervene and arbitrate in the disputes and conflicts that inevitably occur in such societies. Crucially, the moral certainties of the dominant monocultural occupational police culture are all the time more inappropriate in this greatly changed world.[8]

The issue of police occupational culture is important because of the inherent discretion available to an officer in the course of their job. In essence they must transform the 'written law' into 'law in action' and in doing so they act as key decision-makers or gatekeepers to the criminal justice system (McLaughlin, 2001). Under the guidance and control of experienced officers, new recruits are socialised into the real world of practical policework, while junior officers develop their own common-sense theories of 'justice', crime causation and solutions and come to distinguish between 'real' police work ('feeling collars' and 'getting figures') and 'rubbish' or 'dead-end' work (the rest) (Young, 1991). In order to do their job 'objectively' officers depersonalise the public by 'stereotyping', separating and labelling them into categories deemed worthy of police assistance – the community – and the 'others', the 'toe-rags', 'slags', 'scrotes', 'scum' and 'animals'. Some have argued that these stereotypes drive the day-to-day nature and pattern of policework (Smith and Gray, 1985; Young, 1991, 1993). Certainly, these malevolent attitudes towards the public in general and particular groups are the source of many conflictual and counterproductive encounters with the public.

It is clear that taken together these five broad societal developments – the increase in criminal opportunities and motivated offenders, the increasing embourgeoisement and lower tolerance of criminal activities and social disorder, alongside the great expansion in the number of criminal offences on the statute book at a time of increasingly complex social relations – has increased public expectations of the police service to an extent that they cannot possibly hope to meet.

The purpose of this book

We have seen that the public police service has never had a total monopoly on what Johnson and Shearing (2003) refer to as the provision of *security* in society, although as they so rightly observe this public form was the dominant mode of provision when policing was unambiguously acknowledged to be the essential *responsibility* of state government. With the huge expansion in security issues – of both a criminal and public disorder nature – an expansion in the number of organisations providing security has emerged and the predominant concern of this contemporary multiple policing paradigm has perhaps ironically been a return to the original focus of public policing: the prevention of crime rather than the expensive ineffective reactive-cure model that in the intervening years took precedence.

Johnson and Shearing use the term 'security' as the alternative available terminology such as 'social control' and 'dispersal of control' overly suggests to them that these developments have been imposed, albeit perhaps unknowingly, by agents acting in the interests of a dominant order. They quite rightly recognise, in my view, the much wider popular demand for security throughout society with which the left-realist perspective outlined above concurs.

This book builds on the aforementioned themes. Thus there are contributions on 'hard' policing styles in the UK, USA and Germany with discussions of issues of police accountability and human rights. To offer balance there is discussion of apparently 'softer' style policing initiatives such as diversionary schemes for young people and the work of the contemporary probation service. It is not, however, the purpose of this book to simply juxtapose 'hard' and by implication 'bad' policing styles against 'soft' and thus 'good' policing styles. On the contrary, it is the underpinning theoretical thread of this book that policing in the widest possible sense is both pervasive and insidious throughout society. 'Hard' and 'soft' policing styles – regardless of whether conducted by the public police service, the private security industry or social work agencies – are all part of the contemporary all-seeing multiple-agency corporate crime industry. As the Italian Marxist Antonio Gramsci (1977, 1978) and the radical US criminologist Austin Turk (1969) have both observed, societies adopt coercive or 'hard' policing measures when they are under threat from internal or external 'enemies'. Such measures nonetheless become unpopular with the public if used indiscriminately and for extended periods and it will therefore become more difficult to control society. Thus, 'softer' and more subtle measures are preferred as a more insidious form of social control.[9] In reality, both 'hard' and 'soft' measures are invariably used concurrently and compatibly in pursuit of the same crime control goal.

This theme of pervasive policing used here is resonant with notions of the carceral surveillance society devised by Michel Foucault (1980) and developed among others notably by Jacques Donzelot (1980), Stanley Cohen (1985) and David Garland (2001). From this Foucauldian perspective power is not simply conceptualised as the privilege of the state. It is recognised that strategies of power are pervasive throughout society with the state only one location of the points of control and resistance. Foucault observes that particular areas of the social world – and he uses the examples of law, medicine, sexuality – are colonised and defined by the norms and control strategies a variety of institutions and experts devise and abide by (Foucault, 1971, 1976). He argues that these networks of power and control are governed as much by the *knowledge* and concepts that define them as by the definite intentions of groups.

The state, for its part, is implicated in this matrix of power-knowledge, but it is only part of it. In this vein it has been argued that within civil society there are numerous 'semi-autonomous' realms and relations – such as communities, occupations, organisations, families – where certain kinds of 'policing' and 'order' are indeed present, but where the state administration and police force are technically absent. These semi-autonomous arenas within society are often appropriately negotiated and resisted by their participants in ways that, even now, the state has little jurisdiction over.

This book is underpinned by a variation on that Foucauldian orthodoxy. While it is readily accepted that disciplinary strategies are often implemented by professional agents and practitioners with little or no idea how their often humble discourse contributes to the grand overall disciplinary-control matrix, the variation presented here proposes that this perspective does not tell the whole story, for as the left-realist analysis above suggests there are other interests involved, and those significantly are *ours*. Complex, fragmented, diverse societies are also dangerous societies with – and it is becoming increasingly clear – invariably incompatible and often deeply antagonistic worldviews competing for living space whether at the micro (local neighbourhood) or macro (intra-national) level. Visions of liberty and human rights that have provided the intellectual foundations of what many in post-industrial liberal democratic societies have considered during the past quarter of a century to be progressive social movements might well be at odds with more recent notions of safety and increasingly security, a situation undoubtedly intensified by the terrorist attacks on the USA on September 11 2001 and the subsequent atrocities carried out elsewhere in the world. Meanwhile, the huge demand for closed-circuit television cameras (CCTVs) that continues seemingly unabated throughout society has been created by us. When these cameras are to be found operating in virtually every room and public place on this planet, this situation will not have arisen because of some grand master plan – as devised by a Big Sibling in an Orwellian science fiction fantasy – but because of our own personal sense of insecurity that when multiplied many times over has produced an insatiable demand for visible security. It is likely that when that time arises we will have long forgotten – or will simply fail to recognise – our humble contribution to the creation of that overwhelming surveillance monster. In the meanwhile, there has never been a greater demand for the 'Leviathan' even though some of its functions have been outsourced to private organisations. We will revisit these issues in the conclusion.

Contributions to this book

The book is divided into three parts. The first considers the policing of contemporary communities in the context of contemporary debates about 'hard' and 'soft' policing. In the first of these contributions, Andrew Karmen critically examines the ambiguities surrounding the introduction of the Giuliani/Bratton policing offensive during the 1990s. This paper critically examines a wide range of empirical data and reviews the concerns and controversies that have arisen in the aftermath of the changes in policing style and practice introduced in New York City. Alick Whyte follows this by exploring the application of 'hard' policing strategies targeting incivilities in contemporary Germany following the visit of German police chiefs to New York and their favourable impressions of the zero tolerance-style policing introduced there.

Chris Crowther reflects on how the 'hard' policing of a socially excluded underclass has not led to the much predicted escalation of police–community conflict in poor neighbourhoods and suggests two reasons for this. First, a more sophisticated public policy agenda has meant that crime and social exclusion is no longer considered just a problem for the police; it is now the responsibility of statutory, voluntary and private agencies as well as individual citizens. Second, the growing influence of managerialism and the 'what works' agenda has led to a significant reallocation of resources, which makes the regulation of the underclass increasingly difficult. It is therefore considered necessary for a more nuanced appreciation of the complex relationship connecting crime, social exclusion and policing.

Colin Webster observes that zero tolerance-style policing in the British context had been predicated on both nostalgia for – and disappointment in the capacity of white working-class communities to maintain and enforce informal controls on their young people. Subsequently, a similar if implicit logic began to be applied to 'Asian' communities and their young men in particular. Previously the police and others had idealised 'Asianness' as intrinsically law abiding, in contrast to 'African Caribbeanness'. The chapter charts the process of this change in police perceptions of – and actions towards – 'Asian' communities since the 1990s and some recent consequences.

Paul Sparrow and David Webb document the contours of the British probation service – a supposedly traditional 'soft' policing agency – in the twenty-first century. In charting the demise of traditional social work methodologies the authors show how the 'routinisation' of supervision has reduced the probation officer to little more than a criminal justice functionary and reconfigured the organisation around a more clearly defined correctionist orientation.

Mark Button completes the first part of the book with an exploration of contemporary private security, observing a long-established radical social science perception of the industry as a 'hard policing' agency acting in the interests of corporate capitalism in its oppression of the working classes. It is proposed that in recent years, private security has become reconstituted as a 'soft' policing industry directed at prevention rather than detection.

The contributions in the second part of the book explore the policing of a range of contemporary offences. Nick Tilley observes that police 'crackdowns' – acknowledged to be a less emotionally charged term for the kind of 'hard' policing strategies elsewhere termed 'zero tolerance' – may have a bad name but have been shown to work in some circumstances. He explores the conditions in which crackdowns have a useful role to play in crime reduction, describing forms of implementation and associated measures that have been introduced to complement these and to achieve sustained crime falls.

Mike Sutton notes that the application of the market reduction approach (MRA) to theft provides the 'soft' policing strategy of situational crime prevention and routine activities theory with a previously unacknowledged notion of offender motivation. It is a crime control strategy that looks at each of the different markets for stolen goods and then undertakes systematic intelligence-gathering to find out who is dealing in those markets and how they operate. The primary aim is to reduce the motivation for stealing by removing the demand for stolen goods.

Lorna White Sansom considers the recently identified and now widely discovered offence of 'stalking' as predominantly an aspect of domestic violence and deemed worthy of a zero tolerance-style intervention. In January 2000, the British government authorised the launch of the first anti-stalking police unit to tackle the problem by means of intervention and deterrence. The effectiveness of that strategy with regard to different types of stalker is discussed.

Basia Spalek considers the financial services industry – traditionally subject to 'soft' invariably internal policing strategies – and asks whether the major financial scandals that have hit the US could occur in Britain. With the creation of a new regulatory structure it is considered an appropriate time to consider the way in which the financial system is policed and the resultant impact on investors and the victims of financial crime.

Mandy Shaw discusses two offender rehabilitation programmes implemented in the North of England between 1999 and 2001 and which offer certain offenders an alternative to a prison sentence when found guilty of burglary. There is reflection on the role of the police in the complex interplay between the 'hard' and 'soft' elements of the programmes, the nature of the interaction between police officer and offender, and the perceptions of both parties of these different approaches.

The contributions to the third part of the book consider issues of democracy, accountability and human rights. Graham Smith considers recent arguments and reforms surrounding police strategies in the changing constitutional context of the twenty-first century. A critique is presented of the development of the doctrine of constabulary independence and the process by which increasingly remote police services became separated and isolated from the public. Then, with the introduction of measures to rein in police autonomy in the last decade, concerns are raised about the absence of checks and balances in the emerging arrangements for police governance and the onward march to centralised state power. It is argued that although it is possible to distinguish between 'hard' and 'soft' strategies, strict adherence to either philosophy can be disastrous, and pronouncements by Labour ministers in favour of 'zero-tolerance policing' have contributed to the politicisation of policing. Direct comparison is made between the policing offensive in New York City against 'quality of life' crimes and the anti-social behaviour strategy about to be extended in the UK.

John Wadham and Kavita Modi examine the implications of the Human Rights Act 1998 – adopted from European human rights legislation – which places at least theoretically considerable constraints upon the nature of strategies that the police can legitimately introduce. It is observed that the Act does not prevent the police from adopting any particular strategy but all are highly likely to have some impact on human rights. They therefore examine some of the areas where there is a conflict between police activities and human rights.

Roger Hopkins Burke and Ruth Morrill note that the Anti-Social Behaviour Order – a central component of the flagship New Labour criminal justice legislation, the Crime and Disorder Act 1998 – enables local authorities to take measures against individuals behaving anti-socially in their communities. The implementation of the ASBO is examined in the context of the prescriptions of the Human Rights Act 1998 that supposedly safeguards the rights of the individual targeted by the new legislation.

In the concluding chapter, the debate – introduced here – about the nature of policing a fragmented and diverse multicultural post-industrial society is revisited. It is proposed that debates about differentiation and diversity are themselves the product of a moral certainty or confidence in the product of the economic and cultural dominance of the post-industrial West. That certainty, it is argued, has always been mainly appropriate to those 'in-groups' who are part of the paid employment-based consumption sectors. 'Out-groups' termed the underclass or the socially excluded have always been treated with suspicion and been treated differently by the criminal justice system. Recent events have extended that suspicion to encompass a much wider range of sectors and groups. In these conditions, a return to more coercive 'hard' policing strategies has become increasingly likely, if not certain, with inevitably huge restrictions in the civil liberties and human rights afforded to citizens introduced in the name of the greater good but at the same time with the willing acceptance of a security-craving populace.

Notes

1   The political right, usually not opposed to zero tolerance policing itself, points to the successful increase in incarceration – or incapacitation to use their favoured terminology – of a large number of young males as a central reason for this decline in the recorded crime figures.

2   Modernity is characterised by moral certainty. There is a confidence and belief in the explanatory power of grand theories to solve the problems of humanity. A period characterised by moral uncertainty is nonetheless not postmodern. Adherents to grand explanatory theories may have lost their certainty but believe the paradigm can be reconstituted to take care of the problems and the revised version will then have all the answers. Times may be characterised by moral uncertainty but certainty is just round the corner. The postmodern condition is, in contrast, a period characterised by moral ambiguity. This is not simply a period of uncertainty. There is recognition that different discourses (scientific, religious, political, etc.)

might be right for different people in different contexts (see Hopkins Burke, 2001).

3   The Audit Commission (1996) placed crime control as central to the police function which is observed to be: (a) respond appropriately to crime, other incidents and emergencies; (b) maintain public order and tackle anti-social behaviour; (c) reassure the public through a visible police presence; and (d) forge links with local communities to reduce problems of crime and nuisance.

4   Felson's work is based on the USA but the general idea transfers well across the Atlantic.

5   It is interesting to speculate at this juncture whether the eradication of markets for stolen goods would substantially reduce drug-addicted motivation or displace addicts to other means of obtaining cash such as prostitution, both male as well as female.

6   At the time of writing the government has announced plans in the Queen's Speech for a 'crackdown' on domestic violence and is to publish a Domestic Violence, Crime and Victims Bill. Together with Comic Relief, Refuge and the Women's Aid Federation of England, the government is also launching a 24-hour freephone domestic violence helpline before Christmas (BBC News, 2003g).

7   It is of course arguable whether this policing subculture developed as a result of the demands of the job or whether the recruits brought it with them from their working-class backgrounds.

8   There is little doubt that this culture persists among police officers in Britain regardless of attempts to eradicate it. At the time of writing, a number of police officers have resigned and others been suspended after an undercover BBC documentary revealed racism among police recruits. In the film, one recruit admitted being racist and voting for the British National Party, and said Hitler had the 'right ideas'. Home Secretary David Blunkett said the racism was 'horrendous' and urged better training for recruits. Subsequently, no police spokespersons have suggested that these were isolated incidents (BBC, 2003h).

9   Turk (1969) describes the *control of legal images* and *living time* as a form of a more subtle exercise in social control. Legal systems have formal laws, breaches of which are legally punishable, and there are established procedures for exercising those laws. There are also degrees of discretion as to how that law is exercised. Turk argues that it is the subtle interplay of the formal and informal that allows the powerful to manipulate the legal system in their own interests while still preserving an image of due process and impartiality. The concept of the control of living time suggests that people will become accustomed to forms of domination and control, especially if it is maintained and legitimised over generations. New generations will gradually forget that social control conditions were ever any different from those with which they are familiar.

Part 1
Policing Contemporary Communities

Chapter 2

Zero tolerance in New York City: hard questions for a get-tough policy

Andrew Karmen

Introduction

As the twentieth century drew to a close in the United States, an un-predicted, unprecedented, mysterious but most welcomed outbreak of better behaviour swept across the land. Although this sudden and sharp decrease in interpersonal violence and stealing was quite noticeable in most large metropolitan areas, small cities, suburban communities and even rural hamlets during the 1990s, it was most pronounced in New York City. For example, murders in the five boroughs plunged nearly 75 per cent, from an all-time high of 2,245 in 1990 to a 40-year low of 580 in 2002. The rapid improvement in public safety benefited all New Yorkers, but it especially brought relief to the city's long-suffering black and Hispanic residents and recent immigrants concentrated in the poorest and most dangerous parts of town.[1]

Claims and controversies

The reality is that the model that was adopted for dealing with crime in New York City is the very, very best way to assure that you can keep a city safe. It includes relying on CompStat to make your decisions about how to deploy police officers. It also includes putting a lot of emphasis on quality of life, on the broken-windows theory. These are the two major pillars of it. (Mayor Rudolph Giuliani, 2001)

Crime rates for reported acts of violence and theft were slowly subsiding during the early 1990s, but they began to tumble during the administration of Mayor Rudolph Giuliani. The Mayor and his first Police Commissioner, William Bratton, quickly dominated the media's marketplace of ideas by claiming that the NYPD deserved the lion's share, if not virtually all, of the credit for the suddenly safer streets for two reasons: smarter policing strategies and tougher tactics (for example, see Krauss, 1995). The smarter strategies were attributed to the re-engineering of police department operations, technological innovations and increased accountability, usually summarised by the term 'CompStat' (see Bratton, 1998; Maple, 1999; Silverman, 1999; among many other sources). The tougher tactics were a 'zero tolerance' crackdown on even the most minor quality-of-life infractions and stepped-up stop-and-frisk campaigns to ferret out those carrying concealed weapons. This aggressive, proactive approach reportedly enabled the NYPD to 'reclaim public spaces', 'drive drug dealers out of town' and 'get guns off the streets' (as several pamphlets issued by the department during the mid-1990s were titled) (see Giuliani, 1997; Bratton and Andrews, 1998).[2] All other explanations were deemed 'politically incorrect' (except perhaps assigning some credit to a greater reliance on incarceration). The alleged effectiveness of the NYPD's hard-line measures was touted as evidence of the bankruptcy of traditional liberal views (see Kraus, 1995) derived from criminological theories and research: that substantial and sustained inroads could not be achieved without eradicating the 'social roots' that were believed to generate lawbreaking behaviour, particularly chronic structural un-employment; entrenched pockets of poverty; dysfunctional families; and severely limited educational, vocational and recreational opportunities for high-risk youth.

This politicisation of the crime crash (as early as mid-1995) immediately ignited a high-stakes ideological debate about the reasons for the suddenly shrinking violence and theft problem (see Karmen, 2000). When presented with claims, charges and counter-charges, criminologists have a professional responsibility to insist, 'Prove it! Where is the evidence?' Unfortunately for criminologists, the direct impacts of the switchover to CompStat and the implementation of a zero tolerance policy towards minor transgressions as well as gun-toting are difficult to measure because these changes were introduced as a package citywide, and were not tested out separately in some precincts but not in other comparable ones, in accord with the classic scientific method of a controlled social experiment for evaluation purposes. In the absence of any clear-cut experimental and control

groupings of equivalent precincts, the before-and-after (the introduction of CompStat, more stopping and frisking, and zero tolerance)
statistical changes have failed to convince most criminologists that
improved policing deserves as much credit as its advocates insist upon.
Sceptics suspect some mix of other factors probably played an
important role in crime's decline in New York as well as in the rest of
the country: an improving economy; a winding-down of the crack
craze; favourable demographic developments (a decline in the number
of 16–24-year-old males who were out of work and not in high school or
college); and a growing realisation by ghetto youth that drugs, guns
and gangs were misdirected, self-destructive and counter-productive
forms of protest and adolescent rebellion (see Karmen, 2000; Blumstein
and Wallman, 2000). Nonetheless, the media uncritically spread the
word far and wide that improved policing was winning the war on
crime. Representatives from police departments across the country and
around the globe came to take tours of NYPD headquarters and to
attend promotional conferences to learn how they did it (see Gootman,
2000).

Zero tolerance for minor transgressions

Many of the minor violations of law that undermine the quality of life
in big cities are committed by homeless persons, mental patients and
other 'street people' who live much of their lives out in the open in
public places. The presence of a highly visible underclass composed of
the casualties of drug and alcohol abuse, chronic unemployment, abject
poverty, a rapidly rising cost of living and family dissolution is
considered by some to be an intractable problem within any big city's
landscape. Others insist repressive measures can turn the tide and
effectively sweep the streets of undesirables. The pendulum of public
opinion concerning what – if anything – to do about the deviant
behaviour street people blatantly engage in swings back and forth, as
periods of relative tolerance of 'victimless crimes' give way to periods
of intolerance towards 'vice'. Consequently, policies adopted at City
Hall and at police headquarters change periodically, in terms of the
degree to which patrol officers are instructed to either crack down or
ease up on petty violators. As a result, the total number of summonses
and arrests for minor offences rises and falls over the decades.

As soon as Rudolph Giuliani became mayor in 1994, he implemented
his campaign pledge to show zero tolerance for any lawbreaking
whatsoever, even of the most minor violations of municipal ordinances

which previously had been largely overlooked by officers on patrol. Such low-level arrests previously had been disparaged as 'garbage cases' by police management, prosecutors, judges and court administrators concerned about agency budgets and expenditures. But in accordance with the 'broken windows' thesis, strict enforcement was touted as the antidote to the spread of urban decay (see Wilson and Kelling, 1982; Kelling and Coles, 1996).[3] Blatant signs of disorder and disrespect for the law, it was argued, gave off signals that attracted hard-core offenders who then felt emboldened to commit even more serious crimes. Intimidated neighbours subsequently lost their sense of 'ownership' of their immediate environment and their feelings of being part of a 'community'. To escape the dangers they perceived to be lurking all around them, law-abiding individuals tended to abandon public spaces and to retreat behind locked doors (see Giuliani, 1997; Kelling and Bratton, 1998).[4] Order maintenance required that at a minimum, perpetrators of quality-of-life infractions would receive summonses or desk appearance tickets. Others arrested for committing misdemeanours in an officer's presence were put through the system (fingerprinted, booked, jailed and brought before a judge), especially if they were not carrying proper identification papers. Arrests enabled officers to legitimately carry out searches for controlled substances or concealed weapons and to check for outstanding warrants or for violations of the conditions of bail, probation or parole (Pooley, 1996; Maple, 1999). Suspects taken into custody could be interrogated about their knowledge of other criminal activities, especially drug trafficking and gun selling (Bratton, 1998).[5]

Since New York City's zero tolerance approach is being replicated in numerous other jurisdictions throughout the United States and around the world, it is imperative to ask some hard questions about this get-tough approach.

Question 1 *Was the zero tolerance campaign really the primary cause of the dramatic reduction in violence and theft rates in New York?*

The first difficult question that supporters of this hard-line policy must address is, where is the definitive and unambiguous proof that this much praised and widely promoted policy actually works as effectively as is claimed? Supporters of zero tolerance crackdowns argue that as the number of people arrested for minor transgressions soared during the second half of the 1990s, the number of killings, especially those carried out with handguns right out on the street, plunged (see Kelling, 2002).[6] However, certain facts do not neatly fit the hypothesis of such a clear-cut inverse relationship. First of all, killings committed indoors dropped about as sharply as homicides carried out on the street. Also, in several other big cities (especially San Diego and Los Angeles), the murder rate tumbled during the 1990s even though officers did not make more misdemeanour arrests for minor violations. Actually, the NYPD issued more summonses and made more arrests during 1986 and 1987 than during the 1990s, but that crackdown did not stem the rising tide of violence and theft while the crack craze engulfed the metropolitan area. In fact, even with all the arresting that went on in New York City in the latter half of the 1990s, officers in other police departments were more active, in terms of arrests per officer per year (see Karmen, 2000). To date, unambiguous statistical evidence of a relationship between increasing arrests for minor infractions and declining rates of serious offences has not been demonstrated in analyses by criminologists of data from New York City, other major cities and the nation as a whole (see Dixon, 1998; Bowling, 1999; Greene, 1999; Blumstein and Wallman, 2000; Cohen, Kauder and Ostrom, 2000; Miller, 2001; Taylor, 2001).

Question 2 *Did the huge volume of arrests absorb scarce resources and distort the spending priorities of municipal administrations?*

Zero tolerance campaigns are very expensive in terms of police manpower and overtime, court processing, and short-term jail stays. During the eight years of the Giuliani administration, these expenditures had been touted as worthwhile outlays that enhanced public safety (see Edozien, 2002) and came under scrutiny only after a budget deficit developed in the aftermath of a recession and the World Trade Center terrorist attack. For example, Operation Condor, a programme that paid officers overtime to work a sixth day per week to make additional arrests for drug and quality-of-life offences, cost over $200 million during the first three fiscal years of the new century (Flynn, 2002).

The advocates of zero tolerance have yet to convincingly explain why an arrest and a brief jail term now function as an effective deterrent that teaches quality-of-life offenders a lasting 'lesson' to not repeat their misbehaviour, when formerly this 'slap on the wrist' approach was disparaged as leading to an ineffectual 'revolving door of justice'. Obviously, punishments do not help lawbreakers with deep-seated problems like mental illness and drug addiction.[7] For example, a journalist discovered that one 40-year-old woman had been arrested 229 times since 1983 for soliciting. Another 45-year-old streetwalker

27

had been busted 121 times since 1987, and a male prostitute had been arrested 113 times since 1983 (McPhee, 2002). These kinds of 'garbage cases' are treated in an assembly-line fashion in the lower courts, where it is said that the inconveniences and indignities connected to the processing constitute the punishment.[8] The deluge of arrests for petty offences overwhelmed the lower courts, resulting in overcrowded calendars and backlogs, sloppy case handling and low-quality legal representation by overworked and underpaid lawyers assigned to defend indigents (see Rohde, 1999). Even though the resolution of these cases might not accomplish much, costs mount.[9] An analysis of the municipal budget over two decades (from the late 1970s until the late 1990s) revealed that spending for criminal justice (for policing, prosecution, courts, jails and legal representation for indigents) in-creased sharply (up 35 per cent) while government outlays for social services stagnated in New York (see Jacobson, 2001).

Therefore, the second hard question can be re-phrased as 'Could the time and money spent on handling these deeply troubled chronic offenders within the criminal justice system have been invested more productively in prevention activities and rehabilitation services?'

Question 3 *Did the arrest campaign damage the educational, housing and employment prospects of a huge number of New York City residents?*

During the eight years of the Giuliani administration, NYPD officers made about 1.5 million misdemeanour arrests. Since some people were taken into custody repeatedly for quality-of-life offences, the actual number of people who ended up with criminal records for arrests and convictions would not be as large as 1.5 million. But the question arises whether all this discretionary arresting marred the employment prospects of a large proportion of the City's workforce. 'Rap sheets' are serious impediments to securing gainful employment in decent jobs, especially in post September 11 New York, where a cottage industry performing background checks on job candidates and current employees has sprung up to serve security-conscious employers, even for menial positions paying the minimum wage (see Newman, 2002; Port and Zambito, 2002). Since joblessness, sub-employment and economic marginality are major risk factors for recidivism, is it self-defeating to repeatedly stigmatise petty offenders?[10]

Many of the misdemeanour arrests were for criminal possession of controlled substances. Young people with drug convictions can lose their eligibility for financial aid to go to college under legislation passed by Congress in 1998. If rigorously enforced, this draconian law will hurt the chances of upward mobility mostly for poor and working-class youth dependent on the government for tuition assistance (Editors, Baltimore Sun, 2002). Similarly, a unanimous US Supreme Court decision in 2002 authorised public housing authorities to evict entire households for the drug offences of one member, including 'innocent' tenants who knew nothing about the involvement of other people residing in their apartments. The New York City Housing Authority, which is the largest provider of shelter to low-income families in the country, hailed the decision as strengthening its policy of zero tolerance for drugs and violent criminal activity (Carey, 2002). Ironically, most of the misdemeanour arrests for drug possession during the quality-of-life campaign were for marijuana smoking: nearly 60,000 arrests were made in 2000, compared to a mere 500 or so in 1993 before the crackdown began, according to the NYPD's annual Complaints and Arrests Statistical Reports.[11] Ironically, as efforts to snuff out pot smoking in New York City were intensifying, the 'war' against marijuana was de-escalating in other metropolitan areas, especially in England and Canada.

In sum, tough question number three asks whether the harshness of the zero tolerance crackdown will turn out to be counterproductive in the long run if it drives already marginalised people even deeper into lives of desperation and deviance, thereby ensuring the continuation of a 'dangerous class' within New York City.

Zero tolerance for carrying concealed weapons

Whether or not to arrest the perpetrators of minor acts that undermine the quality of life in urban settings can be a matter of discretion for individual officers, and in the aggregate can reflect the changing priorities of policy-makers and the public. But illegal gun-toting is intolerable because of the potential for murder and mayhem, so whether to arrest people who carry concealed handguns cannot be a decision left to an officer's judgement. The real controversy revolves around the best ways to disarm criminally inclined predators without simultaneously alienating law-abiding people. Unleashing aggressive stop-and-frisk squads can easily provoke hostility from the communities the police are supposed to protect and serve. To fight crime effectively, police departments need to cultivate good relations with their constituents in order to maximise victim and witness cooperation with investigations by locating and apprehending suspects, by securing evidence to gain convictions and by convincing jurors of the trustworthiness of officers' testimony at trials. Officers need the support of the public in order to receive the pay they deserve from taxpayers, enhance their personal safety from attack and minimise the job-related stress they are subjected to from hostile encounters. Members of low-income minority communities tend to be especially in need of the protection and services offered by local police departments because they are disproportionately targeted by the predatory street criminals in their midst. Therefore it is in the best interests of both police departments and communities of colour to forge and maintain close working partnerships whenever possible (see Purpura, 2001).

Concerns that pursuing heavy-handed proactive anti-gun strategies could undermine good working relationships with minority communities have been voiced for decades, starting with the President's Commission on Law Enforcement and the Administration of Justice's Task Force on Police (1967: 23), which noted that:

> It is probably true that an aggressive program of preventive patrol does reduce the amount of crime on the street, although there has been no careful effort to measure the effectiveness of this technique. It is also apparent, however, that aggressive preventive patrol contributes to the antagonism of minority groups whose members are subjected to it. A basic issue, never dealt with explicitly by police, is whether, even solely from a law enforcement point of view, the gain in law enforcement outweighs the cost of community alienation.

In the midst of a wave of disorders that swept through many big city ghettos, the National Advisory Commission on Civil Disorders (1968: 100) argued that police agencies could not effectively preserve the peace and control crime without securing greater public support for law enforcement initiatives. In a footnote, the Commission (1968: 303) entertained the possibility that '[M]any departments have adopted patrol practices which ... have replaced harassment by individual patrolmen with harassment by entire departments'. Indeed, when in 1968 the United States Supreme Court handed down its landmark decision, *Terry* v. *Ohio*, Chief Justice Earl Warren noted that some officers used stops-and-frisks as a means of racial harassment, and that this abuse of authority could be a major cause of antagonism towards the local police department in some communities. But the Court's majority rejected the amicus brief of the NAACP Legal Defense and Education Fund that was filed on behalf of the many innocent persons whose cases never came to court because nothing incriminating was discovered when they were questioned and searched. The brief had claimed that blacks were much more likely to be stopped and frisked than whites, and that racial prejudice on the part of the police was a major cause of escalating tensions between officers and some members of African-American communities (see Schwartz, 1996: 326–37).

The ongoing debate over the benefits versus the costs came to a head during the late 1980s and early 1990s when violent crime rates soared throughout the country, fuelled in part by an explosion of confrontations on inner-city streets between members of gun-toting, crack-dealing crews. In 1992, the Kansas City (Missouri) Police Department agreed to carry out an anti-gun experiment. In certain sectors, selected officers were instructed to step up their reliance on stops-and-frisks and car stops in order to seize illegally concealed firearms. The crackdown seemed to reduce the amount of shootings and other gun-related crimes. But the researchers (Sherman et al., 1995) cautioned that '[intensified] gun patrols ... could conceivably have negative effects on police–community relations ... [and] could even provoke more crime by making youths subjected to traffic stops more defiant of conventional society'. One member of the Kansas City gun experiment research team (Shaw, 1995, quoted in Schwartz, 1996: 319) warned that 'Such hostility adversely affects police work in many respects, e.g., by making citizens unwilling to assist the police or even report crimes to the police when victimized ...'

A greater reliance on the tactic of detaining and questioning individuals and patting down the outer surfaces of their clothing for weapons predictably will have a racially disparate impact. '[I]nnocent people will be stopped. Young black and Hispanic men will probably be stopped more often than older white Anglo males or women of any race', a prominent advocate (Wilson, 1994: 47) conceded. But, this respected criminologist insisted, more police pressure was needed 'if we are serious about reducing drive by shootings, fatal gang wars and lethal quarrels in public places.'

In 1999, a tragic incident heightened concerns over whether the Department's anti-gun policies were tacitly encouraging plainclothes and uniformed officers to use the highly controversial practice of racial profiling. Four officers of the NYPD's elite Street Crime Unit fired 41 bullets at an unarmed West African immigrant in front of his home when he made what they perceived to be a 'suspicious movement' (he was reaching for his wallet, presumably to identify himself). The officers of this now disbanded unit, whose motto was 'We Own The Night', aggressively sought out gunslingers by acting upon their 'reasonable suspicion' that the persons they questioned and patted down might be involved in criminal activity (see Kocieniewski, 1999; Roane, 1999). The ensuing controversy compelled the NYPD to reveal that these plainclothes officers had stopped and frisked at least 18,000 people (mostly young black and Hispanic males) during 1997 and another 27,000 in 1998. Since many officers did not fill out the required paperwork routinely, the actual number of people accosted and searched might have been as much as five times greater.[12] Street Crime Unit members reported that they felt under great pressure to meet an informal quota of at least one gun arrest and seizure per month. As a result, they found it necessary to 'toss' many innocent young men who fit a crude profile until they caught one with a concealed handgun (see Emery, 1999; Roane, 1999; Spitzer, 1999; Gross, 2001; Rashbaum, 2001b).

To repair some of the damage, the NYPD initiated a politeness campaign entitled 'Courtesy, Professionalism, and Respect' (CPR). It became incorporated into the recruitment process, officer training, executive development, citizen contacts and CompStat monitoring of civilian complaints (Silverman, 1999). Officers were instructed to address even arrestees as 'Mr' and 'Sir', to explain to the public the reason for stops and to apologise for any inconvenience the interventions caused. In addition, Mayor Giuliani appointed a taskforce to investigate ways to strengthen ties with alienated communities, but he did not implement many of its recommendations. In response, a coalition of civil rights and civil liberties groups in the City called for the imposition of a federal monitor to oversee the patterns and practices of NYPD operations, a move that the Mayor and the Police Commissioner insisted was unwarranted. However, an inquiry by federal prosecutors in Manhattan concluded that members of the Street Crime Unit had indeed engaged in racial profiling (Rashbaum, 2000). In 2000, the oversight function of the Civilian Complaint Review Board (CCRB), which investigates accusations that officers were abusive or brutal (for example, during stops), was strengthened, after a study commissioned by the City's Public Advocate branded it as ineffective as a source of deterrence and discipline. In 2001, in response to strident complaints about racial profiling, the NYPD implemented a revised stop-and-frisk reporting form. Officers were instructed to check off why they stopped passers-by. The categories included inappropriate attire for that day's weather, actions indicative of engaging in a drug transaction, refusal to comply with the officer's directions, unusual nervousness, presence in an area that has a high incidence of reported offences of the type under investigation, proximity to indications of criminal activity (such as bloodstains or ringing alarms), and showing a suspicious bulge/object (Lombardi and Weir, 2001). In addition, police commanders were instructed to attend monthly meetings with precinct community councils and neighbourhood leaders and to measure progress by conducting periodic surveys of local residents (Lefkowitz, 2001). The head of the City Council, calling for 'transparency' to augment trust and accountability, urged the NYPD to issue regular reports on the race of people stopped on the street, and the distribution of frisks, traffic stops, arrests and misconduct complaints by precinct (Lueck, 2001). Opinion polls were scrutinised to monitor the level of the public's approval for NYPD operations in general, and whether New Yorkers believed that officers often engaged in profiling and brutality, as well as what specific actions were considered objectionable (see Rashbaum, 2001a). However, after the terrorist attacks of September 11, the NYPD enjoyed a groundswell of public appreciation and support, and public criticisms of questionable tactics rapidly diminished.

Question 4 *Did the stepped-up use of stop-and-frisk tactics effectively deter gun toting?*

The major justification for the increased reliance on stop-and-frisk was to help get guns off the street via confiscations, the incapacitation of gunmen through mandatory sentences and deterrence of would-be gun-carriers. Yet very little evidence has been gathered to test this hypothesis.

After 1993, uniformed officers, precinct anti-crime officers and plainclothes members of the Street Crime Unit made many more stops-and-frisks. Armed robberies, shootings and gun murders, which were slowly subsiding, dropped rapidly. However, it is not clear how much credit for these improvements goes to the increased use of this tactic. When the new anti-gun strategy was first implemented, it was expected that gun arrests would soar. But they continued to fall, as they had since 1990. In fact, gun arrests dropped each year throughout the 1990s, in tandem with gun crimes. Furthermore, even when the Street Crime Unit was at its peak manpower in 1998, it only accounted for less than 20 per cent of all gun arrests, so it is far from obvious that the surge in stops-and-frisks had such a decisive incapacitative as well as deterrent effect (see Karmen, 2000).[13]

Question 5 *Did the NYPD's zero tolerance policies to reduce disorder and weapons carrying undermine good police–community relations?*

According to former NYPD Commissioners Bratton (Bratton and

Andrews, 1999) and Safir (1997), not taking action against quality-of-life infractions and gun toting actually undermines good police–community relations. Before 1994, they argued, minority communities suffered from 'under-policing', which fed the perception that the police really didn't care about neighbourhood problems. The findings of a July 2001 poll that documented widespread support for strict enforcement, especially among the City's Black, Hispanic and Asian residents (see Kelling, 2002), lends some support to this contention.

But an alternative interpretation of events predicts that zero tolerance policing tends to result in systematic harassment of targeted groups, an accumulation of grievances and perceptions of persecution, and a consequent backlash of resentment against the police (see Dixon, 1998; Emery, 1999; Greene, 1999; Noel, 2000; Wynn, 2001). Community opinion can be divided, journalists have discovered, and individual reactions can depend on the residents' social class and age and direct personal experiences with both criminals and police officers (see Barstow, 2000). Overall, there are good reasons to hypothesise that the cumulative effects of repeated hostile encounters can undermine confidence and trust in a government agency with the ostensible purpose of serving and protecting.

The possible forms that the alienation of inner-city residents may take include a reluctance to report victimisations, a reticence to supply information to detectives investigating serious offences, an un-willingness to testify as witnesses for the prosecution, a tendency of jurors to disbelieve police testimony at trials and a loss of interest in joining the NYPD.

Some relevant evidence exists about the relative willingness of victims to report crimes to their municipal police. The US Department of Justice's National Crime Victimization Survey (NCVS), which does not routinely use sub-samples that are large enough to permit inter-city comparisons, did carry out a special, intensive study for the first time in 20 years in 1998. In a city-level survey, NCVS interviewers discovered that New Yorkers were more reluctant to bring their problems to the attention of the police than residents in any of the other eleven cities in the study. Specifically, only 32 per cent of the respondents who revealed themselves to be victims of violent crimes reported their personal experiences to the NYPD during 1998, compared to 58 per cent of victims in Springfield, Illinois, 50 per cent in Washington, DC, and 35 per cent in all 12 cities combined (including New York). Similarly, New Yorkers told the NYPD about 29 per cent of the property crimes they suffered, whereas the police were informed of about 47 per cent of the incidents by victims in Savannah, 45 per cent in Kansas City and 34 per cent overall (Smith, Steadman and Minton, 1999). Only 29 per cent of the sample of residents (not just victims) of New York City reported that they had any type of contact with police officers (including casual conversations), which was the lowest level in the 12 cities surveyed by the Justice Department (MacFarquhar, 1999).

Ever since the 1964 Harlem uprising, NYPD commissioners have conceded that, to be more effective, the racial and ethnic composition of the department needs to more closely resemble the characteristics of the residents of the neighbourhoods they patrolled (Pooley, 1996). Diversifying its workforce could help to secure the cooperation that is essential for effective crime-fighting, since it is members of the most afflicted communities who must report incidents, volunteer eyewitness descriptions, hand over evidence, give anonymous tips about wrong-doing or the whereabouts of fugitives, testify for the prosecution and serve as impartial jurors. Before the start of the crackdown, the NYPD had made the least progress of any of the ten largest US police forces, in terms of integrating its ranks with members of minority groups. Not much had changed by the late 1990s, despite the opportunities for taking affirmative action offered by an expansion of the ranks up to an all-time high of over 40,000 sworn officers. The NYPD remained among the least racially diverse of the forces serving the nation's ten largest cities. Whites made up 67 per cent of the sworn officers but comprised less than 40 per cent of the City's residents. The under-representation of black and Hispanic officers was especially pronounced in the higher ranks (Wilgoren and Cooper, 1999).

As the 1990s drew to a close, officers complained that the drive to punish minor infractions undercut their exercise of discretion and made them feel unpopular, even despised in the neighbourhoods they aggressively patrolled. As a consequence, morale deteriorated, many veterans retired early or simply quit in disgust (Flynn, 2000b). As the new century began, police departments in many cities faced a recruitment problem (see Associated Press, 2000). Because young adults residing in the five boroughs showed little interest in signing up for the exam and entering the academy, the NYPD found it necessary to search far and wide for suitable candidates. Recruiters visited distant military bases and Ivy League campuses. The Department waived fees to take the police exam, extended deadlines and added substitutes for the educational requirement of 60 college credits (Rashbaum, 2001c). Although the sources of the problem were not at all unique to New York City, the question arises whether the NYPD's recruitment difficulties were more acute because police–community relations were under greater strains due to the zero tolerance crackdown and the stepped-up stop-and-frisk campaigns. Were substantial numbers of otherwise qualified candidates turned off from a career in law enforcement because either they had been stopped and frisked in an abusive manner or issued a summons or even arrested for a minor quality-of-life infraction? Deeply alienated young men and women of colour even may have felt that joining the NYPD was working for the 'enemy' – the 'army of occupation' sent in by outside interests to repress 'ghettoised' populations justifiably angry about injustice and discrimination – a view limited to radical circles in the 1960s.

Asking the right questions

Zero tolerance has become an extremely attractive political buzzword that has transcended the confines of criminal justice and is now advocated in a wide variety of contexts, from schools to international confrontations, to garner broad support for get-tough policies. That is an unfortunate development because the effectiveness of zero tolerance measures against quality-of-life offences and gun toting remains debatable, while the social costs these hard-line approaches impose are becoming increasingly evident as the answers emerge to the questions posed above.

To avoid some of this collateral damage, new ways of disarming criminally inclined individuals without demeaning innocent, law-abiding persons who fit the same profile must be devised. That line of inquiry invariably leads to the issue of how minority youth as a group might be mistakenly characterised as troublemakers by officers. Unavoidably, that raises the controversy over allegations of double standards and selective enforcement, disagreements about what constitutes racial profiling, interpretations of the meaning of the legal term 'reasonable suspicion' and complaints about abuses of power, brutality and overly intrusive frisks. Surveys, interviews and focus groups could explore what impact, if any, the negative experiences of minority residents (especially male Black and Hispanic teenagers and young adults) had on subsequent attitudes and behaviour. For example, with regard to stops, respondents could be asked what they were doing at the time they were questioned and searched. Were they given an explanation, or an apology, or were they arrested, and if so on what charges? Did they feel they were singled out because of 'racial profiling'? How were their cases handled in court? Did they deem the incidents to be so embarrassing, infuriating and/or physically abusive that they filed or considered filing civilian complaints and, if so, on what grounds? Parallel questions could be asked about summonses, desk appearance tickets and arrests for minor quality-of-life infractions. Even-handed research projects could also explore how the police are negatively stereotyped by minority youth and how officers' legitimate concerns for their own safety dictate the need for weapons pat-downs. A reasonable goal could be to develop practical measures to minimise the personal tensions, group conflicts and mutual recriminations that surround stops-and-frisks.

As for quality of life infractions, research questions should centre on better ways to reduce and prevent disorderly behaviour in public. Besides tackling the root causes of delinquency, deviant behaviour, addiction, mental illness and homelessness, what are required most of all are not just creative and constructive alternatives to prosecution and incarceration for low-level offences – but imaginative and cost-effective alternatives to arrests.

Notes

1   Members of America's minority communities tend to suffer disproportionately from the economic losses and social costs that the street crime problem imposes on poor and working-class neighborhoods. For example, an analysis of murders in New York City revealed that about 85 per cent of the victims and as many as 95 per cent of the arrestees were residents of black or Hispanic descent during the period 1978–98 (Karmen, 2000).

2   After about two years, the Mayor pressured the Police Commissioner to resign because of their competition over who deserved credit for devising these strategies (McQuillan, 1997).

3   Years before the term 'broken windows' was coined in 1982, the main arguments of this thesis, and many of the same examples of casual disregard for the law that were singled out repeatedly in speeches by Mayor Giuliani and Commissioner Bratton almost twenty years later, were anticipated by a precinct captain in Manhattan:

> I believe the erosion of the quality of life in our town began when our 'system' demonstrated its inability to cope – not with murderers at the top of the scale but with the petty violators at the bottom. Once the word was out that the 'system' could not and would not effectively deal with the graffiti artist, the drunk in the hallway, the aggressive panhandler, the neighbor with the blasting radio, the habitual peddler, the petty thief, the late-night noisemakers, the garbage picker, vandals, desecrators, public urinators, kids under 16, litterers, careless dog owners, and on and on … once that word

was out, the seed was planted that has since blossomed into a full-grown disrespect for our laws. (Rosenthal, 1993 [1977]: 23)

4 The criminologists who developed the broken windows thesis have expressed reservations about the implementation of 'zero tolerance' crackdowns (see Kelling, 1998; Wadham, 1998).

5 The time was not right, politically, to even test out the broken windows thesis shortly after it was put forward in a widely read magazine article during the early 1980s. The surge of arrests that would accompany a zero tolerance crackdown could spark bitter controversy. The office of the US Attorney General reviewed a proposal by the National Institute of Justice to launch a campaign against quality-of-life offences in Newark and Houston and 'took one look at the idea of order maintenance and canceled the experiment. It was just too politically volatile even for a conservative Republican administration to deal with', according to one of the architects of broken windows, George Kelling (quoted in Nifong, 1997). The implementation of a pilot test had to be shelved until an adherent, William Bratton, was appointed Chief of the Transit Police during the administration of Mayor David Dinkins.

6 The NYPD made over 200,000 misdemeanour arrests per year in the late 1990s, as compared to only about 130,000 in 1993 before zero tolerance began, according to the Department's annual Complaints and Arrests Statistical Reports.

7 As many as 20 per cent of all US jail and prison inmates may be seriously disturbed, according to a study by Human Rights Watch (Butterfield, 2003).

8 The rights of arrestees for misdemeanours were repeatedly violated by police and corrections officers who compelled them to submit to degrading strip-searches in front of other detainees, according to several successful lawsuits in recent years (Glaberson, 2003).

9 These costs will rise. The fees paid to private attorneys who defend indigents arrested for misdemeanours were raised from $40 an hour to $60 an hour as of 1 January 2004. The insultingly low fees failed to attract sufficient lawyers, so individual attorneys represented hundreds of poor people at a time, undercutting their ability to mount a competent defence for their indigent clients (Saulny, 2003).

10 The Police Commissioner and the Mayor in Baltimore asked the City Council to authorise officers to issue civil citations for petty crimes rather than making arrests which are more expensive and stigmatise offenders with criminal records that hurt employment prospects ('Baltimore Police ...', 2003).

11 In 2000, an undercover officer, seeking to catch street-level dealers, shot and killed during a scuffle an innocent and unarmed man he mistook for a marijuana peddler. In the aftermath of a large turnout for the funeral of this victim of racial profiling and arrest quotas, a simmering controversy over the zero tolerance crackdown directed against pot smoking flared

up, but no change in the policy took place (see Flynn, 2000a; Shapiro, 2000).

12 One former member of the SCU estimated that for every report the unit filed, they made 30 additional unrecorded stops (Dwyer, 1999). The entire force filled out about 150,000 stop-and-frisk reports (UF250s in police parlance) during 1998, but the actual number of potentially hostile contacts with the public must have been much larger (Celona and Neuman, 1999).

13 Commissioner Safir publicly credited the unit with making about 40 per cent of all the Department's gun arrests (Kocieniewski, 1999). However, the detailed breakdown of types of arrests accomplished by different units indicated that the SCU accounted for just 18 per cent of felony-level dangerous weapons arrests, according to the NYPD's 1998 Complaints and Arrests Statistical Report.

Chapter 3

Policing incivilities in Germany

Alick Whyte

Introduction

Public incivilities[1] – graffiti, vandalism, (invariably drunken) loutishness, drug dealing and (particularly aggressive) begging – are part of
everyday life in contemporary society. These are often trivial
inconveniences which offend not only our sensibilities but our instinct
for order. Occasionally, nonetheless, they cause actual discomfort with
fear of an environment or situation and affect our confidence in going
about our daily business (Hopkins Burke, 1998c). They are similar in
nature and extent in Germany as they are in the UK and the USA
the two constituencies previously discussed extensively in the
criminological literature (see, for example, Kelling and Coles, 1996;
Hopkins Burke, 1998a). This chapter discusses the nature of the
response – and the methods employed – by the authorities in Germany
to the problem of incivilities. It is nevertheless influenced by events in
the US and UK.

Public order, zero tolerance policing and 'broken windows' theory

'A place for everything and everything in its place' is the
housekeeper's physical manifestation of a deeper psychological
preference for predictability and control. This tidiness becomes a
moral command: It is bad to be 'out of place', that is different.

People who are dirty and different are bad. (McCoy, quoted in Kelling and Coles, 1996: 38–9)

Germans have been traditionally and widely considered 'orderly'. By this is meant a sense of correctness with everything in its proper place. While this was probably the case in respect of the generation immediately following the Second World War this is clearly not so today. Modern German youth – very much like its cousins in the UK and the USA – has lost much of the uncritical respect that its parents had for the symbols of authority such as the police officer, ticket inspector, game keeper and park warden. Indeed many public incivilities can be best understood in the context of a tacit – or even overt – defiance of authority.

Policing in modern Germany is predominately a decentralised affair. The Western Allies established the nature of policing in each of their occupation zones, and the British wished the German police forces in their zone to be modelled very much along the lines of the decentralised county and borough forces of England and Wales. The Cold War, however, prevented this approach being taken, and national forces such as the *Bereitschaftpolizei* (Bepo), an armed response force, and the *Bundesgrenzschutz* (BGS), a force to control the borders with East Germany and the Soviet Zone of Berlin, were established on a national basis. This was done despite the misgivings of many of the population who remembered the terror instilled by the centralised police apparatus of the Nazi era. With the exception of the railway police – which was a national force for practical, geographical reasons – the Federal Republic of Germany otherwise adopted a police system based upon the *Länder* or counties with control vested in the local authorities of towns and districts who were in turn responsible to the minister of the interior of the relevant *Land*. This system continued with the reunification of Germany in 1990 and the restoration of the *Länder* of the East.

The style of policing introduced to respond to the growing problem of incivilities in Germany was very much influenced by the zero tolerance policing first introduced in New York City in 1993 and later in various constituencies in the UK. Introduced by William Bratton, Commissioner of the New York Police Department (NYPD) and championed by the charismatic mayor, Rudolph Giuliani, the zero tolerance style of policing involved a crackdown on all types of offences, no matter how trivial, but particularly those which caused annoyance to the public. It is an approach to policing influenced by the prescriptions of 'broken windows theory' where it is argued that the existence and escalation of incivilities in a neighbourhood lead to crime, the arrival of which leads to further incivilities. The solution to the problem involves environmental management strategies seeking to remove the evidence of incivilities, for example by cleaning up graffiti and other signs of vandalism (Kelling and Coles, 1996).

Following implementation of the anti-incivilities strategy in New York City, Bratton took credit for a major reduction of crime that subsequently occurred in the city and which suggested that the tactics worked (Hopkins Burke, 1998b: 12).[2] Considered from this perspective, public incivilities are seen as offences that, albeit minor in the individual incidence, nonetheless pose a serious threat to the 'quality of life' in their totality. As Waddington (1999: 33) observes: 'It requires that the broader context is appreciated; what might in isolation be a minor delinquency may be part and parcel of a living hell when minor delinquencies are heaped one upon the other.'

Zero tolerance and implementation of 'broken windows' theory in Germany

Notwithstanding subsequent academic criticisms of zero tolerance policing,[3] a general interest arose worldwide among police services in a strategy that appeared to deliver results. A group of senior German police officers visited New York in 1997 and upon their return reported enthusiastically to the Federal Minister of the Interior on the apparent success of the New York police, quoting falling crime statistics as proof of its effectiveness in the fight against crime (Kant and Pütter, 1998). The Minister of the Interior, Manfred Kanther, then proposed to the ministers of the interior of the *Länder* that a number of German cities be selected for the long-term experimental introduction of a similar initiative. The focus of the strategy would be the prosecution of all offences – including minor ones – found to be particularly repugnant to the public. All criminal justice agencies were to form a *Sicherheitsnetz*, a security network, as the mechanism through which the new order would be established. Most importantly, where existing budgets could not meet requirements, these would be enhanced from Federal resources. Special attention was to be paid to railway stations and their surrounds, and where normal police establishments were insufficient they were to be reinforced using the Border Police, the *Bundesgrenzschutz* (BGS) which had subsumed the duties of the railway police. Since reunification in 1990, the BGS had played an important role in controlling the flood of immigrants from Eastern Europe. Kanther emphasised that where serious offences were involved, it was important that public prosecutors and alien registration authorities adopt a hard line by exercising their powers to withdraw rights of residence to foreigners.

The interior ministers eventually met to discuss this proposition in February 1998 with only Saarland and Brandenburg declining to take part. The other *Länder* cooperated with Kanther's suggestions to a greater or lesser degree with modifications to accord with their own existing policing policies. Two *Länder* are here selected as examples: Berlin and North Rhine-Westphalia.

The former was selected for the experiment because of its long established cooperation with the BGS dating from the days of the divided city and the Berlin Wall. The experiment was entitled *Aktion Sicherheitsnetz*, 'Operation Safety Network'. In November 1997 the *Landeskriminalamt* (CID) set up a coordination centre for the operation based on three existing 'combined search and investigation groups' already operating against smugglers of illegal immigrants, graffiti and the forging of tickets for the city's public transport system. New safety strategies for the railway stations and their surrounds were devised with an emphasis on combating offences such as graffiti and vandalism, travelling without a ticket, drug offences, breaking open automatic vending machines and – inevitably – offences against the regulations for aliens. The central objective of the combined operation was to rejuvenate feelings of safety among the public and to assist this end BGS establishments were increased from 350 to 500. The first *Aktion* took place between January and February 1998 and was officially pronounced a success In one single seven-hour period 165 persons were searched, 78 received official warnings for minor offences and 17 were arrested for assault, resisting arrest, drug offences and offences against the regulations for aliens. Subsequent operations produced comparable results (Innenministerium des Landes Nordrhein-Westfalen, 1998: 12).

North Rhine-Westphalia (NRW) initiated its own version of the 'Safety Network' – *Ordnungspartnerschaft* – 'Partnership in Public Order' and went further than Kanther had proposed. Six cities were selected for the experiment – Bielefeld, Dortmund, Hagen, Düsseldorf, Krefeld and Köln – on the basis that they already had embryo public order partnerships. The intention was to coordinate the activities of the police, public order officials, youth workers, health workers, social workers, BGS, public transport organisations including the railway authorities, law courts and public prosecutors, schools and drug abuse counsellors in a comprehensive multi-agency strategy. Once again the objective was to engender a feeling of public safety and the starting point would be the eradication of crime and public discomfort around railway stations. The activities of individual authorities were to be coordinated with those of private individuals, the visible presence of public order officials increased in public places and the threshold of intervention generally reduced.

Progress was achieved remarkably quickly. As recommended by Kanther, priority was given to cleaning up the railway stations and the surrounding areas in the six cities selected as models. Drug dealing in these environs was a major problem, and Düsseldorf main station provides a good example of how it was tackled.

The main railway station in Düsseldorf, the capital city of NRW, is a modern construction built on the ruins of its bombed predecessor and following the standard German pattern of main line railway platforms above the main concourse with those of the metropolitan and regional network located below. The concourse and the immediate surrounds of the station with its overhead railway bridges and pedestrian under-passes had become a focus for the homeless, beggars, alcoholics and drug addicts. By 1996, about 300 people were involved in drug dealing and use on visible public display to passengers and passers-by at any one time. This created a feeling of unease among the people who lived near the station and the owners of nearby business premises, to say nothing of the 150,000 daily passengers (Innenministerium des Landes Nordrhein-Westfalen, 1998: 12).

An *Ordnungspartnerschaft* was formed consisting of the Federal and regional railway authorities, the *Ordnungsamt* (the division of the city council responsible for public order), the Public Prosecutor's Office, police headquarters and the BGS. The aims of the strategy were: to reduce public drug dealing and the open abuse of drugs; to expel non-local drug users from the area; to offer help to local drug addicts; and to improve conditions in the station for passengers, the public and business people.

The initial phase consisted of direct action against the drug pushers and abusers by a special police group using regular police officers augmented by Bepo, the readiness police. In a sustained operation the police group arrested scores of drug offenders. Where prima facie cases were established, the Public Prosecutor's Office pursued these with vigour and the accused were remanded in custody without exception. Others without a valid reason for remaining within the precincts of the station were issued *Aufenthaltsverbote* (orders forbidding them to return to the area on pain of arrest and prosecution for criminal trespass). The operation was prolonged but extremely successful in that it cleared the station of 'undesirables'. At the same time, a drugs aid centre funded by the city health department was established near the station and was used by local users as a refuge. Medical care – including support for a methadone programme for heroin addicts – plus a welfare service, mainly for young, female addicts, was implemented.

German Railways introduced a 'Three S's' programme: **S**afety, *Sauberkeit* (Cleanliness) and **S**ervice which remained in place beyond the period of the initial police actions against drug users. This involved using a private security firm to look after the safety of passengers. Debris such as litter, spills or dog excreta was cleaned up quickly, and undesirables made to feel unwanted, moved on or reported to the police. The regional railway company employed a private security service to patrol rail and bus routes particularly known for drug trafficking. A 'Night Owl' service was introduced whereby passengers on late-night trams could ask the driver to order a taxi – by radio – to meet them at a designated stop. This has proved particularly popular with women (Innenministerium des Landes Nordrhein-Westfalen, 1998: 14–17).

The general public in Düsseldorf were justifiably pleased with the results of this *Ordnungspartnerschaft*. The main station is a safer place, and those who use it feel more secure. Of course, the operation displaced the drug problem to an extent, and many of the dealers and users are pursuing their activities elsewhere. Nevertheless, the extent of drug use in the vicinity of the railway station has been drastically reduced if not eliminated, and the participants in this partnership have demonstrated how effective coordinated action can be in making a major public place not only safer in practical terms but in creating an environment in which those who use it legitimately actually feel protected. The operation has never been formally terminated and is periodically resurrected whenever the authorities consider that the area around the station is in danger of declining towards its former unsavoury condition.

A similar *Ordnungspartnerschaft* strategy was implemented in Krefeld between the police and the local tram company to combat loutish, foul mouthed and sometimes violent behaviour by youths. Police headquarters organised a training programme for tram company officials and drivers using psychologists and teachers which gave instruction and practical exercises in avoiding and de-escalating conflict situations. Together, the police and the tram company mounted regular patrols, particularly on the late-night trams. Patrols intervened in incidents of 'loutishness', arresting those involved where the circumstances were justified but more often issuing a warning or a *Platzverweis* – a formal prohibition from using the tram system for a specified period, on pain of prosecution for criminal trespass. The police further cooperated by having officers themselves use the trams to and from duty and wherever practicable in preference to official duty vehicles (Innenministerium des Landes Nordrhein-Westfalen, 1998: 22–3).

A different form of *Ordnungspartnerschaft* strategy was undertaken in Köln aimed at the maintenance of safety in its 560 public children's playgrounds. Volunteers, mainly parents of young children who use the playgrounds, have undertaken supervisory duties, reporting defective swings and roundabouts, graffiti, fouled sandpits or other playground areas and keeping observations on adults using the playgrounds for drug and alcohol abuse. The partnership involved the Child Welfare Authority of Köln city, the police and the volunteers, and the outcome was playgrounds in which children have serviceable attractions and clean sandpits, are undisturbed by drug and alcohol users and drunks and where relations with those living close to the playgrounds are friendly (Innenministerium des Landes Nordrhein-Westfalen, 1999: 16).

The above three examples of successful *Ordnungspartnerschaften* can be compared to the Crime and Disorder partnerships introduced in England and Wales following the Crime and Disorder Act 1998 (the flagship criminal justice legislation introduced by the newly elected New Labour government and which is discussed in detail elsewhere in this volume).

Graffiti has been a problem in Germany since the mid-1980s originating in major cities such as Munich, Frankfurt am Main, Berlin and Düsseldorf. The graffiti subculture was adopted from across the Atlantic and the street gangs of New York and employs the same American-English terminology such as 'pieces' and 'tags'. Its manifestations are similar to those in other countries consisting mainly of spray painting any available surface including walls, buildings, tramcars and trains. Indeed, as in other countries, a small number of 'pieces' have come to be accepted as works of art. The Berlin Wall became a world-famous exhibition of graffiti, many poignant, some artistic and it can be said that Germany helped further the notion of graffiti as art. (As a surface the Wall was ideal; four metres high and 107 km long).

Not everyone considers graffiti to be art and there have been various campaigns aimed at participants undertaken by partnerships consisting of the police and various municipal organisations. Strategies have been aimed at schools and youth organisations and have focused on prevention by informing young people of the consequences of being convicted of spraying public or private property. Like the UK, Germany is a country where there is great enthusiasm for 'do-it-yourself' decorative work, so store managers have been advised by the police to restrict paint spray sales to supervised areas to prevent theft by graffiti sprayers. Target hardening is practised in various forms using special paints and surfaces and by cleaning off graffiti whenever detected.[4] But the only deterrent to hard-core exponents has been found to be prosecution and punishment.

Prosecutions are pursued in accordance with both the German Penal Code and legal precedents relating to criminal damage if incidents concur with the following. First, the fabric of the item has been found to be substantially damaged or its (technical) usefulness materially and lastingly impaired. Second, cleaning of the item leads to substantial damage. Third, alteration of the external appearance is deemed to detract from the aesthetic purpose of the item. Graffiti sprayers are unable to resort to the defence of the basic right to free expression or freedom of artistic demonstration laid down in the *Grundgesetz* (Basic Law) because the latter expressly excludes artistic activities on third-party property against the wishes of the owners. Civil actions provide deterrence. The owner of defaced property has a three-year period in which they can submit a claim for damages (he or she will be notified of criminal prosecutions by the Public Prosecutor who may prosecute such offences in the public interest). Damages can be awarded against an individual or against members of a 'crew' collectively and payment – with interest – can be pursued for a period of up to 30 years. Much emphasis is placed upon such penalties by the authorities and they feature prominently in social programmes involving parents, teachers and pupils as well as leaflets published by the major cities and distributed through youth organisations as a deterrent to would-be paint sprayers. Victim–offender confrontation has had some success, particularly when combined with an order requiring the offender(s) to restore the graffiti daubed surfaces to their original condition.

Other measures adopted to deter graffiti do not differ from those adopted in other countries and which are described by Barker and Bridgeman (1994). These have included allowing paint sprayers to decorate walls (or even derelict railway carriages) with the consent of their owners and even enter legitimate competitions for graffiti artists. However, these are rare as there are few volunteers who wish to have their property adorned with graffiti. In Munich a legal spraying project resulted in a 35 per cent *increase* in defacement of telephone boxes, railway platforms and letter boxes in the surrounding area (Landeskriminalamt Nordrhein-Westfalen, 1998: 18).

Vandalism – or the wanton destruction or damage of third-party property – afflicts Germany in much the same way as other Western European countries. The usual method of dealing with the problem in these countries is by fine, probation or community sentence. The *Ordnungsamt* in Düsseldorf has sought to identify motivation for vandalism with a view to its prevention and observes it to be a predominantly urban phenomenon mainly carried out by young men while their targets usually meet three criteria. First, the owners or injured parties are invariably not known to the perpetrators with the implication that the 'threshold of restraint' (*Hemmschwelle*) is low. Second, the vandalised object particularly 'attracts destruction' (*zerstörungsfreundlich*), that is its damage or destruction attracts attention, such as breaking glass. Third, the objects concerned are unsupervised – or have no capable guardians to deter the vandalism (Cohen and Felson, 1979) – so the risk of being caught in the act is substantially reduced.

Prevention of vandalism initiatives in North Rhine-Westphalia have closely followed the prescriptions of 'broken windows' theory with its central notion that neighbourhoods may decay into crime and disorder if damage is not repaired quickly and the area well maintained (Wilson and Kelling, 1982). Increasingly close cooperation between municipal authorities, private businesses and individuals in reporting damage to buildings and fixtures has resulted in swift repair which has had the outcome of deterring further vandalism. The faster damage is repaired, so it would appear, the greater has been the 'threshold of restraint' among vandals to repeat the destruction. Other established tenets of situational crime prevention are followed, that is objects attractive to vandals are designed to be as resistant as possible (see Clarke, 1992). For example, public telephone facilities in German city centres are spartan, constructed of stainless steel and containing no glass regardless of the exposure of the user to the elements. Moreover, the contemporary universal enthusiasm for cellular telephones has very much reduced public telephone usage and therefore the necessity for such facilities.

Vandalism has been the target of many *Ordnungspartnerschaften* partnerships in other North Rhine Westphalian cities, particularly in Gummersbach, Hagen and Düsseldorf. These strategies have centred largely on projects managed by the police, schools and youth authorities but have had limited success. Much emphasis has been placed upon local community responsibility and this may have had a more long-term – but difficult if not impossible to measure – influence than the regular reminders sent to school children warning them of the penalties for criminal damage. The involvement of citizens in projects to report vandalism – that is, reporting suspicions as well as simply objects observed to be damaged – has also had success. An example is the *'Hinsehen statt Wegsehen'* ('Pay attention instead of looking away') project promulgated through the local newspaper in an inner-city centre which provided the police with a wealth of data on suspects. Cooperation between public transport employees, street cleaners and local firms renting advertising space in bus shelters – who undertake responsibility for cleaning them – and the police has been similarly productive.

Offences of both vandalism and graffiti can be made the subject of victim–offender confrontation and mediation resulting in discontinuation of prosecution or mitigation of sentence. German public prosecutors may discontinue prosecutions if recompense has been made to the satisfaction of the victim. Frequently, the victim will formally withdraw their complaint after compensation has been paid which effectively bars further proceedings. The German Penal Code allows a reduced sentence to be imposed or even waived where the perpetrator has made every effort to reach agreement concerning compensation with the victim or shown that he or she has expended personal effort or suffered a degree of sacrifice towards compensating the injured party. This approach has had some success in the prevention of repeat offending but some have criticised its limited use. Miers (2001: 37) concluded that while victim–offender mediation was an available remedy, it was rarely invoked on account of 'the negative attitudes about its value and place within the criminal justice system that are held by the police, prosecutors and lawyers alike'.

Begging in itself is not a criminal offence in Germany but when accompanied by threats it can be dealt with by application of the Penal Code under which threatening behaviour (*Bedrohung*) or coercion (*Nötigung*) are criminal offences.[5] Thus overt acts of aggressive begging can be handled as a straightforward criminal offence by the police or the civilian wardens of the *Ordnungsamt* (the latter are discussed below). In reality, begging is usually compounded by loutish, often drunken behaviour of groups of workless individuals frequenting the streets. Having exhausted their supplies of alcohol, they resort to begging to replenish them. Both in the UK and in Germany, the presence of such individuals, particularly as a group, is viewed as alarming by the public and frequently forms the basis for demands for more visible policing in city centres (see Hopkins Burke, 1998c, 2000,

2001: 226–8). As long as the behaviour of these groups does not amount to threat or coercion, it would seem that nothing can be done. However, each *Land* has a plethora of local regulations which extend to city, town and even community ordinances, in effect by-laws. Lying down in public is considered to be a personal need and as such not an offence whether accompanied by alcohol or not (except in Munich where a city ordinance expressly forbids this). This notion of 'personal need' can be compared to the difficulties experienced by authorities in the USA where citizen's rights lawyers have defended the right of street dwellers to publicly exercise their 'personal needs' such as public urination and defecation or sleeping next to live rails in the subways (Kelling and Coles, 1996: 38–69). However, in Germany, if such behaviour extends to the obstruction of traffic then action can be taken under the traffic laws. Moreover, some farseeing municipalities have used their responsibility for street maintenance to override the 'special needs' of people to lie down and have declared the practice to be no longer acceptable. Cases brought before the courts can create precedents for taking legal action. For example the Saarbruchen Regional Court ruled that lying down to consume alcohol was a public right which was abused if a group engaged in this activity spread out unreasonably and blocked access to a public passage or pedestrian underpass. There are therefore a number of ways in which legal action can be taken against those who attract public opprobrium in this manner. But by far the most effective means of dealing with this problem has been by the issue of a *Platzverweis*, a verbal warning by a police officer, or an *Aufenthaltsverbot*, a written warning by the local authority, which requires the individual to leave the area immediately and forbids them from returning to the area in future. Unfortunately, many do return whereupon more permanent action becomes necessary.

Thus far, the more common public incivilities have been discussed together with the ways in which the German authorities deal with and have responded to them. The *Ordnungsamt* is a very important division of local government which deals with all aspects of public order and local organisation ranging from veterinary services to public parks. It is subordinate to the *Land* minister of the interior who also controls the police. This allows a very close interdependence of departments without any dispute about which department is to take the lead; the task is coordinated by officials from the *Ordnungsamt*. It is an approach rather different to collective decision-making in UK multi-agency problem-solving undertakings where a chief constable 'can continue to maintain the exclusive right to refuse to be bound as others might be and assert full (and unique) "independence" on policy matters' (Savage, 2001: 78).

The *Ordnungsamt* is part of a long established German policing tradition. It undertakes tasks concerning public safety and well-being that were the responsibility of the police service up to and during the Weimar Republic. Hence fire precautions, safety, environmental matters, market trading and black market prevention, hotel and guest house registration and regulation, supervision of hygiene regulations and many other areas in which the well-being of the citizens are concerned fall within this remit. This explains why the *Ordnungsamt* is so well equipped to coordinate operations to suppress or eliminate public incivilities. There is no need to seek cooperation among local government departments and the police or to agree targets and audit results. The *Ordnungsamt* is the ultimate organiser and coordinator and reports directly to the minister of the interior.

A further development introduced under the direct control of the *Ordnungsamt* in Düsseldorf is the *Ordnungs und Servicedienst* (OSD), the public order service. Resulting from the successful and ongoing operations against drug use around the main railway station, it was proposed that much of the burden imposed on the police and BGS could be reduced by a patrol force. Administratively it was relatively simple for the *Ordnungsamt* to consolidate the external elements of a number of its departments – among which were hygiene control, commercial regulation and gardens, parks and cemeteries – in order to form such a force. An experimental deployment for a period of one year confirmed its usefulness and it became established as a department (Section 5) of the *Ordnungsamt* in 1999. In 2000 it was further augmented by volunteers from within the *Ordnungsamt* following public pressure upon local government for a greater police presence on the streets and again in October 2001 by the addition of a dog section (which also enforces the implementation of new legislation concerning the control of domestic dogs in NRW). Supervision of the main railway station remains the principle commitment.

Unlike the German police, members of the OSD are unarmed – although discussions are underway regarding the issue of batons and mace or pepper sprays – and do not have formal police powers of arrest. However, local by-laws afford them extensive powers of arrest and search. They are trained by the police and at the local government training institute. They wear a distinctive blue uniform and badge – the police throughout Germany wear dark green – and have distinctive blue and white liveried vehicles with blue emergency beacons and two-tone sirens. They patrol the inner-city areas daily – principally during the evenings – and are particularly useful in controlling order during major public events such as *Karneval* and the enormous fair held annually next to the Rhine near the city. In the UK, civilian wardens are established in some areas under the control of the local authority to deal with environmental problems such as graffiti, dog fouling and litter. They identify and report their findings and carry out many community tasks which would otherwise occupy police time. They are certainly a useful source of intelligence to the police. Community support officers are a new development in Germany and one that has caused considerable controversy among the police service because they are required to deal directly with the public in matters of public order and may be given additional legal powers. It can be seen that members of the OSD have considerable authority and are in effect unarmed police auxiliaries. Indeed, they are controlled by the local police commander.

Conclusions

Clearly there is no difference between the types of public incivility experienced in Germany and Britain. Deterioration in respect for authority may be seen as particularly contrary to the German tradition of order but it is a reality of contemporary life. Public opinion polls and self-report studies conducted in Britain (see Hopkins Burke, 1998b) show a widespread public enthusiasm for more uniformed police on the streets. In England and Wales, the Crime and Disorder Act 1998 formally placed responsibilities on local authorities and police to audit local crime and disorder problems and produce strategies for solving them in consultation with both statutory and voluntary organisations. Germany did not require legislation to achieve this outcome. Because of the organisation of public order departments in the German *Länder*, a direction from the appropriate minister of the interior appears to have sufficed to achieve a very successful number of partnerships in public order which have solved a number of problems involving public incivilities. Moreover, in Germany the *Land* minister of the interior's control of both the police and the public order department ensures that there is no conflict over coordination and direction of such undertakings.

The public demand for more uniformed presence on the streets has already been met in some areas of Britain by the provision of community wardens by local authorities who have no enhanced powers of arrest. The provision of community support officers as ancillary to the police will increase this presence. In Germany the creation of what amounts to an auxiliary police force from within the public order department in Düsseldorf and now other cities in

Germany has been widely welcomed. However, this force, while unarmed, has considerable powers to arrest and search, many of which derive from local by-laws.

In final conclusion, the nature of incivilities is very similar in both Germany and the UK. However, while the problems may be the same, the German approach to their solution appears more directly organised and has been introduced without the need for specific legislation.

Notes

1   Alternative terms to 'incivilities' used in the literature are 'anti-social behaviour', 'quality-of-life issues' and 'minor disorder incivilities' (see Bland and Read, 2000: 5).
2   It should be noted that this was achieved with an increase in the NYPD establishment of 7,000 (see Hopkins Burke, 1998b).
3   Critics have noted a failure to establish a causal link between implementation of strategy and reductions in crime and an illiberal targeting of the socially excluded (see, for example, Pollard, 1997; Crowther, 1998, 2000; Bowling, 1996, 1998a).
4   Target-hardening strategies are a crucial element of situational crime prevention (see Clarke, 1992). Strategies involve the introduction of physical barriers to protect property including locks, bars, screens, fences and other forms of alteration to the physical environment (Crawford, 1998: 67).
5   Coercion under the German Penal Code is widely construed. For example, if a driver flashes his headlights and/or sounds his horn to persuade the driver in front of him to move over, he or she commits the criminal offence of coercion.

Chapter 4

Over-policing and under-policing social exclusion

Chris Crowther

Introduction

Some academics and policy-makers have argued that hard styles of policing – such as zero tolerance policing – may criminalise a socially excluded underclass through the escalation of police–community conflict in poor neighbourhoods (Pollard, 1997; Crowther, 1998). However, with hindsight it can be observed that these accounts focused too much on the potentially adverse effects of this type of approach to policing marginalised and fragmented communities. This chapter argues that these commentaries require some critical reflection because the application of hard-style policing has not resulted in the predicted further criminalisation of the excluded society. This is for two reasons. First, under New Labour it is generally accepted that crime, disorder, anti-social behaviour and social exclusion are no longer just a problem for the police. The popular refrain of many senior police officers throughout the late 1980s and 1990s that the service alone cannot be responsible for addressing the relationship between poverty and crime has now been recognised by politicians (Reiner, 2000a; Crowther, 2000a). The statutory requirement for 'joined-up', cross-departmental policy and practice attests to this, in particular the Crime and Disorder Act 1998 (Home Office, 1998a), the Crime Reduction Programme and the Social Exclusion Unit. Multi-agency partnerships are now pre-requisites for the development of community safety and crime reduction initiatives at a local level. In short, crime reduction is now the responsibility of statutory, voluntary and private agencies as well as individual citizens. Second, the growing influence of managerialism and the 'what works' agenda has led to a significant reallocation of resources, which makes the regulation and any coercion of the underclass increasingly difficult (Fionda, 2000). It is therefore necessary for a more nuanced theoretical appreciation of the more complex relationship connecting crime, social exclusion and policing (Crowther, 2002).

The chapter has two core sections. The first outlines the current agenda in crime and public policy; the second reviews a range of contributions which have theorised the relationship between the police, policing, crime and the excluded society.

In the first section, the promise of New Labour to be 'tough on crime and tough on the causes of crime' is contextualised. During two successive New Labour administrations 'joined-up' government has been pivotal at central and local levels. For example, there are the activities of the Social Exclusion Unit and the Regional Development Agencies. These organisations are connected with the Crime and Disorder Act 1998, in particular the Home Office's Crime Reduction Programme and the local community safety partnerships and crime reduction partnerships distributed throughout England and Wales. The government demands that all of these innovations need to be evidence-based, satisfy the requirements of the 'what works' agenda (Davies, Nutley and Smith, 2000) and fulfil the aims and objectives of the new public management or the 'three "Es"': economy, effectiveness and efficiency (Clarke and Newman, 1997). The observation that it is too early to audit the effectiveness of these anti-social exclusion and anti-crime and disorder strategies still applies (Crowther, 2002: 201) but there are also some unresolved theoretical debates. The key trend throughout this period is that the boundaries separating criminal justice and social policies are officially recognised as being far less clear-cut than they were under the four Conservative governments who held power between 1979 and 1997.

The second section contains a critical assessment of a range of theoretical perspectives that have focused on the policing of an underclass. This is attempted through usage of the notion of the police-policing continuum (Crowther, 2002b), an idea which attempts to establish connections between what may be characterised as neo-Marxist/neo-Weberian (Crowther, 2000b; Reiner, 2000b) and Foucauldian explanations of crime and crime control (Feeley and Simon, 1994; Johnston, 2000; Stenson, 2000a). These typologies are ideal-types and they undoubtedly share common characteristics but at the same time there are crucial differences.

Neo-Marxists and neo-Weberians concentrate most on the *police* as a specialist, formal state apparatus endowed with the legitimate use of force that is charged with regulating a structurally excluded under-class. The police are the 'thin blue line' responsible for crime reduction, order maintenance and quasi-social service tasks thus combining harder and softer styles of policing. It is recognised that the police and other governmental organisations do work alongside each other, but when they do the former expend their energies on influencing and controlling the agenda (Gilroy and Sim, 1987). Crucially the police mandate is seen to be an extension of state power with the organisation oriented towards maintaining the stability of a political economy, which operates to sanction the interests of the powerful ruling elite to the disadvantage of members of the working and under classes.

Foucauldians have tended to work more closely with notions of police and policing in terms of *Polizeiwissenschaft* or 'police science', which connotes more general forms of administration and regulation. Instead of focusing on the clearly delimited and specialised task of crime reduction, policing is seen to focus on the issue of general social order, including the provision of security, welfare in its widest sense, and general social stability and economic prosperity (Dean, 1999). Furthermore, the police as well as other governmental agencies under-take these functions, and their respective activities frequently interpenetrate each other. The Foucauldian framework has obvious merits as an analytical tool for interpreting the current legislative and policy frameworks in crime reduction and community safety, where many agencies beyond the central state participate in social control. The work of anti-crime and disorder partnerships, for example, has resulted in the simultaneous fragmentation and division of the specialised roles of agencies such as the police, local authorities, housing, social security and health.

The way forward

As in the 1980s the police currently work in partnership with other agencies in crime reduction, providing further evidence of the develop-ment of a new policing complex – or the police-policing continuum – where the role of the service is being displaced, supplanted, strengthened or complemented by the activities of non-police agents and agencies. This is also an example of 'responsibilisation' and 'governance at a distance' (Garland, 2001) whereby non-statutory agencies (i.e. Safer Cities, Crime Concern UK and the Jill Dando Institute of Crime Science) and private citizens (e.g. Neighbourhood Watch) are expected to contribute towards the 'war on crime'. Due to limited resources those policing activities carried out by non-police agencies are also increasingly relatively short-term and targeted initiatives which displace – and are displaced by – other policies. The 'net widening' scenario outlined in the 1980s by Foucauldians (Cohen, 1985) and neo-Marxists (Brake and Hale, 1992) has not happened. The conflicts between social, political and economic priorities in the prevailing political economic environment – characterised in terms of the shift from the Keynesian Welfare National State to the Schumpeterian Workfare Post-National Regime (Crowther, 2000b; Jessop, 2000) – rarely results in an overarching strategy of inclusion or exclusion through policies of care or control and discipline. The rhetoric of 'joined-up' thinking is rarely realised in policy and practice. For instance, the many policies and strategies mentioned above do not operate in all areas and nowhere in the UK would communities receive all the support and service. Consequently, there is still scope for neglect and abandonment (Crowther, 2000b).

Crime, social exclusion and public policy

Social exclusion: the policy agenda

The notion of social exclusion is a variation on the theme of other ideas referring to poverty such as the underclass and social deprivation. There are also multiple methods of defining, conceptualising and measuring exclusion. Even though the terminology may vary there is a familiar set of social problems, illustrated by Rahman et al.'s (2000) inventory of social exclusion that includes households with a lone parent; those dependent on Income Support, Jobseeker's Allowance and low paid workers; local authority and housing association tenants; large families; separated/divorced households; families with a child under 11; adults living in one-person households, including single pensioners; children; young people; those who left school at 16 or under and women. Significantly, crime and disorder are omitted from this list, but they are central to other analyses (Young, 1999).

Once social exclusion has been recognised there are different perspectives on the dynamics causing the problem. For some commentators there are two distinctive approaches, the structural and behavioural (Crowther, 2000a), but Levitas (1998) provides a more helpful threefold typology: the redistributionist discourse (RED), the social integrationist discourse (SID) and the moral underclass discourse (MUD). Levitas (1998: 7) observes that:

57

a redistributionist discourse (RED) developed in British critical social policy, whose prime concern is poverty; a moral underclass discourse (MUD) which centres on the moral and behavioural delinquency of the excluded themselves; and a social integrationist discourse (SID) whose central focus is on paid work.

The influence of these discourses changes across time and space and each one has its unique consequences for policy-makers. The four successive Conservative regimes between 1979 and 1997 appropriated and supported a media-led moral underclass discourse. The election of New Labour in 1997 signalled a slight shift of emphasis towards a social integrationist discourse, which embodies a 'joined-up' understanding of the main causes of poverty and crime. The best method of solving social exclusion, it is argued, is inclusion or integration into paid employment through holistic, cross-departmental and multi-agency strategies and policies, including initiatives such as New Deal for Communities, Sure Start and Connexions. There are now nine Regional Development Agencies (RDAs) charged with developing strategies of economic and social regeneration (Percy-Smith, 2000). Some of the available evidence indicates that these anti-exclusionary policies have started to improve the material conditions of some poor people, but low income and multiple deprivation remain potentially persistent and intransigent problems (Department of Social Security, 2001; Rahman et al., 2001).

New Labour's multidimensional response to social exclusion and crime is underpinned by a distinctive moral and political philosophy, which holds in high regard the basic principle that every citizen must exercise personal responsibility in exchange for rights. According to this communitarian philosophy the main right is to act responsibly by taking up opportunities in the fields of education and employment. State support in the form of welfare services is restricted and targeted towards individuals and families who are not able to fulfil these fundamental responsibilities. The essential tenets of New Labour beliefs are predicated on the assumption that social exclusion will not be reduced by transferring income from the rich to the poor. In an interview prior to the general election in June 2001 with the journalist Jeremy Paxman, Tony Blair stated that New Labour is not specifically committed to narrowing the gap between the richest and poorest in society (BBC News, 2001c). However, the government does take crime, disorder and social exclusion seriously.

New Labour politicians have also denied the traditional political-left shibboleth of a strong causal link between exclusion and crime. It thus follows that the crime problem will not be overcome by the implementation of redistributive policies. The 33 per cent fall in crime rates – averaging out at 6 per cent per year – between 1995 and 2000 as recorded by a recent British Crime Survey goes some way towards vindicating the New Labour approach (although the crime decrease has not been across all offences, some having experienced less dramatic rates of decrease with others having actually increased) (Kershaw et al., 2001).

Crime reduction: the policy context

It was back in the early 1990s that the Morgan Report (Home Office, 1991b) raised the profile of the notion of community safety, but it is in more recent times that it has been formally recognised by policy-makers (Hughes, 2002). The Home Office defines community safety as

> an aspect of 'quality of life' in which people, individually and collectively, are protected as far as possible from hazards or threats that result from the criminal or anti-social behaviour of others, and are equipped or helped to cope with those that they do experience. It would enable them to pursue and obtain the fullest benefits from their social and economic lives without fear or hindrance from crime and disorder. (Home Office, 1998a: 7)

Community safety therefore refers to issues other than crime, such as the 'chronic' social conditions brought about by anti-social behaviour, as well as low-level disorder and incivilities which cause people to fear for their own safety. Behaviours such as hate crime and racist violence, the supply and misuse of drugs and phenomena including consumer protection, fire prevention, road safety, household safety, social exclusion, as well as mental health and public health are all community safety issues. It is for these reasons that some scholars have talked about the displacement of social policy through crime policy and the increasingly indistinct boundaries between police and policing activity (Stenson, 2000b). It is not the police alone who respond to these 'joined-up' problems, and the roles and responsibilities of statutory, private and voluntary agencies are continually being renegotiated along the police-policing continuum. For instance, initiatives and interventions now cut across the different government departments and focus on social exclusion, school performance, drug-related crime, economic regeneration and the promotion of family life. This is consistent with the assumption that the causes of crime include associating with delinquent peers, poor school performance and persistent truanting, poor parenting, poor housing and general poverty (Percy-Smith, 2000).

The government passed into law the Crime and Disorder Act in 1998, followed by the launch of its Crime Reduction Programme. The latter is coordinated by a Crime Reduction Task Force whose membership includes representatives from police forces and local and central government. The Task Force gives Regional Crime Reduction Directors a national focus through advice, support and guidance in relation to matters like target setting, the best ways of enlisting different agencies and the identification and dissemination of good practice. The Regional Directorates inform what occurs locally at the level of Community Safety Partnerships and Crime Reduction Partnerships.

The Crime Reduction Programme is required to use resources prudently, initially to slow down, but eventually to halt, the long-term growth rate in crime (Reiner, 2000b). It is concerned with five broad themes: working with families, children and schools to prevent young people from becoming offenders in the future (i.e. the Sure Start Programme); developing products and systems which are more resistant to crime; tackling crime in communities, particularly high-volume crime such as domestic burglary; more effective sentencing practices; and working with offenders to ensure that they do not reoffend (Home Office, 2000e: 59). Recent initiatives have included the installation of CCTV systems in high-crime areas, tackling school exclusions, burglary prevention and reduction, targeted policing, tackling domestic violence and improving the information available to sentencers (Home Office, 2000e: 59).

Sections 5–7 and 116 of the CDA provide a statutory framework for the police, local authorities and other stakeholders to translate these centrally determined aims and objectives into practice at the local level (Home Office, 1998a). As an ideal-type there are three elements: first the partnership group – assistant chief constable (police), chief probation officer; chief executive local authority, director of social services, director of education, voluntary sector, transport and magistrates; second the publicly accountable bodies – police authorities, health authorities, elected members of local authorities, probation committee; third the working groups – street robberies working group, car crime working group, domestic burglary working group, anti-social behaviour working group, racial harassment working group (Home Office, 2000e: 59).

These local partnerships conduct audits of local crime and disorder problems, including community consultation, and set out the main priorities, objectives and targets of Community Safety Plans. The rationale of these audits is to produce information about the scale of, the impact on and cost of each crime and disorder related problem for communities. This information enables participating agencies and groups to discover those problems they share in common and the best method of deploying resources to resolve them. This is known as 'local solutions to local problems'. These audits are used to formulate effective crime prevention and community safety strategies derived from a basic problem-solving structure. Crime and disorder are not actually defined in the CDA but burglary, racially motivated crime, witness intimidation, fear of crime, domestic violence and repeat victimisation are all designated as requiring special attention. Consideration would also be given to multi-agency strategies to tackle youth crime, to take action against drugs misuse and to create partnerships to crack down on general crime and disorder problems at a local level (Home Office, 1998b).

The above are required to tackle crime and its structural or social and individual or behavioural causes. However, each programme has to satisfy the principles enshrined in the new public management by proving that they are 'cost effective', provide 'value for money' and evaluated according to their effectiveness, efficiency and economy (Faulkner, 2000). The influence of these principles in the public sector can be traced back to the 1980s. Since then agencies have increasingly been required to adopt more business-like styles of service provision in order that they are able to deliver more economic, effective and efficient services. These are the 'Three Es'. Their significance can be seen through the emphasis now placed on value for money, performance targets and auditing, quality of service and consumer responsiveness. The introduction of market and private sector values constrains professionals through the introduction of national standards and objectives, systems to measure financial accountability and increased external scrutiny and monitoring (Crowther, 2000a).

The 'Best Value' initiative is an example of public managerialism. Since the passing into law of the Local Government Act (2000) local authorities have been required to develop more robust and effective mechanisms to consult members of the public to inform the planning and delivery of services. Best Value needs to base its service provision on the basis of a review of the so-called 'Four Cs': challenge, comparison, consult, competition (Newburn, 2002). Let us consider challenge first. It is no longer acceptable simply to provide a service, but it is also required to know why and how it is being provided. Comparison refers to the indicators that need to be developed so the performance of different agencies can be compared. The views of service users and suppliers are important. Performance targets are based on consultation with taxpayers and the users of services. Finally, competition is the mechanism used to deliver effective and efficient services (Newburn, 2002).

The Crime and Disorder Act 1998 – in conjunction with the three 'Three Es' and the 'Four Cs' – have ensured that crime reduction and community safety is no longer a job for the police alone. This is also resulting in major changes in policy-making, including the increased potential for competition and conflict between agencies.

The police, policing and the excluded society

Neo-Marxist and neo-Weberian explanations

Neo-Marxist and neo-Weberian social scientists are markedly different in their theoretical orientation, but both share a common analysis that the core roles and responsibilities of the police are to maintain existing political and economic structures, and that this involves watching the usual suspects or the underclass. Many of these critical accounts have been written in response to the policing of the inner- and outer-city riots in 1981/85 and 1991 which provided apparent evidence that the police force was collaborating with an authoritarian capitalist state to criminalise and demonise the poor (Hall et al., 1978; Campbell, 1993). The Scarman (1981) inquiry into the Brixton disorders recommended that the police should adopt a less authoritarian and coercive response, i.e. hard-style policing, and concentrate more on community-based policies including inter-agency communication, i.e. soft-style policing. Significantly both have been criticised because they are ultimately anti-democratic, unaccountable, unjustifiably aggressive and result in net widening and the dispersal of disciplinary mechanisms and controls (Cohen, 1985; Brake and Hale, 1992). The police and other statutory, private and voluntary agencies with which they work allegedly regulate poor communities through repression, surveillance and control.

Most of this work details the deployment of law enforcement strategies against criminogenic groups and spaces, and though it provides a compelling explanation of certain elements of police–community relations, it overstates the capacity and commitment of the police to exercising its legitimate force, for example hard-style paramilitarist policing (Waddington, 1994). The outcome is that other areas of police work have been given insufficient attention. First, there are policing tactics such as police–community consultation and multi-agency partnerships which are not dependent on the direct use of force. Second, there are the neo-liberal and 'third way' political rationalities associated with the New Public Management (O'Malley, 1997; Faulkner, 2000; Fionda, 2000; McLaughlin and Murji, 2001) that have reduced the resources available to the police so that they are in a position to exert their power and control over the underclass.

The brief history of the police and the underclass discussed above has been analysed in light of the ongoing structural transition of the Keynesian Welfare National State (KWNR) into the Schumpeterian Workfare Post-National Regime (SWPR). This example of the 'regulation approach' may be applied to assess current developments in policing in the context of a globally driven transformation of the process of capital accumulation. These developments in the global economy have impacted unevenly on national, regional and local economies, communities and neighbourhoods. The consequences of this ideal-typical representation of the substitution of one state form by another for the police are as follows.

Since the late 1980s the police have gradually ceased to receive the unconditional support of government (Rose, 1996) mainly because of the anxieties of New Right and neo-liberal politicians about UK economic performance and its inability to compete with other national economies in the global marketplace. The primary cause of the lack of UK competitiveness was attributed to the Keynesian Welfare National State, of which the police are a part (Crowther, 2002). In order to remain economically competitive with other economies across the world it was considered necessary to substitute the demand-side orthodoxy of that approach with the supply-side measures discernible in the emerging Schumpeterian Workfare Post-National Regime, thus prioritising economic policy over social policy. The outcome was in some – but not all – instances, reduced investment in the infrastructure, not the disappearance of the welfare state per se. The main trends have included rationing, targeting, privatisation, civilianisation and a general lack of investment in the infrastructure (Hay, 1999; Jessop, 2000).

The precise relationship between the political and economic changes discussed above and the police service is not entirely clear, but it may be argued that there is a connection between the gradual materialisation of the Schumpeterian Workfare Post-National Regime and the neo-liberal principles of the New Public Management, which were introduced to reorganise and restructure the police to ensure more effective, economical and efficient performance and service delivery (Fionda, 2000). It is also necessary to note that police and policing policies at the local level are framed in terms of centrally determined priorities. For example, New Labour's 'Third Way' version of the New Public Management (McLaughlin and Murji, 2001) underscores the CDA 1998 and the Crime Reduction Programme, and influences the direction of policing at a local level through the anti-crime and disorder audits and community safety and crime reduction partnerships. The police service now devises increasingly targeted tactics which cannot be easily compared to the authoritarian and coercive strategies mobilised in the 1980s – such as the use of the 'sus laws' and paramilitary-style tactics – which criminalised a frequently racialised working-class city (Keith, 1993). Contemporary police strategies include problem-oriented policing (POP), intelligence-led policing and 'crackdowns' like zero tolerance policing, which are relatively intensive but short-lived interventions (Jordan, 1998). These examples of hard-style policing sometimes permit the police to impress their sovereignty in particular streets and neighbourhoods. In contrast to the 1980s the end product is not the mass criminalisation and control of entire communities. Nowadays the police are more likely to be accused of abandoning, under-policing or under-protecting minority ethnic groups (Bowling, 1998a) and women (Campbell, 1993). Notwithstanding these problems, the police service at least aspires to operate ethically, to police by consent and to be democratically accountable to the diverse communities they serve (Neyroud and Beckley, 2001).

This section has argued that the worst-case futures imagined by critical criminologists have on the whole not been realised. It does not follow that criminologists need to become either complacent or un-critical, but rather to attempt a synthesis of neo-Marxist/neo-Weberian and Foucauldian perspectives.

Foucauldian accounts of hard and soft policing

Foucauldian criminologists are indebted to Ulrich Beck's (1992) highly influential text *Risk Society*, and like many other social scientists which have embraced his work, have accepted his central thesis that the notion of risk society has replaced that of social class as a legitimate explanatory tool. Rather than focusing on the material aspects of the political economy, Foucauldian writers consider crime control policies to be the outcome of a range of discursive and political rationalities. Feeley and Simon (1994), for example, have described how the logic of actuarial justice informs different strategies of risk assessment and management, which are mobilised in order to regulate a hazardous and dangerous underclass. Other analysts, which are referred to below, draw on the governmentality literature (Dean, 1999). Here the focus is on the politically constituted, differentiated and hybridised networks of statutory, voluntary and private agencies. In contrast to neo-Marxists, subscribers to the governmentality perspective reason that these networks do not serve the unitary and powerful interests of a political economic elite. However, some contributors do concede that the police do from time to time impose sovereign control over socially excluded places and populations (Stenson and Edwards, 2001: 74).

Feeley and Simon (1994) provide an interesting application of the concept of actuarial justice to explain criminal justice policy in the United States. With liberal conceptions of justice the central objectives are to ascertain the guilt, responsibility and obligations of individual suspects and criminals as part of a more general aim to reform and reintegrate them into society. In the final part of the twentieth century the relevance of these principles to penal policy were increasingly questioned. Actuarial justice is more concerned with formulating 'techniques for identifying, classifying and managing groups assorted by levels of dangerousness' (Feeley and Simon, 1994: 173) thus jettisoning the goals of rehabilitation and punishment that were the central focus of the Enlightenment. The administration of justice does not take into account the idiosyncrasies of individual cases but is based on an initial calculation or assessment of the risks or hazards posed by particular 'groups' and 'aggregates' such as 'permanent-marginal' underclass-type groups. Once this assessment has been completed strategies are developed to ensure that dangerous and unruly groups are managed in crime-ridden territories thus keeping other geographical areas crime free. As the issue of social class is not at the forefront of Feeley and Simon's (1994) analysis, it does indicate, however, that some categories of offender purportedly share in common a predisposition to specific types of behaviour. The potential for targeting the socially excluded is therefore ever present.

The discussion now proceeds to consider how risk assessment and management may result in the segregation of problematic and troublesome populations. Systems are implemented to gather the data required to inform and harmonise the risk management strategies of the different agencies involved in community safety and crime reduction (Hebenton and Thomas, 1996: 435–6). The realisation of security through 'risk management' is, however, seldom straight-forward because local intelligence systems are not adequately equipped to actively assess, monitor and keep track of all offending groups. Moreover, the multi-agency networks coexisting along the police-policing continuum – e.g. the police, education, probation – rarely act and think in a systematically joined-up way.

Ericson and Haggerty's (1997) pioneering text is partly based on a characterisation of the police as 'information brokers' who cooperate with other statutory and commercial agencies such as welfare organisations and insurance companies to identify the crime risks faced by society and the necessary course of action to control and govern crime problems. Police are in the business of processing and repro-ducing knowledge for security through information technology systems, hierarchical bureaucratic structures and techniques of surveillance. Prudential and actuarial models are used to calculate and measure the risk of particular types of crime and disorder and the scale of harm or loss they cause. The use of scientific knowledge makes it possible for different groups of experts to classify, target and finally exclude crime-prone classes of people. In a similar vein, Crawford (1997) contends that agencies appeal to the principles of actuarial justice when they are gathering the crime data which informs the working of anti-crime and disorder partnerships, such as in-capacitation and community-based punishments.

The above analyses are not without critics, though. MacVean (2001) has argued that the prudential paradigm is of limited use because knowledge about risk is finite, is intertwined with ignorance and uncertainty and is more or less incalculable. It is clear that police officers operate with a diversity of risk management strategies; some are attached to more traditional and specialised police activities like the investigation and detection of crime, whereas others form part of policing activities undertaken by multi-agency partnerships.

Ultimately Ericson and Haggerty (1997) have ended up con-ceptualising risk assessment and management as ideal-types. To counter this deficiency MacVean (2001) calls for an appreciation of the extent to which different strategies are combined, thus producing hybrid forms of risk management. It is imperative that analysts do not assume that the models of risk found in policy statements are implemented as intended by legislators in a top-down fashion. Policy statements necessarily interact with traditional police practices and procedures and the array of policing strategies constitute the post-CDA 1998 police-policing continuum. In the last analysis the rarefied con-ceptions of risk formulated by policy-makers are hybridised beyond recognition in practice.

Final words

The purpose of this chapter has been to review ongoing developments in police policy and practice in relation to whatever is meant by social exclusion. The aim has been to delineate two perspectives, the neo-Marxist/neo-Weberian and Foucauldian, which have explored to varying degrees the uneven impact of hard-style and soft-style policing on a structurally disenfranchised and disillusioned underclass in the context of a police-policing continuum. Neo-Marxist and neo-Weberian narratives are overwhelmingly preoccupied with globalisation and its influence in terms of the restructuring of national, regional and local economies. These accounts assert that there is a relationship between a mature capitalist system of production and the criminalisation of economically redundant and generally unproductive groups. Foucauldians, on the other hand, have redirected their attention towards discursive practices and political rationalities such as risk, thus rejecting explanations couched in terms of social class.

The endnote of this article is that both approaches err on the over-optimistic and over-pessimistic side in relation to the police and policing being effective as mechanisms for care and control. The policing of the socially excluded and the political economic conditions under which this takes place is entering a period of uncertainty which renders implausible the view that that the police enact the wishes of an authoritarian state. The police no longer act alone in the police-policing continuum because a disparate collection of statutory, not-for-profit, voluntary and commercial agencies are required to join up their services with the police services throughout England and Wales. The effective delivery of joined-up policies is no longer just about care and control or a balance between the two, but one that needs to be aware of the under-policing in certain domains.

To even begin to offer an explanation of the situation described above attention needs to be directed towards the tension between objectives and priorities fixed nationally and the sometimes competing demand for local solutions to local problems. Many structural arrangements at national, regional and local levels advance the twin goals of reducing crime and disorder and social exclusion, but the outputs and outcomes of these structures are not easily summarised. The main reason for this is that resources are increasingly scarce, and all participating stakeholders have to compete under ever more discriminatory and difficult conditions such as 'what works' and 'Best

Value'. The government vision that there are joined-up solutions to interconnected problems is arguably right, as is its commitment to tackling crime, disorder and social exclusion through cross-departmental and inter-agency coordination and collaboration. The problem is that as policing – or the delivery of services intended to provide economic security and social welfare – is now performed by a range of different agencies, the competition for funding and entrenched professional cultures will compromise serious attempts to further reduce crime, disorder and social exclusion.

Chapter 5

Policing British Asian communities

Colin Webster

Introduction

A recent comprehensive review of evidence about policing British minority ethnic communities concluded that there is 'a widespread tendency for black and Asian communities to receive greatly inferior treatment by the police ...' and that 'ethnic minority communities are considered to be "suspect populations" in a way which transcends their class position and is defined specifically by police officers in terms of "racial" characteristics as individuals and as a collective' (Bowling and Phillips, 2002: 166). Yet as the authors and others (see Smith, 1997a) show, the position of Asians is more mixed, ambiguous and complicated than this conclusion allows. Although police racism towards Asians is evident it takes a different form from racism directed towards African/Caribbean people and this is reflected in different contact and conflict between the police and Asian people. The growing paradox in the policing of British Asian communities is that on the one hand community members seek more effective policing to reduce crime and disorder while on the other Asian communities have become increasingly perceived as sources of criminality and disorder. This and other paradoxes will be explored in the context of a combination of risks faced by Asians who experience some of the highest levels of racist violence, criminal victimisation, fear of crime, ethnic segregation and multiple deprivation in Britain.

The hidden history of Asian–police relations

In claiming that Asian experience has been differently positioned to the kind of visceral hostility[1] that is more typical of relationships between African/Caribbeans and the police, this chapter does not want to give the impression that all has been well between Asian communities and the police. At times police deployment and targeting in relation to Asians generated high levels of conflict from the 1950s (Pearson, 1976; Webster, 1995, 1996; Bowling, 1999). This backdrop dispels myths of deference and quietism applied to Asians, and emphasises the scepticism that Asians have felt towards the ability of the police to protect Asian communities from racist violence, crime, racial discrimination and disorder. An important consequence has been high levels of community self-reliance, self-defence and resistance towards racism, crime and disorder.

The history of Asian–police relations can be said to occupy four overlapping periods. The first period involved the policing of Asian workers involved in strikes against workplace racial discrimination from the late 1950s to the late 1970s (Race Today Collective, 1986). This period was characterised by complaints by Asian workers over poor wages and the segregation of Asians onto night shifts and complaints by whites that Asians were responsible for the decline of the cotton industry and its occupational culture. Cars toured these areas demanding an end to 'Asian imports' and white hostility centred on perceived competition between locals and migrants over jobs, housing, women and girls, which laid the grounds for 'Paki-bashing' (Pearson, 1976).

The second period from the early 1980s involved policing politically organised Asian young people defending their areas from incursions by far right organisations (Race Today Collective, 1986; Independent Black Collective, 1986). This period was also marked by campaigns against the policing of immigration law. It can be characterised by the arrest in Bradford in July 1981 of twelve young Asian men on charges of conspiracy to manufacture petrol bombs. They produced a successful defence that they were defending the Asian community from threats by far right organisations to march through an Asian area (Race Today Collective, 1986; Independent Black Collective, 1986). The acquittal of the 'Bradford 12', as they became known, in April 1982 marked a key moment for the Asian Youth Movement of the late 1970s and 1980s in places like Bradford and Southall (CARF/Southall Rights, 1981) where 'self-defence' became a *motif* among Asian young people faced with racist violence. However, unlike today, Asian young people then sought and won wide political alliances and support for their actions.

The third period from the early 1990s involved policing racist violence producing among other things a marked increase in the reporting and recording of Asian on white racial incidents (Webster, 1995, 1996, 2002; FitzGerald, 2001). The policing of public order situations in which the police have been pitted against groups of 'rioting' Asian males marks the recent and current period. Each period constituted a particular relationship to the police as governors, arbiters and enforcers of public order and marked a shift in that relationship. The recent periods are discussed below.

Between blacks and whites: evidence on the policing of Asians

Studies from the 1970s to the present appear to show that when Asians come into contact with the police whether as victims or witnesses, when they report crime, seek information, or as suspects, their position in terms of the treatment they receive and their perceptions and experiences of the police tends to fall between those of blacks and whites or are similar to whites, with African/Caribbeans receiving the worst treatment and being most hostile to the police. When we turn to criminal justice outcomes, although there has been an 80 per cent increase in the South Asian male prison population compared to an increase of a third for white males and a doubling of African/ Caribbean males between 1985 and 1999. Among Asians this increase began from a low base when Asian males were underrepresented in prison compared to their numbers in the general population. Currently the Asian prison population is proportional to their numbers in the general population (from 2 to 3 per cent over the period). What is particularly significant though is the doubling of Muslim, particularly British Pakistani, prisoners between 1990 and 1999 (Bowling and Phillips, 2002; Desai, 1999; Home Office, 2000a).

Attitudes towards the police, whether derived from direct or indirect contact with them, are different between white, black and Asian. Waddington and Braddock (1991) found that 'cultural attitudes towards the police' varied in that both white and Asian groups of young people contained those who viewed the police as either trusted guardians of law and order or bullies whereas the study's black sample almost exclusively regarded the police as 'bullies' in uniform. These two fundamentally different conceptions of what the police are – their role and function in society as either trustworthy and efficient or epitomised in terms of arbitrary authority and racial discrimination – arise from the ways in which the police are viewed in using their discretion as impartially administered and thus conferring institutional authority or not. We are nevertheless left wondering why black compared to other young people came to reject police authority.

Gordon (1983) concluded that although there was a strong perception within particularly African/Caribbean neighbourhoods that they were 'over-policed' (i.e. harassed and subject to racist abuse and brutality by the police), this was much less the case among Asians including Asian young people. Other national and local studies of attitudes towards the police (Southgate and Ekblom, 1984; Jones et al., 1986; Painter, 1989; Mayhew et al., 1989; Crawford et al., 1990; Skogan, 1990a; Southgate and Crisp, 1992; Jefferson and Walker, 1992; Mayhew et al., 1993; Aye Maung, 1995; Smith and Gray, 1983; Sims and Myhill, 2001; Home Office, 2001a) in different contexts of contact have consistently found that either Asians disapprove less of the police than African/Caribbeans or whites, or tend to hold views which place them between African/Caribbeans and whites in their disapproval ratings, although some studies lump Asian and African/Caribbean together and take insufficient account of age and few disaggregate 'Asian'. Similarly Asians were less likely to believe that police misconduct occurred frequently compared to whites and African/Caribbeans.

Studies of police-initiated contact can permit inferences to be made about police attitudes towards and different treatment of minority ethnic groups (Bowling and Phillips, 2002; Landau and Nathan, 1983; Gordon, 1984; FitzGerald and Sibbitt, 1997; Phillips and Brown, 1998; Bucke and Brown, 1997). Overall, Asians were stopped and searched by the police to a lesser extent than blacks, but more than whites. However, the most common reason for searching black and Asian people is for drugs, and taking account of wide variation between police force areas, the latter were more likely to be stopped for this reason than any other group (Home Office, 2000c). Arrest rates for Asians were generally greater than for white people but below that for black people although this varies according to their representation in the local population and the location of the police station (Phillip and Brown, 1998). Of those arrested, whites and Asians experience similar cautioning rates, higher than for blacks, although some studies have found that Asians were significantly less likely to be cautioned than white suspects (Phillips and Brown, 1998). Black and Asian people are over-represented in arrests for fraud and forgery and drugs (Home Office, 2000c).

Summarising other aspects of police processes, both blacks and

Asians are more likely to seek legal advice and less likely to admit the offence for which they have been arrested compared to whites, there is some evidence of a more punitive police response towards black and Asian juveniles for certain offences including public order and violence against the person offences, blacks and Asians were less likely to be cautioned than whites and both black and Asian suspects are more likely to be refused bail compared with white suspects. However, black suspects were significantly more likely to be remanded – held at the police station prior to court – than either white or Asian suspects. Finally, although there is little doubt that immigration policing under the 1971 Immigration Act has historically been 'a major source of suspicion and mistrust between the police and minority communities' (Bowling and Phillips, 2002: 130; see Gordon, 1984) its effects on established British Asian communities is likely to have waned after successively restrictive immigration and nationality legislation, albeit now retargeted to other groups such as asylum seekers.

Although concern exists in respect of stop and search, particularly in relation to drug searches, and more punitive treatment of some Asian juveniles after arrest, the general picture is unclear about whether racial discrimination or different treatment of Asians on grounds of race or ethnicity is as significant for Asians as it has been for Africans/ Caribbeans. A clearer picture may emerge when studies begin to disaggregate 'Asians', particularly Pakistanis and Bangladeshis living in poor neighbourhoods, and particularly those affected by the disorders in Bradford in 1995, Oldham, Burnley and Bradford in spring and summer 2001 and elsewhere (see Desai, 1999; Alexander, 2000a, 2000b; Webster, 1996, 1997, 2002). It is likely, though, that earlier studies are out of date and that since the mid-1990s police racism towards Asians may have intensified in the context of recent disorders and growing anti-Muslim feeling (see Miles and Brown, 2003).

Asian fear of crime, offending, victimisation and policing

The disorders of June 1995 involving large numbers of Asian young men in the Manningham area of Bradford were triggered when two police officers intervened against a 'noisy group' of young Asian men playing football in the street, entered a house and allegedly knocked down an Asian women in a struggle, during which three young men were arrested (Bradford Commission, 1996). The report of a local community organisation concluded that the disorders occurred in the context of a 'severe loss of confidence in the police' and provocative and unreasonable police action (Foundation 2000, 1995). Unlike the Bradford disorders of 2001 the 1995 disorders were at the time widely seen to be primarily anti-police riots. My own inquiries of participants and local observers, although anecdotal, supported this view but in a paradoxical way. Curiously, Asian young men claimed that the police had for years tolerated and neglected high levels of prostitution, street drunkenness, rowdiness and abusive and intimidating behaviour by whites coming into the area from outside, all of which were deemed an affront to the mostly British Muslim Pakistani and Bangladeshi populations living there. Despite or because of the occurrence of public disorder their resentment towards the police seemed to rest on a perception of them as being unable or unwilling to maintain order and civility on the street or address their concerns about crime.

Their particular concern to protect Asian women from affronts to public morality and propriety was perhaps perversely linked with the action that had sparked off the disorders, which in their eyes demonstrated disrespect among police officers towards Asian women. Somehow this was also linked with the inability or refusal of police officers to rid the area of street prostitution, which they themselves were doing as vigilantes driving prostitutes out of the area. Indeed many of the latter have since left the area.[2] Moreover, there is evidence that considerable 'white flight' or 'fright' has occurred (Webster, 2002) in part, according to anecdotal evidence, because white and black women living in the area have been perceived as prostitutes and harassed by some Asian young men. Regardless, the imagery is unmistakeably that of high levels of distrust and hostility towards the police and their ability to tackle incivility in the area.

As well as acting as proxies for adult concerns and anxieties about crime there is plentiful evidence that young people suffer a heightened sense of defending their areas against perceived threats from without while at the same time this reinforces ethnic and other forms of identity within areas. At the same time young people experience a heightened fear of certain places or people which reflects their higher rates of everyday violence and crime compared to adults, although this varies according to age, gender and ethnicity (Suttles, 1968; Anderson et al., 1994; Aye Maung, 1995; Hartless et al., 1995; Brown, 1994a, 1994b, 1995a, 1995b; Loader, 1996; Webster, 1995; Pain, 2003). Whether as young people or adults, Asians, particularly British Pakistanis and Bangladeshis, suffer greater risks of victimisation than any other group (FitzGerald and Hale, 1996; Percy, 1998; Kershaw et al., 2000). It has become a criminological orthodoxy that the victimisation of young people is ignored or not taken seriously by the police and other adults whereas their offending behaviour is exaggerated. What then is the situation of Asian young people?

The Keighley study (Webster, 1995) was undertaken in the period leading to the 1995 Bradford disorders and was of an adjoining town. It asked young people about their fear of crime, victim experiences and offending, and was predicated on a *belief* among local agencies and the police that offending among young Asian males was increasing. It surveyed 412 13–19-year-old males and females, 7 per cent of the white and 10 per cent of the Asian age group living in the town. Many of those surveyed, both white and Asian, had – or their families had – been victims of crime with a third of the Asian and white sample having been victims of crime. Among Asians 37 per cent had experienced personal violence and 40 per cent vehicle damage; among whites 62 per cent had experienced personal violence, a third had their family's vehicle stolen and a third had a vehicle deliberately damaged. A third of the Asian males and 40 per cent of white males said they had experienced racial violence and a similar percentage of Asians to whites – over 60 per cent – had experienced racial insults. It would be mistaken to underestimate the influence of these levels of cumulative violence and abuse on young people's fear of people and places (see Butler, 1997). Fears and anxieties occasioned by such incidents were reflected in young people's 'fear of crime' and the ways in which they identified crime as the main 'problem' in the area. Although both white and Asian young people reported high levels of worry about crime, the latter were particularly worried about crime and becoming victims of crime. Most marked was the ways in which they took precautions when going out, restricted their journeys after dark and avoided certain areas compared to whites.

Although nearly two-thirds of Asian victims of crime and 43 per cent of Asian victims of racial violence had reported or someone on their behalf had reported their victimisation to the police, in only 18 per cent of cases of racial violence had the police apprehended a suspect compared to a 100 per cent apprehension rate when the victim was white. It is difficult to infer the obvious conclusion because too few whites reported racial incidents to the police. Generally whites were more satisfied than Asians with how individual officers treated them with a third of Asians saying that they were dissatisfied and half that they were very dissatisfied with the way the police had dealt with the problem. Nevertheless half of Asians stated that they knew the community police officers in their area, which they said had an effective presence and thought that they had a good understanding of the problems in the area. This is partly accounted for by the leisure involvement of Community Officers with Asian young people through a large local youth work project.

In respect of self-reported offending many (mostly males) had offended although the majority of this offending was not serious and was occasional. Rates of offending among Asian young men was found to be very significantly lower than for white young men across most offences, a finding supported by other self-report studies (Graham and Bowling, 1995). However, a group of persistent and serious offenders was found both within the Asian and white samples although it was proportionally smaller among Asians compared to whites.

The survey suggested that Asian young people perceive the police as unlikely to be sympathetic to them as victims. Yet they were also more worried about becoming victims of crime and were more likely to report their victimisation. Does the same 'vicious circle' of victimisation and reporting apply to Asian young people as that uncovered by Anderson et al.'s (1994) Edinburgh study of white young people? Which is the important factor here, youth or ethnicity? Young people generally are reluctant to report their victimisation to adults or the police. Instead they employ peer support as a means of security, self-reliance and self-defence that relies on the 'solidarity' of those it protects (loyalty and not 'grassing'). To 'break with this is to threaten the whole basis of the strategy – and with it the personal and collective safety of all' (Anderson et al., 1994: 152). The consequence is that in developing their own strategies for coping with crime and policing in an attempt to reduce the impact that crime has on them without reference to the adult world, young people risk exacerbating and inflating its importance. At the same time a 'vicious circle' is set in train whereby because young people are not taken seriously by adults or the police, or are even held in some way responsible for their victimisation, they do not report, their victimisation remains hidden, adult and police incredulity increases, the police are deprived of the information they require to successfully investigate crime, and faced with this situation, the police are left to resort to the very adversarial methods that contributed to this lack of information in the first place (Anderson et al., 1994: 158). Loader (1996) has noted this vicious circle effect, adding that the frequency with which the police move on young people is matched only by the rarity with which young people call the police as victims of crime. When evidence that the police consider young people in public places as their 'property' (Reiner, 2000), judge them in terms of respectability and ethnicity, question and apprehend them on suspicion of technical delinquency and generally routinely supervise their use of public space, then the circle is closed (Loader, 1996). One can wonder whether in the eyes of some police officers the relative willingness of Asian compared to white young people to report to them their victimisation itself reinforces police attitudes of disbelief in the veracity or seriousness of Asian young people's experience of crime and racist violence compared to whites. Nevertheless, on balance the processes described by Anderson et al. and Loader are likely to be compounded in a situation where Asian young people feel isolated by white hostility and possess a heightened sense of defensive territorialism (see Webster, 1996).

Although evidence has been available for some time that (some) police officers hold stereotypes of Asians (Cain, 1973; Graef, 1989; Keith, 1993, 1995a, 1995b; Webster, 1997; Desai, 1999; Bowling, 1999), it has not been clear whether these incorporate the *belief* that Asians offend more or less than other groups or offend more than they were thought to have done in the past. Nevertheless, Cain (1973) found that police officers believed that Asians tended to be regarded as devious, liars and potential illegal immigrants, and significantly as a police officer in Graef's (1989: 131, cited in Bowling and Phillips, 2002: 158) study put it: 'That's a problem with Asians: they make so many allegations that are totally a pack of lies'. Hitherto low levels of offending among Asians (see Rees et al., 1979; Stevens and Willis, 1979) were explained by virtue of strong informal controls said to inhere in 'Asian culture and family life' creating a criminological and police consensus about the law-abiding nature of 'Asians' (see Webster, 1997). For example, Mawby and Batta (1980) argued that offender rates among Asians were much lower than would be expected given the high crime rates of comparable deprived groups (working class, poor, inner city, etc.), and that this was because of the cultural strengths of Asian communities. Moreover, contemporaneous research on young Asians (Anwar, 1976; Brah, 1978), despite discovery of cultural stress and conflict between the generations, seemed to confirm this view. Wardak (2000) in a more sophisticated and focused study examined the decisive influence of community institutions in the Edinburgh Pakistani community in discouraging or controlling deviance and delinquency, cultural institutions that paradoxically had grown in importance in the face of white hostility and high levels of deprivation.

Webster (1997; also see Keith, 1993, 1995a, 1995b; Desai, 1999) has argued, however, that there has grown a tide of both local and national media and police portrayals of Asians, particularly young Asian males, as disproportionately involved in drugs, crime and public disorder. These representations provided the stage on which public discourse about the alleged involvement of Asians in lawlessness changed.

Through community consultation between the police and community elders and/or 'representatives' parental anxieties about indiscipline and a loss of authority and control over young people found expression in the collusion of police and elders to create an impression of growing lawlessness. An ultimately colonial ideology of 'Asianness' as embodying *both* deference/order *and* deviousness/disorder, and a disillusionment with an idealised view of Asian family and communal life in the face of racist violence and social and demographic change, had served to 'construct British Asian criminality' in the minds of the public, the police, the Asian parent culture and increasingly white young people as Asians increasingly defended themselves against racist violence. The historical link between Asian and white colonial memories and the present is discontinuous and complex. Colonial traditions of policing, especially in 'oriental' India where governance relied on 'inviting' the colonised, who were supposed to police themselves, to collaborate with the colonisers, cannot be reduced to simple brutality and exploitation (see Lea, 2002; Cashmore and McLaughlin, 1991; Said, 1991, 1993; Schwartz, 2002; Hall, 2002; James, 1997). Nevertheless there *is* a sense in which police (and Asian) idealisation of Asian culture[3] and its supposed strengths has led to the expectation that Asians police themselves in the face of the risks of victimisation and criminality associated with modernity, creating the perverse and unintended consequences described here.

Policing 'Asian' youth: racist violence, drugs, disorder and public space

The immediate events leading to the serious public disorders that took place in Oldham, Burnley and Bradford in spring and summer 2001 appeared to be a confused series of well publicised violent 'racist' clashes and attacks against people and property involving Asian and white young people. The context was a climate of fear and rumour within Asian communities that the British National Party (BNP) and/or the National Front (NF) were going to march into Asian areas despite banning orders authorised by the Home Secretary. The NF had visited Oldham from all parts of the country to demonstrate their 'support of the white population against racist attacks', and the relative electoral success of the BNP in Oldham and Burnley (OMBC and GMP, 2001; Clark, 2001) seemed to affirm significant support for ideological racism. The overall effect was to alert Asian and white young people to the possibility of being attacked and the need to defend themselves and in some cases attack others. I have attempted to analyse the contexts, conditions and causes of the disorders and official responses to them elsewhere (Webster, 2003). Here I want to focus on the policing dimension and implications for the policing of Asian communities.

Official local and national reviews and reports on the disorders (Ouseley, 2001; Ritchie, 2001; Clark, 2001; Cantle, 2002; Denham, 2002) were generally uncritical of the police in terms of either any historical role they might have played or in their operational handling of the events themselves. Indeed the police were mostly praised for their actions in what were very difficult circumstances for them. In Bradford alone 326 police officers were injured (Denham, 2002). Nevertheless, Denham (2002: 12) conceded that there were 'weaknesses and disparity in the police response to community issues, particularly racial incidents.' He also noted that 'the approach taken and the quality of policing that ethnic minorities experienced varied across the country' (2002: 18). Significantly, and consistent with the argument begun in the previous section, most of the reports emphasised that their consultation with local Asian communities had revealed that most people, including young people, want the police to be more evident on the street and have a stronger and more visible role. Local perceptions were that the police had tolerated virtual 'no-go areas' in respect of tackling drugs by colluding with non-intervention in relation to inner-city drug sale and use on the street, and had underestimated the extent to which 'low-level' persistent offences and harassment creates fear of crime and lack of public safety. Meanwhile it was felt that Asian young men in gangs remained untouchable (Cantle, 2002; Ouseley, 2001). Indeed the police report and inquiry into the Burnley disorders argued that drug-related criminality within an Asian and a white group rather than racism sparked the disorders (Clark, 2001).

This recurring theme in the policing of inner-city Asian communities – that in effect they are under-policed rather than over-policed and that the police seem unwilling or unable to enforce the law against prostitution, drug dealing, anti-social behaviour and low-level per-sistent offending – sits uneasily alongside perceptions of the inadequacy of police responses to racist violence (see Bowling, 1999) and the punitive criminalisation of large numbers of Asian young men involved in the disorders. In terms of policing policy Cantle (2002) asserts that minority communities must face the fact that over time the police have adopted a toleration of certain types of criminality. Both Cantle (2002) and Denham (2002) argue that 'policing deeply fragmented communities poses particular challenges' and local com-munities cannot leave that responsibility for law enforcement to the police alone, while at the same time the police require understanding, confidence and support. Finally the reports point to the need for local Crime and Disorder Reduction Partnerships to be effective in reducing crime and fear of crime, that community policing remains central and that officers should engage with disaffected young people and try to develop them as community advocates (a 'youth parliament' has very recently been set up in Bradford).

While it is true that the underlying structural issues that in combination disaffect Asian young people and lead to public disorder cannot be addressed or solved by policing alone, it is still the case that Asian communities lack faith in the police to protect them from threatened or rumoured incursions into their communities by organised racist far-right groups. This lack of confidence results in Asian young people, who 'police' public space, mobilising to defend their areas from real or perceived threats in ways that are clearly disproportionate to the threat posed and can involve criminality. When this spills over into public disorder situations the police become targets because they are perceived to be symbols of white authority. Although belonging to a minority this criminality reinforces within the police perceptions of Asian young people as a 'suspect population' requiring control rather than protection (from racist violence and crime).

Community policing has in the past made profound errors in seeking the views of unrepresentative adult 'community leaders', while ignoring the views of a wider constituency including young people. It was the 'Bradford Race Review' carried out by Sir Herman Ouseley (2001), which set the agenda for how the disorders came to be understood, that pointed to the existence of self-styled and un-representative 'community leaders' who encourage segregation and fear to maintain their power base. Ouseley (2001: 1) argues that there are growing divisions along race, ethnic and social class lines noting 'the very worrying drift towards self-segregation' in a city that apparently 'now finds itself in the grip of fear'. According to Ouseley growing ethnic segregation is partly fuelled by 'self-segregation' based on fear of racist harassment and violent crime, and partly by the promotion and protection of identities and cultures. Examining detailed socio-economic, ethnic, demographic, housing, crime and racist violence data from Oldham, Burnley and Bradford, Webster (2003: 1) concurred with some essential features of this argument arguing that:

> Increasing spatial concentration and segregation within and between working class Pakistani, Bangladeshi and white

communities in the North of England creates a concentration and combination of risks associated with relative deprivation, racist violence, crime and disorder. This development has generated a specific fortress mentality and geography of fear within these communities.

However, he criticised the notion that 'self-segregation' was 'chosen', being more a result of historically inherited constraints on housing choice. Nevertheless, policing can be an important factor in alleviating or at least not exacerbating the more pernicious effects of segregation. After all, Bangladeshi and Pakistani populations live in some of the most multiply deprived and ethnically and socially isolated communities in Britain.

An example of policing Asian communities in Oldham will suffice to bring out some of the complex and pressing policing issues connected to the disorders (see Webster, 2003 for more detail). Oldham stands out in a number of respects compared to other police divisions in Greater Manchester. Firstly, high and increasing rates of crime, especially violent crime, and disorder are concentrated in or are adjacent to areas of growing ethnic concentration and segregation with the highest rates of unemployment and social and economic disadvantage (OMBC, 1999). Oldham has the third highest crime rate for violence against the person in Greater Manchester (OMBC, 2001a). Secondly, it has seen the largest increases in reported racist incidents and, against national trends, the biggest proportion of recorded racially motivated offences have been violent ones with the town having the highest rate of these incidents of all ten local authority districts in Greater Manchester (OMBC, 2001a; GMP, 2000). Thirdly, the majority of victims were white whereas in every other Greater Manchester division the majority were Asian, although 72 per cent of repeat victims were Asian and twice as many perpetrators were white than were Asian. Although more recently half of victims were white and half Asian, of those involving violence 60 per cent of victims were white and 40 per cent Asian. The issue in Oldham thus seems to be the willingness of whites to report incidents against them they perceive as racist and identify the *suspect* as Asian (GMP, 2000), reflecting a perception among whites of an increase in violent attacks upon them by groups of Asians and among the latter that certain areas and housing estates are 'no-go areas' for them.

There is a clearly a pressing need in Oldham to police poor communities generally and racist violence in particular in more effective ways. For example, in response to the *Oldham Independent Review* on the Oldham disorders, Brian Holland (2001: 4), who is Force Race Advisor for Greater Manchester Police (GMP), stated that '... policing takes place in a socio-economic context which is determined by forces and factors largely beyond GMP's direct control' but that nevertheless the policing of locations like Glodwick (where the disorders took place) necessarily requires 'care, attention and sensitivity'. This is fair comment because it grasps the context of policing Asian communities as well as the responsibilities of the police. This context is that racist hostility joins with other factors such as the availability and afford-ability of housing in trapping ethnic and social groups within a new form of poverty, that of geographical immobility. Northern British Pakistani and Bangladeshi populations in particular are increasingly spatially concentrated and segregated in socially excluded areas faced by violence, crime and public disorder. As Modood (1992) and Modood and Berthoud (1997) have argued, social exclusion affecting 'Asians' needs to be disaggregated, and the real divide in terms of economic success and social mobility is between Indians and Sunni Muslims (primarily of Pakistani and Bangladeshi origin).

Conclusion

Combining Ouseley's (2001: 18) examination of factors within and without Bradford Asian communities that have 'fuelled the drift towards segregation, the formation of ghettoes and comfort zones', with evidence presented here, we can begin to see the emergence of not only 'comfort zones' but of novel 'contact zones' (see Hall, 2002) between the police and British Asian communities. These contact zones risk becoming places where at least in part a colonial memory, legacy or nostalgia loaded with racial and ethnic meaning can become played out on the street. Perceptions and resentments among whites and police officers of a supposed 'Islamisation' of areas previously denoting positive qualities such as 'law and order' now connote negative qualities of 'crime, drugs and disorder'. This repositioning of Asian communities and their contact with the police has become a question of power and (loss of?) control. This division or separation of 'good/bad, docile/hostile', non-criminal and criminal (Webster, 1997; Desai, 1999; Hall, 2002; Schwartz, 2002) projected onto Asian communities has and will continue to take place. So far, however, the evidence is mixed about the significance of such change and what the consequences might be.

In part this will depend on contingent and pragmatic issues of police recruitment, perception, operational policy and events, and the balance and mixture of 'hard and soft policing' employed to address contradictory and conflicting demands and criticisms of them. Following the disorders hundreds of Asian young men have received 'punitive' and 'disproportionate' sentences for riot of between four and six years (*The Guardian*, 27 August 2002), men of whom it is said '…gave themselves up, pleaded guilty, had no previous convictions and took good character references to court …' (*The Guardian*, 31 August 2002), and whose pleas that they were engaged in acts of self-defence are rejected by the courts (*The Guardian*, 11 September 2002). Meanwhile the police campaign to recruit Asian officers and the current government talks of 'social cohesion' (Denham, 2002).

At one level whether young Asian men are stopped and searched by the police and generally targeted in greater numbers, especially for drugs, will partly depend on changes in the law and local police policies towards enforcing drug laws (see Kalunta-Crumpton, 1999). At another British Pakistani and Bangladeshi populations are seeing a demographic explosion in the proportion of young men in the age range of peak offending compared to whites and other ethnic groups in a situation of narrowing employment opportunities for this relatively unqualified and unskilled group (Webster, 2003). Overall, the real concern is that the disorders will predispose police officers to make unfounded generalisations about Asian young people as having a predilection to collective violence, and that evidence will be found in high or growing levels of racist and other violence in the context of a demonisation of Islam and an association of Muslim identity with terrorism and disorder. For their part appropriations and interpretations of Islamic identity among some young people may lead to a heightening of a disaffected and embattled sense of collective identity joined with the adoption of masculinist aggressive forms of resolving conflict and dispute found in poor white working-class areas (Desai, 1999; Alexander, 2000b; see Johnston et al., 2000). At the same time Asians living in poor areas are demanding more not less law and order.

A nostalgic and mythical view of the past that projected qualities of internal informal control and order upon 'traditional' white working-class communities in the face of fragmenting modernity (Lea, 2002) has been reworked to apply to the supposed unifying and ordering qualities and values of honour, respectability and prestige (*izzat*) and common socio-economic, geographic kinship (*biraderi*) and caste (*quom*) provenance said to reside in 'traditional' working-class Asian communities. These 'guarantees' apparently no longer apply. In a post-colonial and post Lawrence policing climate police racism *may* have subsided but, as Chan's (1997) study has shown in a different national context, in this respect police reform is fraught with difficulties and can easily be overtaken by events. Miles and Brown (2003) have demonstrated how different forms of racism and the groups targeted by racism change over time and according to context. As Choongh (1997) has argued negative attitudes to poorer minority ethnic areas can lead to aggressive and antagonistic policing strategies that discipline particular segments of the population legitimised in terms of the maintenance of public order, although Johnston (2000: 51) argues that late modern policing combines this disciplinary function with 'policing communities of risk'. Change in the policing of British Asian communities can be characterised as towards a bifurcated approach involving attempts at managing their social integration and 'social cohesion' on the one hand and disciplining and 'distancing' these 'risky groups' on the other.

Notes

1 Bowling and Phillips (2002: 129) amply illustrate the source of this hostility citing pervasive, ongoing targeting of black areas involving 'stopping vehicles "often on a flimsy pretext", persistent stop and search on the streets, commonplace rude and hostile questioning accompanied by racial abuse, arbitrary arrest, violence on arrest, the arrest of witnesses and bystanders, punitive and indiscriminate attacks, victimisation on reporting crime, acting on false information, forced entry and violence, provocative and unnecessary armed raids, and repeated harassment and trawling for suspects.'
2 The Manningham area of Bradford had been the city's 'red light district' for decades and the policing of prostitution raises complex issues. Nevertheless, if such street trade were to be concentrated in a white middle-class rather than ethnically mixed inner-city area residents would insist that the police eradicate it.
3 The whole notion that ethnicity and ethnic difference necessarily equates with different, stable and homogenous culture needs to be challenged (see Barry, 2001).

Chapter 6

Discipline and flourish: probation and the new correctionalism

Paul Sparrow and David Webb

Introduction

It is doubtful that the probation service can continue to claim the exclusive right to be the 'welfare arm' of the criminal justice system. The intellectual, political and professional challenge to the therapeutic discourse that served as the overarching justification for probation's existence during the middle decades of the twentieth century has brought into question, more sharply than ever, the 'traditional' framework adopted by probation officers in their day-to-day contact with offenders.

This chapter explores the issue of enforcement in its historical context and in doing so documents the new contours of probation practice in the twenty-first century. In particular, we show that the recent reconfiguration of the probation service around a much more clearly defined correctionalist orientation has its routes in earlier phases of probation practice. While enforcement is generally understood as a function of the modernisation programme, archival material shows that issues of control have long been an important feature of probation supervision, certainly in the postwar era. In charting the demise of traditional social work methodologies we show how the 'routinisation' of supervision has the potential to reduce the probation officer to little more than a criminal justice functionary. In reducing probation supervision to a series of bureaucratic compliances, we suggest that the power of the probation officer to individualise and contextualise the offender has been significantly curtailed. At a time when faith in the crime-reducing qualities of the probation service is in the ascendancy, we question whether the current approach to enforcement is compatible with our present understanding of what works with offenders.

Probation in a time of tolerance

In the fifteen years following the end of the Second World War the probation service made significant advances in establishing its professional credibility (McWilliams, 1985, 1986; May, 1991). Its right of access to the court process continued to distinguish the profession from the general body of social work (McWilliams, 1981) and its expansion and subsequent success in the field of matrimonial dispute served to strengthen yet further its relationship with the judiciary (Page, 1992). In the face of a rising prison population the process of professionally supervised alternatives to imprisonment appeared to offer an antidote to Britain's embryonic penal crisis. So enticing was the prospect of an expanded role for the probation service that Radzinowicz (1958: x) described in euphoric tones the development of probation as '... the most significant contribution made by this country to the new penological theory and practice'.

The Committee on the Social Services in the Courts of Summary Jurisdiction (1936) and the subsequent Criminal Justice Bill (1938) had formally validated the worth of probation. Many of the committee's recommendations, particularly those concerned with the desirability of training, stood to establish probation work as a profession, and certainly as an occupation for which entrants trained rather than a vocation to which people were called (LeMesurier, 1935; Home Office, 1936; McWilliams, 1985). The declaration of war had, however, delayed any action on the 1938 Bill and despite the substantial escalation in crime rates it was not until 1948 that Britain witnessed legislative implementation of the prewar proposals (Bochel, 1976).

The Criminal Justice Act 1948 effectively resurrected and subsequently implemented many of the issues and recommendations proffered some twelve years earlier. In repealing all previous legislation the new Act has, not unreasonably, been credited with establishing the structure of the contemporary probation service (Bochel, 1976; Page, 1992; Nellis, 2001). In restating the powers of the courts as they related to community sentencing, together with explicit statements concerning the duties of officers, particularly the extension of responsibility for the after-care of prisoners (McWilliams, 1981), the 1948 Act sought to establish a stronger and more elaborate system for the administration of the service (May, 1991). This then was to be the 'golden age' of probation (Page, 1992).

Confirmation of the importance of the probation service's role and perhaps more crucially recognition of its professional status within the administration of criminal justice was to be found in the report of the Morrison Committee (Home Office, 1962: para. 54): 'today the probation officer must be seen, essentially, as a professional caseworker, employing, in a specialist field, a skill which he holds in common with other social workers ...' In recognising the rapidity of change both for the criminal justice system as a whole and for the probation service in particular, the Committee noted the likelihood of ever greater demands being placed on the service in the years to come. In identifying the point of sentence as the critical juncture in the penal process, the Committee reaffirmed the importance of the service's role in the provision of reliable information to the courts (Home Office, 1962) and, of equal importance, affirmed the probation officer as a skilled caseworker. It was this medium which would, ultimately, legitimate the service's claim to professional competence (McWilliams, 1986).

While history quite understandably regards the Morrison Report as the official endorsement of the therapeutic approach to working with offenders, far less is generally made of the Committee's focus on the probation officer as officer of the court:

> It must be added that while, as a caseworker, the probation officer's prime concern is with the well being of an individual, he is also the agent of a system concerned with the protection of society and as such must, to a degree which varies from case to case and during the course of supervision, seek to regulate the probationer's behaviour. (Home Office, 1962: para. 54)

The committee recognised that under certain circumstances the probation officer would be expected to bring to bear the full weight of this authority. The probation officer must, they reported, '... be prepared, when necessary, to assert the interests of society by initiating proceedings for breach of the requirements of the probation order' (ibid.). While recognising the social work foundation of the probation officer's role the Committee noted that the coercive element of the relationship between officer and offender distinguished the probation officer from social workers in other fields. The Committee made no apology for drawing this distinction and went so far as to suggest that the term 'client', traditionally used to describe users of social work assistance, served only to misrepresent the nature of the supervisory relationship. In this respect the Committee considered the term to be '... inappropriate since it obscures the disciplinary aspect of probation by suggesting that the offender's approach to the social worker is wholly voluntary' (ibid.: para. 56). The term, they concluded, ought to be avoided.

Not withstanding the fact that the history of the probation service in the postwar era, and certainly up until the 1970s, has been portrayed traditionally as the period embodying professional discretion, the assumption that 'care' equated to the abandonment of enforcement would be a fallacy. Figures for the 1960s, for example, show the percentage of male probationers who had their order terminated either because contact was lost or because supervision became 'impracticable' increased marginally throughout the decade from 1.8 per cent in 1961 to 2.0 per cent in 1970. Interestingly, the numbers for women in the same period were, on average, approximately one percentage point higher (Haxby, 1978). Although by modern standards these figures are relatively modest (currently breach rates for Community Rehabilitation Orders, previously known as Probation Orders, run at around 7 per cent), they nevertheless confirm that at a time when the casework model was at its height, probation officers did return their probationers to court. These figures become all the more enlightening when we consider that prior to the implementation of the Criminal Justice Act 1991 and the introduction of National Standards, breach action was a matter for the officer's own discretion.

For the probation officer then, the duality of the casework model and their duty to act on behalf of the courts often made for a difficult reconciliation. The coercion implicit, and for that matter explicit, in a court order might well be regarded as the very antithesis of the casework model, emphasising as it does a non-judgemental attitude and a non-directive approach (Oldfield, 2002). However, as McWilliams (1985) points out, the model was often far from an equal partnership between officer and probationer. Since offenders rarely had an insight into the nature of their 'real problems', they often needed to be 'worked on' rather than 'worked with'. The nature of the casework relationship, certainly as it applied to probation, was thus redefined and the power imbalance justified on the grounds that it would, in the long term, work in the best interests of the probationer.

It is clear that in both official reports and in daily practice, the issue of enforcement was something that occupied both the service and the Home Office alike. How then did probation officers and the service to which they belonged square the mantra of 'advising, assisting and befriending' with their duty to act on behalf of the criminal courts?

Ultimately, reconciliation, if it were needed, was to be found in a particular understanding of the authority role. As Timms (1966: 135) notes, '... the exercise of authority is tempered by the discretion allowed to the officer and by his concern to use his authorized powers for his client's benefit'. 'Control' therefore is reconceptualised as concern and thus incorporated into the more generalised and palatable spirit of 'care'. In his elaboration of the casework approach Timms (1966: 136) provides a useful illustration of 'control' as 'care'. The example concerns a young woman in breach of probation for failing to report as instructed:

> In the interview after the hearing Grace was her old withdrawn self. The officer suggested that Grace had not really believed that she would be brought back to court. Grace said nothing. The officer said that it might look as if they were back at the beginning again, but Grace knew really that she was not a frightening giant person (giants had figured in more recent drawings), though she did mean what she said. *She had brought Grace back before the court because what happened to Grace mattered to her*. Grace smiled slightly. (Emphasis added)

According to Timms (1966), therefore, for the probation officer's authority to be legitimate it must be driven by benevolence and unfettered by unnecessarily strict rules of supervision – in essence the probation officer is engaged in a form of 'tough love'.

The proposition that a particular course of action is in the best interests of the offender provides the ultimate defence against the most coercive aspects of probation practice. In the decades that followed, however, two issues would serve to challenge the prominence of the casework model. First, the presumption that professional discretion enhanced the supervisory relationship would be called into question (Bean, 1976; Bottoms and McWilliams, 1979). As the weight of empirical evidence gradually undermined the efficacy of the rehabilitative model the professional competence of the probation officer, so clearly endorsed by the Morrison Report, would be brought into doubt. Second, the desire of probation officers to conceal the controlling aspects of their work under a veil of care would come to be regarded as counterproductive to the public image of the service. Ironically, the coercive aspects of the probation officer's role, which the service had endeavoured to moderate with the provision of care and assistance, would thereafter serve as their new *raison d'être*.

Diversion from custody: probation in a time of transition

Based solely on the accumulation of research evidence, the probation service at the beginning of the 1980s seemed to have a precarious future. The predilection of the service to treat offenders 'kindly' had been proved to be ineffective in reducing crime and certainly out of kilter with a general governmental inclination to roll back the frontiers of the welfare state. Politically the service was seen as being '... committed to "soft" social work values ...' (Mair, 1997: 1002) and organisationally at odds with the newly elected Conservative government's view about the purpose of the penal system (Sparrow, Brooks and Webb, 2002). If a wholesale dismantling of the probation service was mooted as a theoretical possibility in some quarters (Croft, 1978), most accepted that this was neither a desirable nor realistic option. In reviewing the penal posturing that came to characterise the 1980s Garland (1989: 4) observed the dilemma which beset the government:

> For a decade now this administration has associated itself with a penal policy rhetoric which is punitive, hard-line and avowedly tough on crime, but ministers are also aware that the financial and political costs of fully implementing this rhetoric are unacceptably high.

From the mid-1970s onwards the Home Office (1977) had begun to officially acknowledge the necessity of reducing the burgeoning prison population (see Advisory Council on the Penal System, 1977, 1978) and certainly throughout the 1980s it was this preoccupation which would serve to construct a new relationship between the Home Office and the probation service. The Criminal Justice Act 1982 had already begun the process of transforming the probation order into a credible alternative to custody through the provision of additional requirements (Raynor, 1988). The issuing, subsequently, of the Statement of National Objectives and Priorities (SNOP) (Home Office, 1984) served to finally clarify the role of the probation service in the proposed decarcerative enterprise. According to SNOP the overriding priority for the service was '... to ensure that, wherever possible, offenders can be dealt with by non-custodial measures ...' (Home Office, 1984: 5). All other activities not directed to this end, through-care and civil work in particular, would thereafter receive resources sufficient only to meet the minimum statutory requirements of the service. With the re-habilitative ideal officially in decline, diversion from custody offered a new purpose for the probation service, albeit one which was driven much more by the economics of punishment than a belief in the capacity of one individual to affect change in another (McWilliams, 1987; McWilliams and Pease, 1990).

As a sentiment, the prospect of diverting offenders from custody had much to commend itself to the traditionalists within the service. Indeed, the idea that prison represents an inappropriate response to much offending goes to the very core of the probation service's values and purpose. However, as McWilliams (1987) points out, the rationale for promoting the benefits of community-based supervision during the 1980s differed markedly from the justifications proffered during earlier stages of the probation service's development. According to McWilliams (1983, 1985, 1986) the service is to be understood by reference to two earlier periods of development. The first, taking place from the 1870s through to the 1930s, he describes as 'special pleading'. Here the probation service's purpose is to save the souls of offenders through kindly guidance and the spirit of God. During the second phase (1930s–1970s), the period of 'diagnosis', the service leaves behind its theological foundations in favour of 'curing' offenders of their 'psycho-social ills' via the medium of social casework. Although forged from radically different understandings of criminality, the respective phases of 'special pleading' and 'social diagnosis' are unified by an overarching purpose, namely the provision of an individualised response to the perceived needs of the offender with the sole intention of bringing about a cessation in their future criminality.

In this third phase, 'pragmatism', the service continues with its historical legacy of providing supervised alternatives to custody, but this venture is undertaken without '... any transcendental *justification* ...' (McWilliams, 1987: 114, original italics). The service ceases to legitimate itself with claims of rehabilitative efficacy and instead becomes an integral part of a government-led strategy which aims to distribute offenders throughout the range of court disposals. Thereafter, suitability for probation intervention is based not on an assessment of need, but rather on tariff position.

While in practical terms SNOP achieved only marginal success as probation regions effectively usurped the Home Office's drive for uniformity with a range of locally agreed priorities (Lloyd, 1986), the document nevertheless gave a very clear signal concerning the future direction of the probation service. In the years following SNOP the criminal justice community was witness to a multitude of policy papers (Home Office, 1988, 1990a, 1990b, 1991a) which both reaffirmed the government's pledge to reduce the prison population and placed the probation service at the centre of this enterprise. Notwithstanding political inclination, the availability of community-based sanctions does not in itself provide a guarantee that the prevailing judicial preference for imprisonment will be displaced. Certainly in part this is because alternatives to custody are rarely used in that way, but rather become alternatives to other alternatives (Cohen, 1985; Raynor, 1988). As Garland (1989) quite rightly observes, welfare-based approaches to offending in Britain have tended to be directed at minor or first-time offenders, a one-off opportunity not to be repeated in the event of the offender not taking the chance of reformation. The presumed problem with community sanctions then was that they lacked the punitive edge of imprisonment and as such failed to offer an attractive alternative to sentencers. For the probation service to truly challenge the judiciary to think of punishment beyond custody, community-based sanctions would, of necessity, have to become '... more explicitly punitive in their content and – most importantly – in their public imagery' (Garland, 1989: 4).

Collectively, the array of discussion and decision papers produced during the late 1980s and early 1990s sought to create a new framework for sentencing and within this to reconfigure the probation service around a more clearly defined Home Office agenda. As McWilliams (1987: 99) noted:

> ... until relatively recently the officer and the service of which he was a member were virtually synonymous: the large measure of consensus about the probation system, its purpose and its tasks meant that the probation officer encapsulated the probation service *in propria persona*; for most purposes the probation officer *was* the probation service.

But this was not the kind of service that the Home Office had envisaged for the 1990s and as such McWilliams (ibid.) conceded in his analysis of developments at the time that:

> It is clear that such an understanding of the probation officer does now not hold: simply it is not possible to comprehend the modern service purely, or even mainly, by reference to its officers. The probation officer today cannot be understood without the service policy within which he or she operates.

The legislative strategy of the 1980s had been focused on pulling offenders back from the brink of custody. While the forthcoming Criminal Justice Act 1991 shared this goal, its mechanism for increasing the proportionate use of non-custodial penalties differed radically from its antecedent legislation. Despite the hopes and aspirations that diversion from custody would reduce the numbers of offenders being sent to prison, the government had to concede that, despite their best efforts, they had failed to convince sentencers that non-custodial sentences were real punishments. In the wake of the diversion from custody enterprise, however, the courts would be encouraged to think about punishment in a different way. Thereafter punishment was to be redefined in terms of degrees of restricted liberty, the level of restriction being dependent on the seriousness of the offence committed. Community penalties would no longer be 'let-offs', but rather the level of surveillance that they offered would be 'commensurate' with the nature of the offence. As Brownlee (1998b: 18) has argued, the 1991 Criminal Justice Act effectively:

> ... brought together the themes and philosophies that had been emerging in government thinking throughout the 1980's, among them the primacy of retribution as a justification for punishment, 'loss of liberty' as a unifying principle in sentencing, increasing 'bifurcation' between violent and other types of offenders and the encouragement of greater resort to non-custodial sentences by introducing statutory restrictions on custody while making available 'tougher' community-based sanctions.

Probation in a time of intolerance

In its original incarnation, the Criminal Justice Act 1991 appeared to have the potential to stem, once and for all, the inexorable rise in the prison population. Attempts during the 1980s to divert offenders from custody had relied, broadly speaking, on a strategy of enticement and, as a consequence, had failed. By contrast the 1991 legislation sought to tackle the issue of sentencing head on, by effectively limiting the judicial power to impose custodial sentences. Early indications all pointed toward the success of this legislative flagship. The combined impact of legislative restrictions on imprisonment and the strategic repositioning of community sanctions to capture mid-range, frequently custodial, sentences had brought about a fall in the proportionate use of immediate custody and a rise in the proportionate use of community penalties (Home Office, 1993; Worrall, 1997; Brownlee, 1998b).

Despite the apparent merits of the 1991 Act, however, any retrospective analysis of its impact is forced to concede that this systematic approach to diverting offenders away from custody was relatively short lived. Subsequent legislative amendments in the form of the Criminal Justice Act 1993 and the Criminal Justice and Public Order Act 1994 effectively ensured that thereafter courts punished offenders harshly and for the most part by resorting to custodial penalties. In light of the 1993 amendments in particular, Ashworth and Gibson (1994: 101) concluded that '... policies based on mature reflection, consultation and research findings were abandoned in an instant in one of the most remarkable *volte-faces* in the history of penal policy in England and Wales'.

The immediate impact of dismantling the 1991 sentencing framework was to bring about a sharp (and sustained) increase in the number of offenders sentenced to custody. By 1995 the use of immediate custody for indictable offences in all courts had risen to 20 per cent, the highest recorded figure over the preceding 20 years (Brownlee, 1998b). More generally, however, this new direction in penal policy signalled the resurrection of imprisonment as the only 'real' punishment. If the government had earlier sought to place community supervision at the centre of its new sentencing arrangements, a return to the primacy of the prison did not provide an avenue for the probation service to retreat into its traditional role of providing welfare-orientated services to petty, but 'needy', offenders. Within a political climate which had sought to redefine the offender as a rational decision-maker and deny the possibility of a community dimension in sustaining criminality, the probation service continued to suffer the worst effects of a penal climate which was driven by belief in deterrent-based punishment. As Garland (2001: 137) observed in his review of the incoherence which came to characterise penal policy at this time:

> The once-dominant welfarist criminology that depicted the offender as disadvantaged or poorly socialized and made it the state's responsibility, in social as well as penal policy, to take positive steps of a remedial kind ... has become increasingly irrelevant to policy-makers ...

If there had been any doubt remaining, collectively the publications *Strengthening Punishment in the Community* (Home Office 1995a) and *Protecting the Public* (Home Office 1996) provided further confirmation that the government continued to view the probation service as ineffectual and its offices as wedded to social work values. In the perceived absence of a credible alternative, the government persisted with their claim that prison was an effective means of reducing crime and challenged all other disposals to mirror, as far as possible, the conditions of the custodial environment. For the probation service this was the culmination of an attack on its traditions which had begun at least a decade before.

If, during the 1980s, SNOP had been intended as the genesis for a new direction in probation practice, its subsequent failure provided an important lesson for the Home Office in the difficulties of managing change within the probation service. With both probation managers and main grade practitioners marked out as having deliberately undermined the government's drive to modernise (and toughen) the service (Sparrow et al., 2002) the Home Office initiated an alternative means of ensuring that, certainly during the 1990s, probation practice would reflect much more closely the intention of government policy. The Criminal Justice Act 1991 had introduced, for the first time, a set of National Standards (Home Office, 1992) which dictated, if not the nature of contact, then certainly the frequency of it. The imposition of centrally determined terms and conditions for engaging with offenders marked the beginning of a new and fundamentally different relationship between the Home Office and local probation regions. The tradition of allowing services the latitude to adapt policy to the peculiarities of their region was officially at an end.

As far as the government was concerned supervision was un-attractive to sentencers because probation officers could not be relied upon to ensure that their offenders abided by the terms and conditions of their orders (see Ellis, Hedderman and Mortimer, 1996). The solution therefore, was to remove the discretion which, in the view of the Home Office, probation officers used to justify their failure to return re-calcitrant offenders to the courts. Ultimately, National Standards provided a much-needed degree of reassurance to the Home Office; thereafter they would no longer be the unwilling recipients of benevolent but misguided probation officers. As we have argued elsewhere (Sparrow et al., 2002), the introduction of National Standards had as much, or even more, to do with bringing probation officers' practice into line with Home Office demands as it did with making the offenders' supervisory experience a recognisable punishment.

Subsequent editions of National Standards (Home Office, 1995b, 2000f) have further reduced probation officer discretion and ensured that the elective power to enforce has become an obligatory duty (Raynor and Vanstone, 2002); currently, a second missed appointment without a valid reason triggers breach action. As the monitoring of the probation service's adherence to ever stricter reporting instructions has become embedded in the Home Office's quality assurance procedures, so compliance has increased. Indeed, at the end of ACOP's three-stage audit of enforcement standards (Hedderman, 1999; Hedderman and Hearnden, 2000), Hedderman (2001: 17) concluded, 'it is worth noting that, no matter how it is measured, compliance has gone up'.

Despite the obvious rise in the importance attached to enforcement in probation practice, it is still the case that relatively little attention has been paid to the impact of breach action. According to Ellis (2000: 6) currently, enforcement '... lacks clear theoretical underpinnings and evidence that it is effective'. Moreover, he suggests that 'Compliance levels alone tell us nothing about whether a change was achieved with offenders on community orders' (ibid.). The lack of attention paid to this issue is all the more surprising when set within the context of the 'what works' debate which has dominated probation research over the last decade (Farrell, 2002). Thus, while the desire to find and implement programmes which demonstrably reduce offending behaviour has become a preoccupation for the Home Office, the impact of increasingly onerous standards of reporting has apparently failed to attract the same degree of interrogation. Recent Home Office statistics show that in relation to probation orders (now community rehabilitation orders) the rate of breach for failure to comply with the requirements has begun to increase in recent years. During the period 1989 to 2000 the rate of breach increased from 3 per cent to 7 per cent. By way of contrast the number of offenders whose orders were terminated early for good progress during the same period declined from 12 per cent to 8 per cent (Home Office, 2001c, 2002f).

According to Ellis (2000: 6) if an increasing proportion of the probation service's caseload is likely to be returned to court for breach, then the service has a responsibility to know whether '... current enforcement policy and practice works toward or against effective practice ...' Traditionally, the value of breach has rested on four key principles: first, that it is good for those on the receiving end; second, that the consequences for the offender are unlikely to be serious; third, that fairness demands it; and finally that the credibility of the service is positively correlated to it (Drakeford, 1993). Not only is it doubtful that any of the above stand up to scrutiny but seeing breach as a con-structive action with minimal risk to the offender is, at best, a precarious strategy. Indeed as Drakeford (1993: 296) eloquently points out, 'the endurance of the therapeutic view of breach is one of the minor marvels of the age'. Bringing an offender back to court for wilfully disregarding the opportunity provided by the original sentence in-evitably places them at risk of additional penalties. Thus 'the notion that breach is a no-cost option is as perilous as it is ill-informed' (ibid.).

As the number of offenders appearing before the courts for breach has increased, questions are beginning to be asked about the utility of an enforcement policy that is driven by uniformity alone. Raynor and Vanstone (2002: 104) have suggested that at a time when the average completion rate for probation programmes is low '... there is a need for an approach to enforcement which makes a positive contribution to motivating offenders to complete programmes rather than terminating orders and risking imprisonment'. Above all, it is certainly possible that the Home Office's belief that the credibility of the probation service is enhanced by the number of offenders it returns to court might actually be false (see Home Office, 1995a, 1996). Drakeford's (1993) fear is that an increasingly public display of failure, far from affirming the punitive credentials of the probation service, might actually reveal it as an ineffective institution. 'Credibility [he suggests] will have become culpability as the service is rightly blamed for shortcomings of its own making' (Drakeford, 1993: 297).

Conclusion

Ellis (2000) and Farrell (2002) are undoubtedly correct in their assertion that despite the importance attached to enforcement it has received precious little research attention. Only recently have there been calls made to evaluate the consequences of an increasingly strict approach to breach. The possible contribution of enforcement to supervision appears, somehow, to have been lost as both the probation service and allied researchers have become preoccupied with which programmes work to produce the greatest reduction in offending behaviour. At first sight, it would be easy to assume that issues of enforcement are a by-product of the post-1991 era of probation policy, but, as we have shown, this is certainly not the case. Enforcement and the problem of its appropriate application are as old as probation itself (see Page, 1992). The issue then is not whether breach should be a part of the probation officer's armoury but rather what the purpose of breach should be, how and when it should be used, and what outcome should the probation service be seeking when returning offenders to court.

In considering the changing contours of probation practice and as a consequence the role of enforcement, Garland's (1989) distinction between punitive and constructive approaches to punishment offers a useful framework for analysis. Put simply, punitive approaches '... express anger, resentment, hostility and seek to ensure denunciation, retribution and usually deterrence ...' (ibid.: 8). By contrast, constructive approaches '... express sentiments such as compassion, understanding, forgiveness and aim to promote prevention and reform' (ibid.). While these two approaches may occasionally converge, '... at heart they embody different values, different sentiments and different visions of the purposes and objectives of punishment' (ibid.). Our suggestion, therefore, is that what we have seen in terms of enforcement is a shift from a constructive approach where breach was conceptualised, rightly or wrongly, within a framework of assistance, to a position where enforcement is the defining feature of a punitive approach to community supervision. It is clearly possible to level a whole raft of criticisms at the discretion afforded to probation officers during earlier stages of probation practice and in particular at the period which McWilliams (1986) described as its diagnostic phase (see Bean, 1976). Certainly it would be difficult to argue that during this period there was any consistency in the application of enforcement standards. It is not our intention to counter these criticisms, but rather to question the emerging orthodoxy that seeks to construct breach as an exclusively punitive sanction and reduce enforcement to a series of administrative technicalities (see Sparrow et al., 2002).

At a time when the Home Office has set exacting targets for the recently reconstituted National Probation Service (an increase in the number of offenders completing accredited programmes and a reduction in the rate of reconvictions) the necessity for the service to promote compliance has never been greater. Given that evidence is beginning to suggest that court action alone is unlikely to be the most effective mechanism for reducing absenteeism among probationers, it is perhaps now that the service should consider, firstly, whether there are more effective strategies for facilitating compliance and, secondly, how far breach action might reflect the principles of effective practice.

According to Farrell (2002) a more constructive approach to enforcement demands a shift away from the current system which seeks to castigate the non-compliant offender toward an approach which provides incentives for probationers to maintain contact (see also Bottoms, 2001). In Farrell's study it was the prospect of practical help with specific problems that appeared to offer the strongest incentive to attendance. The fact that such assistance was rarely provided led to the conclusion that '... the finding which is most troubling for the probation service concerns the data which suggests that some probationers did not maintain contact because they felt that probation offered them little of much use' (Farrell, 2002: 274). It seems increasingly likely – or at least it is a reasonable inference – that as the probation service has become ever more concerned with its punitive credentials, so it has lost its capacity to engage with offenders on terms which are meaningful for the probationers themselves.

Notwithstanding Farrell's findings, it remains the case that the 'what works' initiative has meant that the way in which the probation service engages with offenders has received considerable attention in recent years. It is also true that the drive toward effective practice in general has done much to revitalise a service that had suffered the worst effects of the politicisation of the crime problem. It is strange, then, that at a time when the Home Office has done much to ensure that rehabilitation is firmly back on the practice agenda, enforcement has remained fixed within a framework that continues to confuse quantity of contact with quality of impact.

Reducing effective practice to a few key principles is no easy task. However, most would agree that robust assessment instruments directing offenders into approved programmes of supervision (group and individual) are among the most significant features of the effective practice agenda. It seems to us, therefore, that it is these principles which should now be informing the debate around enforcement practice. Above all, the 'what works' literature reminds us that a singular approach to supervision is unlikely to meet the needs of a group as diverse as offenders. Increasingly, both the mode and intensity of supervision is a function of an extensive risk/needs assessment. It is our proposition, therefore, that this ongoing assessment process could also form the basis of a more flexible approach to enforcement. The enforcement regime might actually be articulated much more clearly in terms of the risk the offender poses and the outcome of breach determined by any change in risk resulting from supervision already completed. Inevitably, proposals to introduce more discretion into the supervisory process, particularly around that aspect which concerns the most overtly coercive element of the probation officer's role, will fall foul of the charge that discretion equates to inequality. Certainly, there is a body of evidence which suggests that probation officers' discretion has not always served the best interests of the offender (Bean, 1976). There is, however, a distinction to be drawn between discretion based on instinct and impression, which appears to have characterised decision-making during earlier periods of the service's development (McWilliams, 1983, 1986), and the professional competence to apply flexible working practices based on 'best evidence' about what improves offender compliance and reduces reoffending.

Current evidence, based on gradually increasing breach rates (Home Office, 2001c, 2002f) and qualitative accounts of offenders' experiences (Farrell, 2002), indicates first that the present rigid approach to enforcement is unlikely to encourage compliance on the part of offenders and second that the probation service could do more to reduce absenteeism among its caseload. Present thinking provides the clearest indication yet that 'one size' supervision does not fit all offenders. There is little reason to assume therefore that one approach to enforcement would be any more successful. We conclude our contribution to this debate in much the same way as Farrell (2002) did by drawing on the earlier work of Drakeford (1993: 301) and supporting his call for '... less coercion and more consideration ...' in the enforcement process, since, as he warns, a 'good' probation officer is not necessarily a breaching probation officer.

Chapter 7

'Softly, softly', private security and the policing of corporate space

Mark Button

Introduction

Since the modern private security industry began to emerge in North America in the late nineteenth century there has been a critical view on its legitimacy and role. This perspective is less dominant today, but frequently arguments are raised of private security as 'private armies', engaged in political policing and the oppression of marginalised segments of society (Bowden, 1978; Bunyan, 1976; Hunt Saboteurs Association (HSA), 1994; Liberty, 1995; Vidal, 1997). Moreover, there is still evidence to support such perspectives, particularly when the experience of developing and former Communist countries is examined. What these disturbing examples mask, however, is the general emergence in post-industrial societies of a private security industry centred upon the reduction of losses for its corporate clients through preventative strategies and working in partnership with the agents of the state (Cunningham, Strauchs and Van Meter, 1990; Johnston, 2000; and Shearing and Stenning, 1985). This chapter will seek to illustrate this 'soft' approach to policing generally pursued by private security in post-industrial societies. It will begin by theorising the characteristics that distinguish 'hard' from 'soft' policing, applying them to the most dominant theoretical perspectives explaining the emergence of private security. Some of the evidence illustrating examples of 'hard' policing will then be examined, before moving on to demonstrate some of the evidence for the 'soft' approach to policing generally pursued.

Defining 'hard' and 'soft' policing

There has been much written on different models of policing, ranging from 'zero tolerance' versus 'community' policing, 'force' versus 'service' to more specialist debates concerning 'problem-orientated' and 'intelligence-led' policing (Hopkins Burke, 1998a). It is not the aim of this chapter to get embroiled in definitional debates concerning these styles. However, for the purposes of this chapter it is necessary to draw out the key characteristics of the two extremes in the continuum of policing styles vis-à-vis private security in order to examine where private security generally fits. Table 7.1 illustrates the ideal type of what is considered in this chapter to characterise the two ends of the continuum of 'hard' and 'soft' policing by private security.

As with any ideal type there are few examples that conform to all these characteristics, but they do illustrate the definitive characteristics of the two styles. This chapter will argue that although there are elements of the 'hard' approach to policing found among private security firms operating in the UK, more generally the private security industry operates at the 'soft' end of the continuum. Before we consider the evidence for this it is first important to understand the theoretical bases for the emergence of private security as these are central to interpretations of the style of policing.

The emergence of private security can broadly be divided into 'fiscal constraint' theories and 'structuralist' or 'pluralist' theories (Jones and Newburn, 1998). The latter view the emergence of private security as linked to the growth of mass private property and systems of private justice. Fiscal constraint theories explain the growth of private security

Table 7.1 Characterising 'hard' and 'soft' approaches to policing by private security operatives

'Hard' policing	'Soft' policing
Confrontation	Consensus
Detection	Prevention
Reactive	Proactive
Rigorous enforcement of the law and regulations	Discretion and desire to avoid criminal justice system
Politically motivated	Non-political
Threat to the state	Support to the state

in terms of the inability of the state to meet the demand for services which has led to the private sector filling the gap. In the case of policing, demand for the services of the public police has outstripped the resources that are available and as a consequence the private sector has stepped in to fill some gaps in provision. Within this perspective two distinct schools can be distinguished: the radical and the liberal democratic. Broadly the former views private security as pursuing 'hard' methods and the latter a 'soft' approach. Evidence for these two styles will now be considered.

A legacy of 'hard' policing in private security

The 'radical' perspective views the growth of private policing as an inevitable consequence of the crisis of capitalism where the state draws in the private sector to strengthen its legitimacy (Spitzer and Scull, 1977; Weiss, 1978; Couch, 1987). Much of the literature associated with these views centres on the emergence of industrial capitalism in the USA around the end of the nineteenth and early twentieth centuries. In a number of areas the development of the coal, iron and steel industries took place in rural areas where the state was not well established. Industrial militancy threatened the corporations of the time and as a result companies resorted to private policing to maintain control. The private services went well beyond keeping the peace and also sought to ensure the working classes remained obedient. The companies would draw upon their own private forces, but also made use of contractors for investigations and policing industrial disputes – most famously Pinkerton. Central to these views is an assessment of private security as pursuing a 'hard' approach to policing, emphasising their threat to the state, political motivation, confrontational style and reactive approach.

Companies like Pinkerton provided a range of services that included general property protection services and a range of strike-breaking services such as labour espionage, strike-breakers, strike-guards and strike missionaries (those who were paid to convince strikers to go back to work) (Weiss, 1978). The policing practices that emerged, particularly during strikes in this period, led to serious confrontations between the forces of capital and labour. There were many disputes where the civil rights of striking workers were violated and where some were even killed. Such were the problems throughout this period that 'private police systems' were the subject of many Congressional reports (see United States Committee on Education and Labor 1971 – a publication of a 1931 report). As the 1931 report argued:

> The use of private police systems to infringe upon the civil liberties of workers has a long and often blood stained history. The methods used by private armed guards have been violent. The purposes have usually been to prevent the exercise of civil rights in the self-organisation of employees into unions or to break strikes either called to enforce collective bargaining or to obtain better working conditions for union members.

This extract is typical of a widespread view in America that considered private security in the 'hard' sense as involving private armies/spies, as a threat to the public interest, as dangerous to society and as a phenomenon that should be restricted in the roles it undertook.

The modern division of American society into the heavily protected enclaves of the rich by private security and police and the exposed slums with limited protection has also been noted by Davis (1990) in his analysis of modern Los Angeles. Many of the private enclaves are protected by perimeter fences, CCTV, access control and security staff and it not possible to enter them without a prior invitation from a resident, thus keeping out large sections of the community. Even in areas that are nominally public, measures have been pursued to keep out the 'wrong' kind of people, such as having to prove local residency to enter a park. Again it is private security personnel who have to enforce such measures. In undertaking these functions in the USA there is little evidence of the systematic violence that takes place in Brazil (which will be discussed later). However, the significant number of security officers carrying arms, many of whom have had only limited training (and it is debatable whether they possess the appropriate character to be armed), has led to frequent accidental and unnecessary shootings. The Rand study during the early 1970s provided numerous examples of security officers using arms when they should not have. They included in Florida a security officer who was suspended after he ordered a life-size dummy to step from the shadows, and when it refused, he shot it with his pistol. In another incident, a boy swimming in a lake refused to respond to a security officer's request to leave and was fatally shot (Kakalik and Wildhorn, 1971d).

A number of writers on policing in the UK during the 1970s were also critical of the 'hard' approach to policing pursued by private security. Bowden (1978: 254) considered private security as 'private armies' and cited the former Labour Party leader George Lansbury who regarded the industry to be the 'the first halting step towards fascism'. Bowden was concerned with the political activities of the industry, particularly those of private detectives investigating trade unionists and political activists. He wrote:

> Of particular concern is the fact that private police forces have been used, and will be used in the future, in Britain, for covert political operations. Their powers of investigation and surveillance are considerable and have been given a boost in terms of information resources that they have available by the recruitment of senior ex-policemen, politicians and even Intelligence specialists onto their staffs. (Bowden, 1978: 256)

Bunyan (1976) took a similar view and highlighted investigators involved in the gathering of information on political extremists and trade unionists for the 'Economic League' (an organisation dedicated to securing information on such groups for the business community). One former private detective from this period, Gary Murray, has illustrated in his memoirs how investigators were used not just by private companies to secure information on political activists and trade unionists but also foreign governments to secure intelligence on their political opponents in the UK, most prominently by the South African government on anti-apartheid protesters. He also offers evidence that the Security Service (MI5) subcontracted some of its work to private investigators (Murray, 1993).

There is also evidence of 'hard' policing in the activities of the private security industry over the last decade in the UK. In evidence to the Home Affairs Committee inquiry into the private security industry examples were given of private security personnel becoming involved in political disputes and in using excessive force. Evidence from the Hunt Saboteurs Association (HSA) (1994) and Liberty (1995) demonstrated numerous accusations of the use of excessive force by 'security' staff. The HSA also illustrated many examples where members had suffered excessive violence from security staff guarding hunts. Allegations included being whipped, kicked, beaten and threatened with knives, spades, coshes and even stun-guns. In one of the most graphic examples a woman protester was allegedly attacked and forced to eat sheep dung by two security staff (HSA, 1994). Private investigators have also been used to gather intelligence on environmental and animal rights protesters (Button and John, 2002). Most notably, McDonald's in the 'McLibel trial' were shown to have used two firms of investigators to infiltrate 'London Greenpeace', to the extent that at some of their meetings there were more investigators than activists (Vidal, 1997).

So far the focus has largely been upon examples of 'hard' policing in the USA and UK in historical perspective with a few examples from the modern era. As an example of a post-industrial country it will be illustrated later in this chapter that generally the norm in the UK is a 'soft' rather than 'hard' approach to policing by private security. There is, however, much more evidence of 'hard' policing in other countries, particularly developing and former Communist countries. At the most disturbing end of the continuum of policing styles private security has been implicated in repressive social control, including organised death squads, most notably in the slums of Brazil. In São Paulo during the last three months of 1999 of the 109 citizens killed by the Militarized Police, 69 were dispatched by off-duty officers working part-time in private security! As Huggins (2000: 121) has argued:

> In Brazil today, death squads continue to operate, paralleled by a growing 'rent-a-cop' industry, with each social control entity directly 'serving' different population segments to the benefit of one over the other. The poor are treated as undifferentiated 'criminals' by death squads and 'rent-a-cops', and richer Brazilians are protected from the poor by their private security forces.

The collapse of the Soviet Union and its satellite countries has also led to the emergence of examples of 'hard' policing by private security personnel. In Russia between September 1991 and June 1992 over 20,000 KGB officers left or were discharged. Many of these personnel moved to the private sector to work for and establish private security operations. Indeed, Volkov (2000) estimates that nearly 50,000 former officers of state security and law enforcement are now working for private security agencies. Many of these personnel have taken the culture and tactics of their old employers to their new private masters.

This section has illustrated a legacy of 'hard' policing in the history of private security along with some more disturbing contemporary examples. However, it would be unfair to categorise the 'hard' approach as the norm in the UK and other post-industrial countries today. As the next section will illustrate, private security is generally more orientated towards the 'soft' end of the continuum than the 'hard' end. To that extent it is useful to view 'soft' policing in terms of Spitzer and Scull's (1977) analysis of the emergence of private policing. They identify three periods which begin with 'policing as piece work', in which they describe a diverse system of entrepreneurs – many holding public offices – selling policing services to clients on a piece-rate basis. In the second stage, which they call 'private policing in the industrial age', they argue policing becomes centred upon establishing a secure environment for capitalism to flourish. With the emergence of worker and trade union militancy private security finds its role in the degradation of the working classes to ensure the smooth running of capitalism. In the third stage, 'private policing under corporate capitalism', they argue private policing has emerged to deal with the consequences of large-scale enterprises employing substantial work-forces. These include fraud, pilferage, sabotage and investigating the character of staff. Many of these functions are those the public sector would be unable and unwilling to undertake. Hence private policing has moved from 'an oppressor' of the labour movement to enforcer of corporate order. This has links to the 'liberal democratic' fiscal constraints perspective which views the emergence of private security as filling the gap in policing in a much more positive way. This perspective and the evidence of the more extensive 'soft' approach used by private security will now be considered.

'Soft' private policing

The 'liberal democratic' perspective views the growth of private security as an inevitable consequence of the inability of the police to satisfy public demands. As a result the private sector has stepped in to fill the gap and uses what are generally considered to be a 'soft' approach to policing. The first and most significant study associated with this perspective was Kakalik and Wildhorn's (1972a, b, c, d, e) research published by the Rand Corporation which illustrated the significant role the private security industry undertakes in policing, particularly in its preventative strategies against crime in corporations. It also emphasised the supportive and complementary role of the industry to the public police and developed the idea of the industry being the 'junior partner' to the police in 'policing'. Shearing (1992) argues that until the publication of the 'Rand Report' the private security industry had either been simply viewed as a potential 'private army' or dismissed as having no importance. This watershed publi-cation turned these ideas on their head viewing private security as a positive asset to society that could be more fully developed and utilised in partnership with the police. This study was accompanied during the early 1970s by a range of further research published in the UK and USA that illustrated the growing importance of private security (Braun and Lee, 1971; Scott and MacPherson, 1971; Wiles and McClintock, 1972; National Advisory Council on Criminal Justice Standards and Goals,

1976; Draper, 1978). Implicit in the 'liberal democratic' perspective is a 'soft' approach to policing characterised by a commitment to partnership between the public and private sectors, an elevation of the status of private security and a focus on prevention rather than enforcement. These characteristics and others will now be explored in greater depth.

Partnership

Central to the 'soft' approach pursued by the private security sector in recent years has been the desire to engage in partnerships with the police combined with an elevation of the status of private security policing. This has been encouraged by the UK government and an increasing number of voices within the police service. At a national level the government has introduced regulation of the private security industry with the Private Security Industry Act 2001, one of the main aims being to improve crime reduction partnerships with the police. The Police Reform Act 2002 has further encouraged partnerships with provisions to enable the police to accredit private security staff in return for the granting of specialist powers to those staff to undertake local policing functions. This can be viewed as a significant elevation of the status of private security in policing. The latter proposals have been heavily influenced by Sir Ian Blair, Deputy Commissioner of the Metropolitan Police Service, who has advocated private security patrols accredited by the police, carrying police radios and working in partnership with them. These proposals do not seek to create a private security industry capable of replacing the police, but rather a junior partner to support and work with the service. This view is strongly encouraged by the most influential voices in the private security industry, as the views of David Dickinson, the chief executive of the British Security Industry Association (the leading trade association for British security companies), illustrate, 'there is a prospect of greater involvement of the private security sector in community safety schemes, but it is vital that we are seen to support the police rather than attempting to assume any kind of law enforcement role' (Dickinson, 2002: 2). Thus it can be seen that the private security industry seeks a role as the junior partner and supporter of the police rather than seeking to replace the public service.

Loss prevention and risk management

One of the defining characteristics of the commercial security industry is its proactive and preventative role. (Johnston, 2000: 130)

Central to the 'soft' characteristics of private security is the focus upon prevention rather than detection (although this is not to say the industry is not also engaged in the latter). This manifests itself in the form of situational crime prevention measures combined with risk management strategies that seek to minimise the risk of losses and manage those that do arise. Measures used focus on surveillance systems and environmental design, the use of security officers and/or closed-circuit television systems (CCTV) (Shearing and Stenning, 1985). Conversely in the public police service it could be argued that – despite an increasing shift towards prevention – the focus remains on the detection or the 'collaring' of offenders (Morn, 1982). This difference was noted by the former chief executive of the BSIA, David Fletcher (2002: 65), commenting on the Police Reform Act 2002:

> ... we are clear that our (private security sector) role remains solely one of crime prevention; not law enforcement. That responsibility should remain solely in the hands of the police, and any extension of civilian powers should be considered with great care.

Private security companies increasingly offer the 'total solutions' package of services. These are usually based upon the application of situational crime prevention measures to an organisation to protect it from crime and therefore losses. To achieve this goal, security officers, products and procedures are used in a tailored package to increase the effort, increase the risks and reduce the rewards from offending. Linked to preventative strategies, sophisticated risk identification and management systems have also emerged. Detailed calculations of the risks of particular crimes are often undertaken and the outcome influences deployment and level of security. Thus once the risks have been identified and quantified they are managed with the aim of reduction. The British Post Office, for instance, has a sophisticated risk model for its post offices to calculate the risk of robbery, burglary, etc. Information on the location, proximity to motorways, number of previous attacks and social indicators – among many other factors – are fed into it and the outcome calculation decides the nature of the security strategy. Many other organisations have developed such strategies with varying degrees of sophistication. The emphasis is upon avoiding risk and the prevention of crime rather than catching the perpetrators.

The focus upon 'prevention' is further illustrated by the training and guidance given to security officers. From the very beginning of their induction training security officers are taught that their role is one of loss prevention. In the opening paragraphs of the *Initial Security's Security Officer's Handbook* (a handbook given to all security staff at one of the UK's largest companies) it is stated, 'companies ... employ security officers to prevent and detect losses by theft, prevent water damage, fire damage and vandalism, prevent wastage and control access/visitors' (Initial Security, undated: 1).

Indeed many security officers find themselves undertaking a wide range of functions that are not 'security' related. These might include switching lights, electrical heaters and other electrical equipment off to save energy. Such additional services are actively marketed by some companies as the extract from the Pinkerton website illustrates,

> Many people know Pinkerton from our 'basic' security officer services. However, Pinkerton also offers a comprehensive range of value-added services delivered by our security professionals. Our officers can provide outsourced services beyond the traditional duties of standing post, making patrol rounds or standard access control. (Pinkerton, 2002)

Security officers may even find themselves supporting 'ordinary' staff in their duties at 'quiet' times. For instance, in one ethnographic study centred on the retail environment security officers were often expected during quiet periods on the night shift to help staff stacking shelves, thereby improving the efficiency of the company (Abu-Boakye, 2002).

Avoiding the criminal justice system

Linked to prevention is a general desire to avoid incidents becoming 'dragged' into the criminal justice system. Instead, private systems of justice are utilised alongside civil remedies with extensive rules and sanctions for their breach often reflecting those of the state (Macauley, 1986). In particular, many fraud investigations do not result in a criminal prosecution but instead measures are implemented to recover the monies lost and terminate the employment of the offender. In a study of private investigators Gill and Hart (1997: 558) found in relation to the investigation of fraud that 'many companies resort to private provision to avoid the need for prosecution (and public disclosure of the case). The investigator's role is to establish the cause of a loss and, if an individual is found to be responsible, provide evidence for the fact'.

The extent to which avoidance of the criminal justice system is pursued is further illustrated by statistics from the annual British Retail Consortium's crime survey. For instance only 55 per cent of customers detained for theft by retailers – usually by security officers and store detectives – are handed over to the police for prosecution and in the DIY/hardware and food subsectors this falls to 36 and 41 per cent respectively (British Retail Consortium, 2002). Such low rates are a reflection of the view that handing over suspects is too onerous and bureaucratic and the costs of such action outweigh any benefits obtained. Indeed, in recent years this lack of faith in the criminal justice system has increased further with the expansion of 'civil recovery' strategies where the costs of dealing with theft are recovered by a civil action against the offender rather than criminal prosecution (Bamfield, 1998).

Image and marketing of private security

A further illustration of the 'soft' characteristics of private security is the image and marketing many companies use. A selective perusal of the literature produced by some companies reveals the 'soft' approaches used. For instance, a company noted above to have a 'hard' approach to policing in the last century, Pinkerton (although now part of the global conglomerate Securitas), in its modern literature exudes the 'soft' approach. One brochure uses the expression 'minimizing business risk in a global environment' on its front cover and states on its opening page:

> The potential for business loss in today's global market is ever expanding. Whether it's from internal employee theft or embezzlement or from external criminals stealing trade secrets, the opportunity for loss is demanding more and more corporate resources.

Another leading UK security company, Reliance Security, states in its advert in the BSIA's 2002–2003 annual directory: by promoting increased understanding of risk management, crime levels can be reduced dramatically. A photograph included in this feature shows two smiling security officers (one black male and one white female) in 'slack' (or non military-style) uniform. Another Reliance advert in the same directory shows a female security officer in 'slack' uniform bending down to talk to two young girls. The use of females (who are a significant minority in the industry) and slack uniforms is illustrative of the desire to promote a 'soft' image to the public, rather than a more traditional male, macho and police-like 'hard' image.

The 'soft' approach is further illustrated by the changing styles of uniform pursued by many security companies in recent years, although there are still a significant number of security companies with 'militaristic'-style uniforms. Many private security staff operating in environments dealing with the public are increasingly wearing blazers, ties and shirts – so called 'slacks' – rather than the traditional police or military-style uniforms. An illustration of this approach is demonstrated by the leisure and shopping complex at Gun Wharf Quays in Portsmouth. Here the security officers are called 'customer service officers' and wear 'slack' style uniforms. Again the focus of the security staff there is to help the customers rather than zealously enforce the law and the rules of the site.

Avoiding conflict

A further illustration of the 'soft' approach to policing generally employed by the private security industry is the reluctance to embrace or demand the use of lethal weapons. Up until the 1950s it was quite common for private security officers to carry weapons in armoured cars transporting cash and other valuables. It was only an incident at the beginning of this decade when a private security officer shot an attacker that the police started to enforce firearms legislation more rigorously, refusing to grant certificates to private security personnel (Draper, 1978). It was also common up until the 1970s for some private security officers to carry non-lethal weapons such as truncheons. In 1973, however, three security officers were convicted under the Prevention of Crime Act 1953 for carrying batons. There was an appeal to the Court of Appeal which failed and since then most reputable companies have agreed that private security officers should not be armed, although in recent years in the UK there have been some vocal calls for private security officers to be armed with non-lethal weapons, most notably from Sir Stanley Kalms (chairman of Dixons) and the managing director of Guardian Security (Plews, 2001). The most influential voices in the industry have resisted these calls for arming security officers. David Cairns (2001: 13), managing director of Securitas, in response to the Plews article advocating the use of non-lethal weapons, wrote:

> Many security officers' primary function is to protect a company's premises or assets, but this doesn't mean that they should put themselves at any unnecessary risk by doing so. … Securitas Security Service employees are actively discouraged from placing themselves in a situation of danger.

In the same edition there was a letter from the then chief executive of the BSIA also opposing the arming of security officers. It is also interesting to note that in the USA, where security officers can be armed with firearms, the numbers of security officers carrying a firearm at least 25 per cent of the time had fallen from 50 per cent in 1971 to 10 per cent in 1981 and was projected at the time to be 5 per cent by the year 2000 (Cunningham et al., 1990).

Conclusion

Policing in contemporary industrial society is characterised by 'fragmentation' where private security has assumed a significant role in terms of size and function (Johnston, 2000; Reiner, 2000). This has stimulated debates in both academia and policy-making circles of the legitimacy, nature and consequences of these changes (Button, 2002). There has, however, been a much longer debate over the growing role of private security and three distinct perspectives have emerged (Jones and Newburn, 1998). The radical stance has generally viewed the emergence of the modern private security industry with concern. Juxtaposing the 'ideal' characteristics of 'hard' and 'soft' policing it can be seen that much of the 'radical' perspective illustrates evidence of the former and the 'liberal democratic' the latter. This chapter has demonstrated that in North America there is a legacy of 'hard' policing and that 'pockets' still exist in varying degrees throughout the world. In the UK, as well as many other post-industrial societies, however, the general orientation of the private security industry has been towards the 'soft' end of the continuum. This can be characterised by an emphasis on partnership with the state police, particularly in a supportive and junior capacity. Private security is also generally orientated towards the reduction of losses for its corporate clients through a focus on preventative and risk management techniques underpinned with surveillance. Linked to these facets it also generally seeks to avoid the criminal justice system and confrontation. The image of private security is also marketed to emphasise these characteristics drawing upon 'soft' images. Thus despite concerns over the growing role of private security, in terms of the UK context there is little evidence of a 'hard' approach or desire for private security firms to move in that direction. However, as Shearing and Stenning (1985) illustrate, this could mask a far more sinister future where order is not induced through an Orwellian state supported by a private security industry, but rather a Brave New World built upon seduction, corporate control systems and consensually based measures.

Part 2
Policing Contemporary Offences

Chapter 8

Using crackdowns constructively in crime reduction

Nick Tilley

Introduction

Police crackdowns describe 'sudden increases in officer presence, sanctions and threats of apprehension either for specific offences or for all offences in specific places' (Sherman, 1990). Crackdowns thus comprise heightened enforcement activities relative to those that normally occur. They do not, of course, necessarily involve only the police – other enforcement agencies may apply crackdowns on their own or do so in conjunction with the police. Crackdowns require the allocation of additional resources in relation to the offences and/or places targeted. They are ordinarily short term. There is, as a rule, a return to background levels of enforcement.

The police (and other enforcement agencies) will rarely if ever have the resources to enforce all laws in relation to all offenders in all places. Decisions on what to prioritise have to be made. A police (or other agency) policy of applying crackdowns and switching their focus around describes one way of allocating enforcement resources. Others might include, for example, focusing consistently on the most costly offences, local residents' chief concerns, government priorities or the local police commander's views of what matters most, or some mixture of all these. The risk of prioritisation is that low priority offences, even if a substantial nuisance, will effectively be decriminalised since they will rarely if ever come to compete successfully with higher priority issues for police attention. In a revolving crackdown approach even quite minor offences can periodically become a focus for concentrated enforcement (Wright, 1994).

Crackdowns may or may not, however, be implemented as part of a coherent approach to crime and disorder problems. They may simply be part of the suite of responses that the police deploy from time to time in response to particular problems that have come to a head, or they may be applied strategically in an effort to achieve longer-term benefits. Applied strategically they may form part of a series of linked measures to address an issue or they may be implemented as stand-alone responses though configured with an eye to having a sustained impact.

Crackdowns have a bad name. They seem to involve the arbitrary application of police authority to particular groups or to those in particular areas and thereby to be discriminatory and unjust. At their worst they can provoke perverse effects, alienating the community and creating mistrust of the police. The Scarman Report vividly describes how crackdowns can backfire (Scarman, 1981). Operation Swamp was followed by riots which spread widely. Lawlessness was generated by the intensified police attention among a disconsolate population that had been socially and economically marginalised. It evidently did so by intensifying community suspicion that the police were persecuting residents on the basis of their race and style of life. The (predominantly white) police went into (substantially black) Brixton, where levels of perceived police legitimacy were already low and targeted their enforcement activities there. Far from containing crime the upshot was a revolt against the police.

Well-targeted crackdowns have, nevertheless, also been shown to be capable of producing rapid falls in crime (e.g. Ross et al., 1970; Homel, 1995; Braga et al., 1999). Moreover the effects have been found often to outlast the direct application of the crackdown (Sherman, 1990). If crackdowns are unconditionally applied then they risk producing unwanted side effects from time to time. If they are eschewed completely, one potentially effective means to reduce crime is excluded. A key issue both for research and practice is thus that of determining the conditions in which crackdowns can produce reductions in crime without the unwanted side effects. This involves asking the realist question, 'In what circumstances and how do crackdowns work for whom?' (Pawson and Tilley, 1997).

Sherman's theory of crackdown

In a seminal paper published in 1990 Sherman lays down many of the key terms used to discuss crackdowns and develops a theory of how they may work (Sherman, 1990). The theory is not articulated explicitly in realist terms but it lends itself to a realist reading. Sherman also reviews the then literature reporting studies of crackdowns and explores in more detail how they have been found to work in practice.

In the left-hand column of Table 8.1 are listed Sherman's main concepts for discussing crackdowns. The middle column briefly explains the meaning of the concept. The column to the right interprets the concept in realist terms. Realists attempt to produce 'context–mechanism–outcome pattern configurations'. These describe the ways in which effects (intended and unintended outcomes) are brought about by the operation of causal processes (mechanisms) in the circumstances in which interventions are made (context). Measures are deemed to bring about their outcomes by activating one or more unseen causal mechanism. They do so by changing the context in which agents act. Mechanisms normally refer to the reasoning and resources of those affected. Thus, to take the first line of Table 8.1, heightened 'presence' of police (i.e. an increase in the ratio of police officers to potential offenders) alters the context for the potential offenders' decisions to offend or not to do so. Looking down the table 'incapacitation' describes a mechanism through which outcomes are brought about, though, unusually, it does not refer to changed reasoning on the part of potential offenders but rather their physical containment. Further down still we find 'initial deterrence decay'. This captures both an outcome (reduced reduction in crime) and the mechanism through which this is deemed to happen – a growing realisation by potential offenders that they had overestimated the increased risk brought about by the crackdown. Here the mechanism does refer to changed reasoning.

Table 8.1 shows how Sherman's concepts capture a range of potential context, mechanism and outcome pattern features of crackdowns. Without compromising Sherman's own discussion at all we might now also want now to add 'Anticipatory deterrence' to the left-hand column. The corresponding middle column would read 'Effect felt before crackdown implemented' and the right-hand column 'Outcome pattern triggered by crackdown-related activity before the crackdown itself is put in place'. Anticipatory benefits often result from media-induced deterrence, where publicity has been given to the measures yet to be put in place (Smith et al., 2002), a pattern noted in one study discussed by Sherman himself.

Sherman develops a quite brilliant crackdown theory. His discussion of 'bluff' highlights the importance of understanding the (unseen) mechanisms producing outcomes. Crackdowns, he suggests, do not do

Table 8.1 Key concepts for understanding crackdowns

Sherman's concept	Meaning	Comments on realist category
Presence	'Increased ratio of police officers per potential offender'	Part of the intervention – change in context
Sanctions	'Any coercive police imposition on offenders or potential offenders'	Part of the intervention – change in context
Media threats	'Announced intentions to increase sanctioning certainty'	Part of the intervention – change in context
Backoff	Crackdown end	Part of the intervention – change in context
General deterrent effect	Reduced participation rate	Outcome and broad mechanism by which it is brought about – mechanism needs further unpacking
Initial deterrence	Crime reduction while crackdown in operation	Outcome during intervention
Residual deterrence	Crime reduction sustained after crackdown terminated	Outcome after intervention ends
Incapacitation	Removal of offender	Mechanism for crime reduction
Crackdown decay	Declining intensity of crackdown	Part of the intervention – change in context
Initial deterrence decay	Reduced deterrence as offenders learn that they had overestimated increased risk	Outcome pattern during intervention and mechanism producing it
Residual deterrence decay	Reduced deterrence as offenders come to realise crackdown and hence increased risk has ended	Outcome pattern after intervention and mechanism producing it

much physically to prevent crimes. Rather, crime falls are effected by changes brought about in the reasoning or perception of the potential offender.

Drawing on Tversky and Kahnemen (1974), Sherman suggests that the key deterrence mechanisms in crackdowns comprise heightened perceived risk and heightened uncertainty over the level of risk that would be incurred by offending. Crackdowns are thus deemed to disrupt the existing sense of risk-level and create uncertainty over it. Potential offenders may then substantially overestimate the actual risk and avoid crime. Repeat random crackdowns, with periods of withdrawal, would fuel this uncertainty, in effect continuously disrupting emerging confidence among the likely offending population. Continuing a given crackdown beyond a certain period, however, will allow a new stable sense of risk to evolve and hence crime could be expected to resume – the heightened uncertainty mechanism is gradually extinguished. The end of a particular crackdown, though, would not necessarily lead to an immediate restabilisation of risk estimates among prospective offenders, especially if the crackdown withdrawal happened unannounced. Sherman suggests that the same volume of resources from the police might be used intermittently in crackdowns to sustain uncertainty as could be used to maintain a given, relatively continuous presence, enabling potential offenders fairly confidently to gauge levels of risk. In the course of his theoretical discussion, Sherman acknowledges variations in the nature of those targeted which will be significant for mechanisms of adaptation to the crackdown conditions. He notes that some kinds of offender will be quicker than others at learning about risk levels and changes in them: highly active criminal populations are deemed likely to learn (and hence adapt) more quickly than less active ones (Sherman, 1990: 11). Sherman also notes that the precise attributes of the crackdown, including its intensity, sanction levels and forms of publicity will be significant for the change mechanisms activated and the outcomes brought about.

To bring home his theory, Sherman cleverly invites us to take part in a thought experiment. He asks us to imagine two approaches by the income tax authorities. In one they focus on those with known tax-evasion risk attributes. In the other they randomise their selection such that half of all taxpayers with a given birthday are audited unpredictably once a decade. His hunch is that with high publicity the outcome of the second approach would be less recovered revenue per audit but greater revenue overall from those not audited. Taxpayers would send in returns that are more honest to avoid the uncertain risk.

This policy we are invited to prefer is counterintuitive. Most would probably conclude at first sight that efficiency and effectiveness are maximised by targeting audit resources on those with attributes most associated with evasion.

Studies of crackdowns

At the level of theory Sherman refers to attributes of the crackdown which change the context for potential offenders, to the causal mechanisms relevant to offending that crackdowns may activate, and to expected outcome patterns in the light of the causal mechanisms activated by the crackdown. He goes on to review studies of crackdowns and their impacts. Matters here become a little more complex.

Five additional change mechanisms emerge, generating their particular crime pattern outcomes:

1   *Adaptation/innovation.* Sherman refers to a study finding offender innovation in the light of the new uncertainties facing them. Drug dealers in New York's Lower East Side responding to a prolonged crackdown were reported to have developed 'new and [less public] marketing strategies that would reduce their risk of arrest' (Zimmer, 1986, quoted in Sherman, 1990: 24). Sherman's point here fits with Ekblom's more general point about the liability of offenders to adapt to preventers' efforts to thwart them, by whatever means (Ekblom, 1997). It comprises an additional explanation for the limited time span for the impact of a crackdown.

2   *Sense of threat/twitchiness.* Sherman refers to Operation Clean Sweep in Washington which targeted drug markets. The numbers of homicides almost doubled (from 148 to 287) and the proportion attributed to drugs went up from 17 per cent to 68 per cent (Molotsky, 1988, cited in Sherman, 1990). The hypothesis is that dealers felt more threatened (hence twitchy) with the crackdown (Reuter et al., 1988, cited in Sherman, 1990). Moreover, the switch to dealing in apartments provoked by the crackdown put more people at risk during shootings.

3   *Sensitivity to publicity/shame.* Sherman notes the sensitivity of some to sanctions and publicity if their offending behaviour is exposed. He speculates that this mechanism may be class (context) sensitive – middle-class offenders being especially susceptible (Sherman, 1990: 25). He takes this to be especially significant where crackdowns

affect more middle-class populations of potential targets, for example where drunk driving is the target offence.

4   *Initial shock/loss of confidence.* Sherman refers to initial shock as an explanation for the short-term effects and long-term decays found across several studies reviewed (Sherman, 1990: 36). Initial shock may not, of course, comprise a separate mechanism but simply be an acute version of uncertainty creation.

5   *Market pressures/need for revenue.* Sherman refers to classic market mechanisms in discussing how drugs supplies are reduced through crackdown leading to a price rise and a consequent need for addicts to raise more money through increased crime (in the case cited, robbery) to 'maintain their habits' (Barnett, 1988, cited in Sherman, 1990: 19).

Sherman also refers to contextual variations in the crackdowns included in his review. These sometimes concern attributes of the areas into which the crackdowns were introduced and sometimes features of the crackdowns themselves. Such variations matter where they create differences in the causal mechanisms that are activated, and hence the types of outcome brought about:

1   *Class variations.* As already mentioned, class variations may be relevant in relation to responses to heightened risk and uncertainty because of differences in patterns of perceived consequences.

2   *Available alternatives variations.* Sherman cites a study in Lynn, Massachusetts where there were readily available alternative locations for drug supplies to street criminals (Kleiman, 1988, cited in Sherman, 1990: 19). There is an implicit contrast with sites without readily available alternative sources.

3   *Dosage variations.* Police presence crackdowns in large areas tend to be relatively dilute. Low-dosage crackdowns have smaller effects presumably because they fail significantly to trigger heightened risk and/or uncertainty over level of risk. This was found, according to Sherman (1990: 19) in Kleiman's studies of the crackdown on drug markets in Lynn and Lawrence, Massachusetts.

4   *Publicity variations.* Sherman cites outcome variations associated with differences in levels of publicity. Sherman refers to a study in Cheshire where an unpublicised but otherwise fully implemented crackdown relating to drunk driving was associated with no change

in numbers of serious crashes. In contrast highly publicised crackdowns in Britain were accompanied by sharp falls at the times when drink-related accidents would otherwise be expected (Ross, 1973, 1981, cited in Sherman, 1990: 26–7). Presumably, only specific-deterrence mechanisms are activated by stops and checks alone, whereas more general deterrence mechanisms are activated where there is also publicity.

5   *Duration variations.* According to Sherman, long crackdowns differ from short ones in the scope for offenders to learn and adapt in the course of them. Short-term crackdowns included in the review showed no signs of deterrence decay, while there were some signs of deterrence decay in most of the long-term crackdowns (Sherman, 1990: 35).

As might be expected given context and mechanism variations in the studies reported by Sherman, differences in outcome pattern are identified also. These include, for example:

- reduction in the number of arrests;
- increased drug prices;
- initial deterrence decay;
- fall then rise in robberies to higher than pre-crackdown levels;
- displacement beyond the immediate locale of the crackdown;
- increased homicide;
- displacement of open drugs market to a closed one;
- geographical displacement of drug market use;
- quick re-establishment of drug market;
- Residual accident fall (deterrence) during drink-driving crackdown back-off;
- fall then rise in subway crime over two years;
- pre drink-driving crackdown, but post-publicity reduction in cars at taverns and hospital admissions from car crashes.

Unsurprisingly, none of these outcomes is found universally. Crackdowns differ in target, implementation and context. Sherman, however, identifies initial deterrence in 15 of the 18 studies covered in his review. This comprises pretty robust evidence that targeted crackdowns *can* produce a short-term reduction in crime, but not that they will always do so. He also concludes that displacement is not an inevitable side effect though he presents evidence that it can happen – it was clearly indicated in four of the crackdowns considered. Sherman found none of the successful short-term crackdowns to suffer initial deterrence decay, though he reports it in most long-term ones where evidence was provided. For all five projects tracking what went on post-crackdown, which had also found an initial effect, Sherman reports residual deterrence during the back-off period. Crime reductions thus normally continued beyond the operating period of the crackdown.

Sherman's findings seem to support the inclusion of brief crackdowns as one potential component of a crime reduction strategy. Indeed, Sherman suggests that benefits might be maximised by the accompaniment of publicity announcing the crackdown but not their ending, and by switching the focus of the crackdown. This will take advantage of anticipatory deterrence and residual deterrence effects extending the period during which impact is felt. These extensions to the period of impact comprise a form of 'diffusion of benefits'.[1] New crackdowns can be initiated intermittently and when crime levels rise again above an acceptable level.

Sherman's case for making use of crackdowns is quite compelling. However, part of the evidence Sherman himself provides, as well as the Brixton experience, suggest that crackdowns are not always benign in their effects. They can sometimes produce unintended and unwanted side effects. This explains, of course, the need for a realist reading of the evidence to determine how they produce what outcomes for whom and in what circumstances. Only with this can informed decisions be made about when it is safe and useful and when it is unsafe or useless to apply crackdown responses to crime problems.

There is a good deal of devil in the detail in individual cases. Sherman summarises one unpublished report, which suggests some complex context–mechanisms–outcome patterns:

Zimmer (1986) has documented how some drug dealers and users responded to the Lower East Side crackdown. She claims, apparently from interviews, that many stayed off the streets at first, waiting for law enforcement to return to 'normal'; some took vacations out of the country. When the crackdown was maintained, she reports, the 'drug sellers' began to re-emerge, developing the new [less public] marketing strategies that would decrease their risk of 'arrest' (1986: 24). Moreover, she claims that the more gentrified areas of the crackdown zone experienced no decay in the deterrence of public drug dealing, which remained suppressed. Rather, despite police concentration of more personnel on the poorer blocks, the greatest visible decay was observed there. (Sherman, 1990: 21–2)

There are several outcomes, mechanisms and contexts here. The outcomes include initial withdrawal of dealers, their changed methods of working and the variations in change in locations of drug dealing within the area covered by the crackdown. Mechanisms include (presumably) heightened uncertainty and perceived risk among dealers, efforts by dealers to spot opportunities to return to previous activities, and their subsequent adaptations in methods of operating to circumvent the increased risks presented by the new conditions. The variation in outcome by sub-area (context) within the scope of the crackdown is unexplained. Perhaps local resident hostility is greater (or perceived to be greater) to dealers contemplating a return.

Zimmer's account suggests that the particular details of any particular location will need to be considered in individual crackdown decisions. The best that social science can hope to offer is some evidence-based theory to inform practitioners and policy-makers about the sorts of details that need to be looked at and why. Before coming to that, though, three further accounts of crime-reduction work involving crackdowns are briefly summarised.

Random breath tests in New South Wales

From December 1982 police in New South Wales were able to pull drivers over randomly to take a preliminary breath test. They did so in large numbers and with extensive publicity. As Homel (1995) put it, there were 'highly publicised and visible random checking procedures applied indiscriminately to the whole population of potential offenders'. About a million tests were made in the first year, in a population of three million drivers. There was no 'back-off'. Many of the ingredients found in successful crackdowns were present. There was a substantially middle-class target group, heavy publicity and significantly increased police activity. Most importantly, the major apparent mechanisms, consistent with Sherman's theory, comprised a plausible increase in risk and the creation of heightened anxiety about whether the risk was high or low on any given occasion (Homel, 1995). No increase in arrests followed, but there was a dramatic and instantaneous fall in fatal crashes (by 22 per cent) and more especially in alcohol-related fatal crashes (36 per cent). The falls have been maintained for at least a decade. Homel argues that 'RBT succeeds not at the level of efficient enforcement of the law but as a *communications exercise*. By removing from the offender all control over risks of apprehension, and by keeping him guessing as to what those risks are at any time, RBT changes in a strategic way the game of "breathalyser roulette" many drinkers engage in' (original italics). In the RBT experiment Homel also notes what he deems to have been crucial contextual conditions. Public views on drinking and driving were changing and citizens were minded to stop. RBT provided a trigger and pretext for initiating changed behaviour. It gave drivers an 'excuse' to stay dry, where they might otherwise have found it difficult to refuse a drink – an interesting supplementary change mechanism. Homel believes that the RBT experience suggests the more general use of a 'keep potential offenders guessing' mechanism.

The Boston gun project

Whereas the focus of the New South Wales RBT was indiscriminate and 'worked' because no one could evade police enforcement attention, the crackdown provisions in Boston 'worked' because potential targets for enforcement attention could reduce risks by behaving in specified ways (Braga et al., 1999). Gang conflict lay behind many shootings in Boston. Operation Ceasefire attempted to reduce them. In this, in the event of an incident a crackdown would be initiated in relation not just to the supposed perpetrator, but to all relevant gang members. The Operation Ceasefire crackdown was implemented by a wide range of enforcement agencies in Boston, not just the police. Moreover, it was highly publicised in meetings with gang members, through flyers and through the media. There was an immediate and dramatic fall in shootings. The mechanisms here relate not so much to uncertainty about enforcement as to a promise over its certainty. Though not in any sense made exempt from normal police enquiries, gang members could avoid bringing sustained broad-based attention to all their activities and ways of life by avoiding engaging in shootings. They did so. Kennedy (1997) suggests that leverage along these general lines could be applied across a range of unwanted behaviours, where classes of offender could avoid inviting wide enforcement attention by ceasing to engage in defined behaviours. In the case of the gangs it is plausible that informal social control by some gang members of their colleagues might have been applied to avoid the generalised police attention. Moreover, the background research to Ceasefire suggested that many gang members would prefer not to carry weapons. They did so defensively. Reduced risk would lead to reduced weapon carrying, and fewer opportunities and temptations to use them. If this is the context for weapons use then success in triggering an initial fall in shootings might be expected to bring further change processes in train consolidating the effects of the crackdown per se.[2]

Crackdown and consolidation in Boggart Hill

In Boggart Hill, part of a local authority housing estate in Leeds, a crackdown was targeted on suspected prolific burglars in the area, with the intention of incapacitating those offenders as well as achieving general deterrence as the crackdown became known (Farrell et al., 2000). In the crime lull achieved through the crackdown, longer-term measures, including for example security upgrades on vulnerable, victimised properties, were put in place to achieve longer-term falls – the consolidation side of the strategy. In this area analysis suggested that the vast majority of offences were committed by high-rate offenders who commit burglaries at a uniform rate. Rates of burglary varied with the number active burglars available to commit them, suggesting that the incapacitation was leading to a fall in burglary. Diffusions of benefit were found in the form of reductions in thefts of vehicles in Boggart Hill and of burglary in adjacent areas – suggesting that the offenders were generalists and also tended to commit their offences locally, though not necessarily exclusively in Boggart Hill.

A revised, realist account of crackdowns

Let us turn now to realist readings of the literature looked at here. Table 8.2 presents a series of context–mechanism–outcome (CMO) pattern configurations that are suggested. It is clear that much of Sherman's original theory remains intact, though it is supplemented with fresh insights from empirical research.

It is unlikely, though, that all significant contexts and mechanisms liable to be activated by crackdowns have yet been identified here. Sherman himself notes one further mechanism not mentioned so far, in a study that took place after his review of literature on crackdowns. He notes illegally held gun seizure in Kansas City, following the intro- duction of targeted patrol (Sherman et al., 1995).[3] In the same study context variation is used to explain the success in using body language cues to spot those carrying concealed weapons in New York City but their failure in Kansas City. Because of enormous differences in population density, in Kansas City people tend to travel by car but in New York they walk. As Sherman et al. (1995) put it, 'The social and physical characteristics of cities vary widely, and these methods may work better in different kinds of communities.'

What we do have so far, however, are the beginnings of a partially evidenced-tested account that may help inform decisions about the propriety and usefulness of crackdowns as part of a crime reduction strategy. The final section of the chapter spells out some possible practical implications.

The place of crackdowns in crime reduction

The potential for crackdowns to produce disastrous side effects speaks in favour of their application only with very great caution. The expense and short-term impact of any single crackdown tells against their use simply as occasional acts of desperation in the face of recurrent problems (Read and Tilley, 2000). The availability of many alternative ways of addressing specific problems, including tactics that do not turn on enforcement at all, suggests that crackdowns, even if potentially effective, may not comprise the only option or the best option (Goldstein, 1990).

Despite these caveats about the use of crackdowns they may still have a place within crime reduction strategies, where problems are serious and the context suggests likely beneficial effects, the absence of countervailing, unwanted side effects and no plausible preferable alternative strategies. There are at least three possible ways they might be used constructively.

1 *To nip problems in the bud*. If a crime problem were emerging and there were grounds for believing it could otherwise become more serious, then a crackdown might conceivably be used to eliminate it early. This is the basic logic of 'broken windows', where a concerted response at a tipping point is designed to avert a spiral of decline into more serious and entrenched problems (Wilson and Kelling, 1982).

2 *To keep offenders guessing in the long term*. Sherman's prescription for sporadic, repeated but unpredictable crackdowns, introduced with publicity and abandoned quietly, is designed to maximise offender uncertainty and the period of crackdown impact. Repetition is designed to maintain significant levels of uncertainty over risk.

3 *To create conditions for longer-term, non-crackdown measures effectively to be introduced*. In some circumstances, crackdowns may provide necessary conditions for the operation of longer-term measures. In the case of the Boston gun project longer-term social measures had not been having a discernable effect prior to Operation Ceasefire.

Table 8.2 Some realist CMO configurations for crackdowns

Intervention	Context	Mechanism	Outcome
Sudden unannounced high police presence in area	Marginal groups, with low levels of police trust, but some internal cohesion	Indignation; provocation; police delegitimation and mistrust	Resistance and riot; reduced cooperation with the police
Well-publicised high initial police presence in area, with quiet withdrawal	High crime transitional area	Increased risk perception; uncertainty over risk	Rapid initial crime fall
	High-rate offenders	Innovation and speedy re-estimates of changed risk	Early resumption of crime as revised risk estimates made; some innovation in MOs; quick initial and residual deterrence decay
	Low-rate offenders	Non-innovation and slow re-estimate of risk and slow realisation of crackdown withdrawal	Gradual initial and residual deterrence decay
Area crackdown on property crimes	High crime proceeds need offenders (perhaps because of drug dependency)	Adaptation to offending patterns to yield equivalent returns	Displacement of offending by place, type or method
Time-limited crackdown on specific behaviour	'Respectable' offenders	Anxiety over apprehension; uncertainty over risk; inability to control risk	Quickly reduced offending; residual deterrence decay

	Plausible messages to offenders	Perceived increase in risk; uncertainty over level of risk increase	Rapidly reduced offending pre (or without actual) crackdown; residual deterrence till absence of reduced risk perceived
Publicity announcing crackdown	Members of groups wanting to be deemed 'respectable'	Anxiety about uncertain and uncontrollable risk of exposure to shame	Rapid fall in targeted behaviour and slow resumption
Randomised enforcement/ crackdowns on individuals, with minor penalties	Members of 'marginal' groups	?Anger at arbitrary, unexpected detection or resignation at penalty	?Violence, compensatory crime, compliance with punishment
Conditional crackdowns, applied to membership group following specified behaviours	Offenders belonging to loose groups engaged in diverse behaviour open to enforcement activities	Perceived heightened group risk and costs of generalised enforcement on members; informal social control within target group	Reduced behaviour activating crackdown
Sustained low publicity, low dosage crackdown over large area	Typical offender population	Crackdown not noticed. lacks/ quickly loses credibility	No change
Crackdown targeted on suspected prolific offenders	Large proportion of offences committed by known regular, high-rate offenders	Incapacitation; general deterrence	Reduction in crime proportionate to supply of high-rate offenders at any given time.

Note: Except for entries marked '?', these are rooted in some evidence, though it is far from conclusive.

The crackdown introduced by Ceasefire may have created conditions in which the social measures in place could begin to have an effect. By breaking the cycle of weapon carrying and weapon use and by providing a pretext for members to leave gangs Operation Ceasefire may have opened the way for social measures to be taken up by gang members (Braga et al., 2000; Bullock and Tilley, 2002). In the case of the crackdown and consolidation strategy implemented in Boggart Hill, there is evidence of the immediate effects of the offender-focused crackdown and of some longer-term victim-focused consolidation (Farrell et al., 2000). Figure 8.1 shows a vicious cycle of neighbourhood decline in one area in Wolverhampton (Tilley and Webb, 1994). Part of the response involved a crackdown on the families intimidating residents, creating a breather while other physical and social measures were adopted in relation to other elements in the cycle. The estate has since ceased to suffer the chronic and widespread crime and disorder problems that had earlier afflicted it. A similar pattern occurred in an estate in Leicester where a crackdown accompanied the introduction of a variety of social measures in a coherent strategy. This evidently produced some sustained effects (Leigh et al., 1998). The random breath testing in New South Wales created conditions in which a growing disposition not to drink could be acted on since the crackdown gave an acceptable pretext to stay dry (Homel, 1995). In regard to drugs markets, May et al. (2000) have argued that success in their disruption through concerted enforcement activities needs to be complemented by treatment services for users and situational measures in the market's locality.[4]

Finally, there may be potential benefits from applying crackdowns to offences characteristically or frequently committed by those who are socially integrated and jealous of their reputations, especially members of the middle classes. Homel's account of the random breath testing introduced in New South Wales suggests that it might be effective. Sherman's thought experiment for tax evasion could, perhaps, become a real experiment. Other offences that might be subject to revolving crackdowns might include, for example, crimes connected with fraud, pollution, breaches of safety regulations at work, internal theft, much domestic violence, false accounting and traffic violations. These are all potentially highly damaging areas of offending. The costs of detection are likely to be high. Police attention is very limited. The characteristic offenders are middle class and value their respectability. The unknown

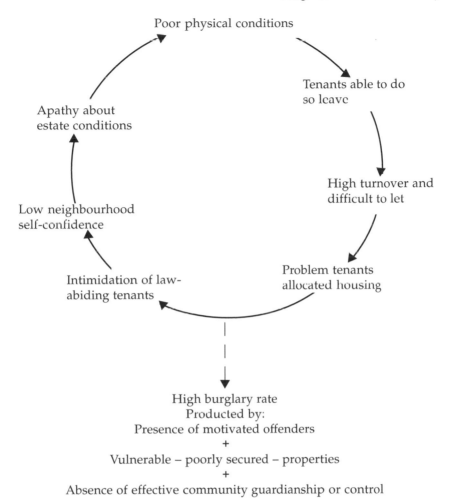

Figure 8.1 Neighbourhood decline in a Wolverhampton estate (from Tilley and Webb, 1994)

risk of exposure as 'common criminals', activated through the certainty of crackdowns but their unpredictable timing, might be very threatening and a substantial disincentive to crime. Moreover, though likely targets might resist the attention of enforcement agencies, their response is unlikely to be to riot. These groups and their likely offences are not, though, those who have so far ordinarily been targeted with crackdowns. Perhaps they should be.

Notes

1 Where the precise boundaries of a crackdown are unknown, there may also be other forms of benefit diffusion, for example by offence or by geographical scope.
2 A strategy was agreed for Manchester that would replicate elements of Ceasefire in Britain. See Bullock and Tilley (2002).
3 This amounts to 'crime resource removal' in Ekblom and Tilley's terms (2000).
4 May et al. (2000) also note, however, innovations in methods of operating the market with the arrival of mobile phones, making crackdowns more difficult.

Chapter 9

Tackling the roots of theft: reducing tolerance toward stolen goods markets

Mike Sutton

Introduction

Most crimes require convergence in space and time of likely offenders, suitable targets and the absence of capable guardians against crime (Cohen and Felson, 1979). Selling or buying stolen goods is commonly known as handling. Handling (knowingly buying or selling stolen goods) is an offence under the Theft Act 1968 and – as a crime like any other – can be explained by Cohen and Felson's model. However, handling is also what might be termed a *precursor crime*, because knowledge of the markets for stolen goods provides the motivation for theft (Sutton, 1995, 1998). Stolen goods markets motivate thieves because most steal goods to sell for cash, whatever they want to spend that cash on. Ground-breaking research reveals that some 29 per cent of arrested thieves are heroin or cocaine users and that these are the most prolific offenders, probably responsible for more than three-fifths of illegal income generated by thieves selling stolen goods in England and Wales (Bennett et al., 2001). It is not surprising, therefore, that so many crime experts now see drug use as the root of theft. However, interviews with prolific thieves (Sutton, 1998; Sutton et al., 2001) also reveal that drug dealers are often reluctant to exchange drugs for stolen goods. Thieves know they can get more drugs if they buy with cash, having first sold their stolen booty, rather than taking the hot goods to their drug dealer where the exchange rate is at best poor and more usually the dealer will not want to know. This means that stolen goods markets play at least as an important part as regular hard drug use in explaining high theft rates and, therefore, represent an important opportunity for crime reduction initiatives.

Market demand for particular stolen items has an essential role in creating two of the three preconditions of theft incidents outlined by Cohen and Felson's model: *likely offenders* and *suitable targets*. Moreover, there are a sizeable number of people who are not particularly capable as *guardians* of law and order when it comes to the opportunity to resist a bargain. This means they are unlikely to be capable guardians of the law in the many places where stolen second-hand or new goods are offered for sale, even if, ironically, they are capable guardians in the places where the same goods are stolen. This can be demonstrated quite simply by the mathematics of the market. The 1994 British Crime Survey revealed, for the first time, the prevalence of handling among people in Britain: 11 per cent admitted buying stolen goods in the previous five years, 70 per cent thought that some of their neighbours had stolen goods such as TVs and VCRs in their homes and 11 per cent had been offered stolen goods in the past 12 months (Sutton, 1998). Put simply, there are more handlers than thieves.

In Britain in 1995, an unpublished document by the National Statistics Office entitled: 'UK National Accounts' reveals, for the first time, a government estimate of the extent of the contribution of the informal economy to the UK economy. The document reveals that thieves selling stolen property may have cleared as much as £1.68 billion (net) and that handlers probably cleared as much as £870 million (net) through selling stolen property.[1] About 18,000 handling cases are sentenced annually, compared with 17,500 for domestic burglary, 13,000 other burglary, 15,000 fraud, 5,500 robbery and 66,500 for shoplifting (Sentencing Advisory Panel, 2001).

Tolerance towards stolen goods markets in everyday life

Marcus Felson is arguably the world's leading writer in the field of crime reduction. In the second edition of his book *Crime and Everyday Life* (1998), he tells us about the existence and influence of pawn shops and other outlets in his own neighbourhood advertising that they buy gold and diamonds and used electrical goods. Indeed, such is the importance now attached to stolen goods markets by Felson that a photograph of a pawn broker's store now features on the cover of the third edition of *Crime and Everyday Life* (Felson, 2002). The everyday examples of crime that Felson writes about in his book add meaning to his writing, because it is important for the reader to see how it is that 'everyday' opportunities facilitate most offending behaviour. Adopting the *Felsonian tradition* this chapter includes one of the author's own recent crime and everyday life experiences:

A week before sitting down to write this chapter on stolen goods markets I was offered stolen goods myself. It had been a while since that's happened, but I've moved recently to a new city and consequently find I've made new friends who don't yet know that I have a thing about *not* buying stolen goods. The person making the offer was a friend of a friend. We were having a glass of wine at my friend's house and remarking on the high price of her wide-screen, surround-sound, digital TV and DVD home cinema system.

At this point I was told that I could have a DVD player, in its original box, brand new, for £50. If I wanted anything else, such as a digital camcorder, I could have one for half the high street price. 'Its OK,' my friend's friend said. 'I'm not sure how it's done but they come from a shop – not out of peoples' houses. And if anything goes wrong with them you can have another or your money back.'

I jokingly asked if this contact could secure for me a half-price plasma screen TV, which at the time of writing tend to retail for around £5,000. My friend's friend seemed quite sure that it could be arranged. At which point, I let her know that I was not really serious and did not think it right to buy stolen goods.

Later that evening we drove my friend's friend and her 6-year-old daughter home to a run-down public sector housing estate in a high crime area of the city. We sat with the car headlights trained on her at her front door as she struggled with the four separate door locks that she had installed to keep the burglars out of her house. Ironic, I thought as we drove away, that she is plagued by fear of thieves because her house contains a lot of desirable in-home entertainment equipment – all of it stolen.

Like many people, who would otherwise consider themselves respectable and law-abiding, my friend's friend insists that the stolen goods she buys as 'bargains' must be new and boxed – and so clearly not from other people's houses. This is not unusual. I have been involved in researching stolen goods markets since 1993, and the distinction between acceptable and unacceptable stolen goods is made many times in the literature (see, for example, Henry, 1976). It also occurs regularly in the course of my own research (Sutton, 1995, 1998).

The purpose of reporting the events that happened to me only recently is to show just how typical such situations are. And the purpose behind writing this chapter in a book on hard and soft policing and zero tolerance is to show just how it is that tolerance towards the question-able provenance of 'bargains' is helping to fuel acquisitive crime rates in the UK and other consumer oriented societies.

Tolerance, the law and crime reduction

Compared with convictions for theft, very few handlers are ever found guilty. One of the main reasons for this is the relative difficulty involved in proving the requirement of section 22(1) of the Theft Act 1968 that someone either knew or believed the goods to be stolen (see Sutton, 1993). Judicial interpretation of this legislation has been such that mere suspicion that goods are stolen is not enough to lead to conviction for handing unless the defendant either knows or is virtually certain that they are stolen goods (Hall, 1952). From this cause, Glanville Williams (1985) stressed the need to understand the legal meaning of 'belief', within section 22, that goods are stolen as '... the sort of belief we would associate with a devout religious believer' not as a belief that goods are probably stolen. In defence of this judicial interpretation, Williams (1985: 433) argues that there are good reasons why the law treats receiving with particular caution because

> ... people must be allowed a margin of safety. If they cannot buy goods that they know to be probably stolen, then they cannot safely buy goods when there is an appreciable possibility that they are stolen, because no one knows when lawyers, judges and juries between them may not turn possibilities into probabilities.

This consideration, above all others, has placed severe constraints on what can be achieved in the way of controlling burglary and other thefts by purely legislative measures aimed at receiving. Even when they have a clear case of guilt before them, the courts are particularly cautious when it comes down to determining the degree of seriousness to be attached to handling. While the criminal justice system has the potential power to treat handling stolen goods seriously – with a maximum sentence of 14 years – only 20 per cent of offenders sentenced for this offence receive custodial sentences. In determining the severity of punishment, courts are keen to distinguish between so-called professional handlers of stolen goods and the 'average citizen' who succumbs to temptation and buys a cheap VCR (see Sentencing Advisory Panel, 2001).

It could be argued that current judicial thinking is not taking account of the fact that research now shows illicit markets not to be simply a downstream consequence of theft but the primary motivation (see Sutton, 1998; Sutton et al., 2001; Felson, 2002; Langworthy and LeBau, 1992). Since the time when Hall and Williams were writing there has been a near doubling in numbers of acquisitive crimes committed and only one or two studies of burglars and thieves have paid any attention to what they actually do with stolen goods (see Sutton, 1998; Sutton et al., 2001). Attention has tended to focus more upon why burglars and other thieves target particular buildings (Bennett and Wright, 1984) or vehicles in particular car parks (Tilley, 1993). However, the reasons why certain houses are burgled or cars stolen from certain car parks – e.g. less risk of detection or apprehension – are not the same as those which influence the decision of an offender to steal particular items. In fact, theft rates have gone up since the time of Jerome Hall's jurisprudential masterpiece, not because our houses and cars are more vulnerable – quite the opposite, actually – but simply because people own many more goods that are worth stealing. This is the case because markets have grown in poorer areas where these goods can be sold by thieves for ready cash.

Research shows that theft has taken off in line with the growth of consumerist culture and clearly increases in the recession periods that follow economic booms (Field, 1990). This is because there has been a rapid growth in ownership of lightweight consumer durables in the past 20 years, and it seems most likely that this has played the most important role in leading burglars and other thieves to assume that many properties contain such goods (Sutton, 1995, 1998; Clarke, 1999). Theft probably happens more in times of economic recession because people still want the expensive consumer goods in the high street but fewer can afford high street prices (Sutton, 1995). It is unlikely that on the whole people become unemployed and, therefore, start stealing more (Field, 1990) but probably that the market for stolen goods expands at such times among those who would buy goods on a *no questions asked* basis.

The rapid growth in the ownership of consumer products has been fuelled by the constant introduction of new 'must have' upgraded models by manufacturers. The constant introduction and technical development of leading-edge items – such as mobile phones, games consoles, TVs, hi-fis, DVDs or PCs – has, in turn, meant that it is quite common to see such used consumer durables offered for sale to those who cannot afford, or do not wish, to buy new. And it is this combination of ready supply of goods with a new and ready market for them which provides offenders with motivation to steal in the first place. It makes breaking into unknown property likely to be worth-while. What we have by way of the cars on our streets and goods in our homes is a kind of *illegal lucky dip* where thieves can easily exchange their prize for cash. So, in terms of embarking upon and sustaining a lifestyle supported by crime, theft is a good bet because there is a high probability of finding valuable goods in homes and cars. This good bet is complemented by the ease with which thieves can convert loot into the cash that they crave to support a drug/party lifestyle. These facts suggest that stolen goods markets are probably a strangely neglected area where crime reduction schemes might prove particularly useful in tackling the very roots of theft.

The current *belt and braces* legislative situation

The rise of the consumer society since the time of Jerome Hall has meant that police forces have had to do what they can to regulate markets for stolen goods and to decrease the burden of proof required to successfully prove guilt under section 22 of the Theft Act. This has been done in the UK by *local legislative stealth*. Both the local Humberside Act of 1982 and the Medway Council Act of 2001, for example, lay down local rules for dealers in second-hand goods that aim to curtail trading among those who deal in stolen goods. The market reduction approach (MRA) (Sutton, 1998; Sutton et al., 2001) is currently part of the routine police work of West Mercia Constabulary (see: http://www.wedontbuycrime.org.uk/news.asp) and as part of this strategy the little used section 27 of the Theft Act of 1968 is being deployed as a routine prosecution measure. This section allows for joint prosecution of those suspected of stealing and/or handling stolen goods. More importantly, however, is the provision that streamlines the process of proving criminal intent of theft or handling for those who have been convicted of either of these offences within a five-year period prior to a current charge and who have within their possession stolen goods from a theft occurring no more than 12 months prior to the current charge. Put simply, with section 27 it is possible, for the purpose of proving that a person knew or believed goods to be stolen, to present evidence of their earlier convictions for theft or handling stolen goods. Whether or not this will prove to be an effective prosecution measure is yet to be determined by those responsible for evaluating the project.

Tackling theft with the MRA

It is essential that we know what happens to stolen goods if we are to seek to reduce motivation to steal. This is because asking the questions who does what to whom, when, in which way and with what effect helps to identify risks from particular offenders in certain situations and identifies threats to the potential targets of their offending. The answers to what might be termed the 6Ws – the who? what? to whom? when? which way? questions – also help us to formulate strategies for dealing with risks. The Home Office Handling Study (Sutton, 1998) set out to answer the 6Ws in relation to stolen goods markets. Undertaking the first ever systematic analysis of stolen goods markets, the study involved 45 in-depth interviews with thieves and fences conducted in prisons, young offender institutions and probation offices, and in the homes of convicted and non-convicted offenders. The study identified five main market types:

1 *Commercial fence supplies.* Stolen goods are sold by thieves to commercial fences (e.g. jewellers, pawn brokers, second-hand dealers) operating out of shops.

2 *Residential fence supplies.* Stolen goods (particularly electrical goods) are sold by thieves to fences, usually at the home of the fence.

3 *Network sales.* Stolen goods are passed on and each participant adds a little to the price until a consumer is found; this may involve a residential fence, and the buyer may be the final consumer or may sell the goods on again through friendship networks.

4 *Commercial sales.* Stolen goods are sold by commercial fences for a profit, either directly to the (innocent) consumer or to another distributor who thinks the goods can be sold again for additional profit. More rarely, such sales are made to another distributor.

5. *Hawking.* Thieves sell directly to consumers in places such as bars and clubs, or door to door (e.g. shoplifters selling clothes or food).

Although the Handling Study found that particularly active fences tend to encourage thieves to increase their offending, it also revealed that stolen goods markets are mainly fuelled by thieves offering goods for sale rather than by proactive demand from dealers. On the basis of the limited evidence available, it appears that offers from thieves to sell stolen goods have the greatest influence on the way that stolen goods markets operate. This is because most dealers and consumers do not actively seek out stolen goods. Therefore these items need to be offered to them in order for them to be able *knowingly* to buy. Stealing to order does go on, and the practice is quite widespread, but it is not as common as what should, perhaps, be called *stealing to offer* (Sutton, 2002). As Marcus Felson (2002) concludes in his chapter on marketing stolen goods: '... offers of second-class merchandise at low prices are exactly what drives crime in local areas'.

In Britain, new knowledge of the practice of stealing to offer was first used to create an initial menu of *situational* tactics designed to reduce theft through the MRA (Sutton, 1998). That menu was then further developed to form the core element of a report that provides a strategic and systematic 'toolkit' for reducing stolen goods markets (Sutton et al., 2001).

In simple terms, the market reduction solution should be arrived at by a process of lateral thinking, which is referred to as *lateral strategy* (Sutton et al., 2001). This involves working back from the particular local crime problem to devise or adopt suitable crime reducing tactics. In many cases police forces and other agencies employed to reduce all kinds of crimes seek to try to apply a *favourite solution*, such as, for example, using property marking in an attempt to reduce all theft problems. Such off-the-peg solutions as this are not likely to be effective in areas where thieves steal marked property, people buy it and the police intercept less than 1 per cent of it (Sutton et al., 2001). Despite this fact, even some UK police forces, that, incidentally, have been granted many tens of thousands of pounds of government money to implement the innovative MRA approach, have found it difficult to break with *favoured practices* and have gone on to spend large proportions of their budget on property marking – including mailing 98,000 ultra violet marker pens to addresses in the Medway Towns (see: http://www.radium.org.uk/news_arch.html). Such spending continues in police forces despite the fact that Home Office (Sutton, 1998) and other research (Knutsson, 1984) suggests that such property marking has never been shown to reduce crime because thieves steal it just the same and handlers buy it. Although property marking is one of the easiest initiatives to undertake, it is unlikely to be cost-effective and should not be undertaken as part of an MRA project unless it forms part of a local strategy that will genuinely and significantly increase the likelihood of thieves and handlers being caught in possession of marked goods. Whether or not property marking in the Medway Towns was a cost-effective tactic when combined with other measures will be determined in the near future by the government-appointed independent evaluators of that project.

The MRA: zero tolerance on handling

In the eyes of most acquisitive offenders, property represents money – hard cash – or else it is stolen to be swapped directly for illegal drugs with drug dealing fences. Therefore, in most cases, unless thieves believe that they can sell what they steal they will not steal it, and if they cannot sell it anyway then they are unlikely to want to risk stealing it again for no reward. If we know this, then it makes sense to increase the risks associated with selling stolen goods and to reduce the rewards. This thinking is at the centre of the MRA.

Tackling stolen goods markets is 'root-level' situational crime prevention

Following research into stolen goods markets and development of the MRA (Sutton, 1995, 1998; Sutton et al., 2001), situational crime prevention and the routine activities theory now pay particular regard to tackling offender motivation. This is a major development because in the past Clarke and Felson's approaches were interpreted by many writers to have, for the most part, 'side-stepped' the question of why offenders *are* motivated. Arguably, Clarke and Felson's work has, in the past, concentrated more upon the opportunities for crime – particularly the opportunities for acquisitive offending (see, for example, Sutton, 1995; Crawford, 1998; Hopkins-Burke, 2001). However, in many cases, opportunity cannot be separated from motivation. To emphasise a point already made, without an opportunity to, for example, easily convert stolen property into cash, or cash in on an offer to buy cheap goods (Felson, 2002), there is little motivation to steal or deal in stolen goods.

More offers to sell to the public stolen goods are made in the poorest areas in Britain (Sutton, 1998) and, as the Handling Study reveals, the more offers a person gets the more likely they are to buy. It was found that 7 per cent of those living in the most affluent areas were offered stolen goods compared to 17 per cent in the poorest areas. Again, the degree to which offers are made influences decisions to buy. It seems that more than half of people conform to the law against handling most of the time, since 56 per cent of those offered stolen goods resisted the temptation to buy. However, the research found that the more offers people receive then the more likely they are to buy: 68 per cent of those offered stolen goods *once* resisted the temptation to buy, 54 per cent of those offered *a few times* resisted, but only 29 per cent of those offered stolen goods on *a regular basis* resisted. That said, it is important to be cautious about interpreting these findings in a simple linear manner. Actual buying behaviour in illicit markets is inextricably linked to the number of offers a person might receive, but the number of offers they receive may also be inextricably linked to what the seller knows about their past buying behaviour.

As the most extreme example of the link between buying habits and receiving offers one has only to look at the way that professional fencing operations work. Professional fences do not have to go out looking for stolen goods; thieves make a beeline for the nearest fencing operation (Klockars, 1974; Steffensmeier, 1986; Langworthy and Lebau, 1992). An interesting example of the way that this can actually get out of control for the fence is described in detail in an important study of a corner shop fencing operation carried out by Mike Maguire and published in the Handling Study (see Appendix 3 in Sutton, 1998).

Avoid bad practice – don't reinvent the flat tyre

Langworthy and Lebau (1992) found that it is a big mistake for police operations to set up sting operations even though fence stings bring the police excellent publicity and meet with widespread public approval (Felson, 2002). Whether run by criminals or set up as stings by the police, local fencing operations increase local theft rates because thieves do not like to travel far with stolen goods in their possession – it increases the risk of being caught – and a 'good and fair' fence will increase the incidence of theft (Sutton, 1998). No one could put it more plainly than Felson (2002: 81) who knows that it is necessary for those who implement law enforcement to take note of the facts learned from research: 'Providing a convenient fence is probably one of the worst ideas that law enforcement has ever come up with.'

Again, it is important to emphasise a point already made: in the light of all the evidence against it, and the scarce resources that it wastes, it is suggested here that property marking is probably the second worst idea that law enforcement has ever come up with (see Knutsson, 1984; Sutton, 1998) and if there were a competition to see which police force could waste the most public money earmarked for crime reduction, a close third would be operations that seek to return stolen goods to their rightful owners; they cost a relative fortune to operate, do not make sense in terms of reducing crime and do not even work (see, for example, Whitehead and Gray, 1998).

The MRA as 'root-level' crime opportunity reduction and situational crime prevention

Situational crime prevention involves the deployment of discrete managerial and environmental change to reduce the opportunities for crimes to occur and is particularly useful for designing solutions to prevent specific crime problems in the places where they usually happen (Clarke, 1977). The MRA builds on this by examining each of the different markets for stolen goods and then undertaking systematic intelligence-gathering to find out who is dealing in those markets and how they operate. By using an array of police tactics and interagency interventions to disrupt and reduce each type of market for stolen goods, the MRA aims to make stealing and dealing in stolen goods more difficult and risky, and therefore a less attractive way to make money. Tackling stolen goods markets with the MRA is not just about seeking to reduce handling offences because the primary aim is to reduce motivation for stealing by reducing dealing in order to reduce both the incidence and prevalence of theft in high crime areas.

The design of the MRA is heavily influenced by the routine activities approach – which is an approach that helps with our understanding of why crime occurs where it does. Routine activities advocates applying lateral thinking ('lateral strategy') to design tailor-made solutions to local problems. Many of the bespoke solutions suggested in the Home Office publication *Tackling Theft with the Market Reduction Approach* (Sutton et al., 2001) employ the situational crime prevention and routine activities approaches. The influence of Clarke's work can be seen in the following attempt to match the MRA to three of the main elements of the situational crime prevention philosophy:

1. INCREASING THE EFFORT OF OFFENDING
Focusing upon the:

Thief:
• Making it as hard to sell stolen goods as it is to steal them.

Dealer (fence):
• Making it difficult to safely buy and sell stolen goods.

Consumer:
• Reducing opportunities to buy and thereby deflecting consumers to legitimate markets – or alternative illegitimate markets where they

will have to work harder to find what they want – to the point where the expense/effort of searching becomes intolerable.

2. INCREASING THE RISKS OF OFFENDING
Focusing upon the:

Thief:
- Making it as least as risky to transport and sell stolen goods as it is to steal them.

Dealer:
- Making it much more risky to buy, transport, store and trade in stolen goods

Consumer:
- Making it much more risky to knowingly buy, transport and own stolen goods.

3. REDUCING THE REWARDS OF OFFENDING
Focusing upon the:

Thief:
- Reducing the price received for stolen goods because they are no longer so desirable – due to impact of moral exhortation and increased risks (no longer a seller's market).

Dealer:
- Reducing the profit margin on stolen goods due to the increased risks faced in inter-dealer trading and the perceived risks that the consumers face. Fewer stolen goods in circulation – no longer core source of income.

Consumer:
- Risks/guilt of purchasing and ownership outweigh the enjoyment of possession and use of stolen goods.

The MRA should be seen as a theft reduction strategy, not simply as a way to reduce illicit trading, because each essential attempt to reduce illicit markets is also essentially targeting both the theft process and loot trading process. To put it bluntly, in the words of the eighteenth-century magistrate Patrick Colquhoun (1796): 'No fences, no thieves.'

How the MRA fits the philosophy of the routine activities approach

1. Motivated offenders:
- Motivated *thieves* (selling stolen goods), *dealers* (buying/selling), *consumers* (buying/owning).

2. Suitable Targets:
- Stolen goods for sale – and when sold, similar goods become suitable targets for theft.

3. Absence of capable guardians:
- Low level of policing (public and private policing or citizen control) of stolen goods markets.

The way forward

Things have changed a great deal since the laws on handling were drafted. The law as it currently stands, and is interpreted, is not enough, since it does not provide the criminal justice system with an adequate means to control crime and punish the everyday dishonesty that encourages it. Perhaps in determining the degree of seriousness to be attached to handling, judges and their advisers should consider the social harm that stolen goods markets do in fuelling both the incidence and prevalence of theft. Given that theft is inextricably bound up with supporting drugs use and drugs markets – which are in turn inextricably bound up with sex markets (May et al., 1999) – this is a strangely neglected area of both criminology and policy-making.

Perhaps it is time to become less tolerant towards the *business of crime*. Fences remain in the community as stalwart businessmen, or as local heroes who can provide the much needed 'bargain' with no questions asked, while their heroin and crack cocaine addicted suppliers – the thieves – are targeted by the criminal justice system and regularly imprisoned. It is hoped that this chapter has gone some way to show how hypocritical and inefficient such a process is in reducing theft. The public and the criminal justice system's traditional tolerance to each of the five types of stolen goods market needs to change in our modern consumer society if we are to move beyond seeing illicit markets as some kind of *Del Boy Trotter/Mertonian safety valve* for a society that is overstressed by a volatile disjunction between goals and means. The reality is much harsher because theft is concentrated in particular areas, and offenders prey more often upon particular people in those areas (see Pease, 1998). Markets for stolen goods are concentrated in the poorest areas (Sutton, 1998; Felson, 2002) and this is probably the most important influence upon prevalence of crime and the incidence of victimisation that is daily visited upon the people who live there – upon their houses, their cars, their businesses and on their persons.

The way forward is to combine a crackdown upon the thieves and the dealers while consolidating on such operations by replacing illicit markets with legitimate alternatives that make it still possible to get a bargain. The Home Office MRA toolkit (Sutton et al., 2001) contains a number of detailed suggestions for multi-agency partnerships to crack down upon and then consolidate to reduce tolerance towards stolen goods markets at the local level. At the time of writing, MRA projects are operating in several police force areas including West Mercia, Greater Manchester and Kent. Whether or not they will be successful in reducing theft remains to be seen. While the MRA represents a sensible and compelling way to reduce theft rates, independent evaluations of these projects are still under way.

Note

1 These figures have been published by the government in another document written by the author (see: http://www.homeoffice.gov.uk/rds/pdfs/r69.pdf).

Chapter 10

Stalking the stalker: a review of policing strategies

Lorna White Sansom

Introduction

> Who taught thee how to make me love thee more,
> The more I hear and see just cause of hate?
>
> (Shakespeare, Sonnet 150, lines 9–10)

Stalking is a phenomenon that has been described as 'a crime of the nineties' (Goode, 1995); however, as the quotation from Shakespeare above indicates, 'longing on a large scale is what makes history' (DeLillo, 1997: 11). Stalking is a social construct, a populist term to describe a spectrum of behaviours that can include surveillance and monitoring, letter and gift sending, nuisance calls and threatening behaviour, all behaviours which separately seem innocuous and harmless, but when incorporated as part of a campaign can be severely damaging for the focus of the unwanted attention.[1]

There are various explanations that seek to account for stalking behaviours grounded in sociology or psychology or a fusion of both, with references made to concepts such as pathologies of love (see Pathé and Mullen, 1997); pathologies of loss and attachment (see Kienlen, 1998 for a more detailed exposition), narcissistic rage (see Meloy, 1998), obsession, acculturisation (see Meyer, 1998) and psychiatric morbidity rates. However, what is apparent from the literature is that it can be multi-causal and multi-motivated, namely that several factors can trigger the stalking, and that within a campaign, a stalker can be motivated by numerous emotions. As McAnaney et al. (1993) note, stalkers have a propensity to 'vacillate between attitudes of love and hate towards the object of attention'.

There is no modal stalker. However, studies have identified them to be typically an unemployed man averaging between 35 and 40 in age, with a school and college education and significantly more intelligent than other criminals. The victim is invariably a woman younger than her pursuer with whom a prior relationship has usually occurred. Mullen et al. (2001) provide a typology of stalkers, namely the rejected and resentful, the intimacy seeker, the incompetent suitor and the predatory stalker. Sheridan and Boon (2002), however, propose the following: ex-partner harassment, infatuation, delusional fixation stalking and sadistic stalking, that is usefully designed to assist in the policing of this behaviour. The infatuated stalker – very similar to Mullen et al.'s notion of an incompetent suitor – is usually non-violent nor dangerous, is amenable to intervention by the police and will usually stop the behaviour once the consequences of his actions on the victim and the implications for himself, if he continues, have been explained. The delusional stalker – divided into two sub-categories, the dangerous and less dangerous – scarcely knows the victim but has an idealised notion about the relationship and tends not to respond to legal intervention, with perceived rejection exacerbating the problem. The authors suggest that this category of stalker can be managed by referral to the forensic psychiatric services. Finally, the sadistic stalker is less likely to know the victim personally who is seen as 'prey' in the most literal sense of stalking. Boon and Sheridan (2002) consider this type of stalker to pose a serious danger to the victim and in such instances the latter should seriously consider relocation. This chapter will focus on the most prevalent – and often most violent (see Zona et al., 1998; Meloy, 2002) form – that of ex-intimate stalking or domestic violence related stalking. As Farnham et al. (2000: 199) note, 'the greatest danger of serious violence from stalkers in the UK is not from strangers or from people with psychotic illness, but from non-psychotic ex partners'.

Legally the behaviour we know as stalking is now covered by the Protection from Harassment Act 1997 and is defined as a course of conduct which occurs on a least two separate occasions and which is known to cause fear and/or distress. Pathé and Mullen (1997: 12) concisely define it as 'a constellation of behaviours in which one individual inflicts on another repeated unwanted intrusions and communications'.

Stalking and domestic violence

Kurt (1995) observes that stalking that should be considered 'a variant of domestic violence'. For as Way (1994: 381) notes, 'stalking is one vicious manifestation of a broader spectrum of violence against women – one part of a multi-faceted whole, integrally linked to the systematic social, economic and political inequalities experienced daily by women'.

There are clear analogies between the two behaviours. US research shows that the majority of stalking crimes are committed by individuals known to their victims. Significantly, persons stalking ex-partners constitute 60 per cent of all cases in the Los Angeles area (Jordan, 1995). It is this category of former-intimate stalking cases that is more prone to culminate in violence and Micken (cited in Beck et al., 1992) estimated that as many as 90 per cent of women murdered by partners may have been stalked prior to their death. Bradburn (1992: 271) notes that, 'approximately 50 percent of all females who leave their husbands for reasons of physical abuse are followed, harassed, or further attacked by their former spouses. This phenomenon is known as "separation assault" ... the broader concept is called "stalking".'

Walker (1979) formulated the 'cycle of violence' theory as an explanation of domestic violence which proposed that women learn helpless behaviour and that is why they do not try to escape or leave abusive situations. Indeed, Coleman (1997) found stalking to be pivotal to that cycle which suggests that men who are abusive throughout a relationship are potentially more likely to subsequently pursue their partner in an aggressive manner. Walker identified specific phases in the build-up to a violent outburst. First, there is 'the tension building stage' during which time minor 'batterings' occur, meted out by the abuser in a conscious manner. Second, there is 'the acute battering incident' or explosion phase, characterised by the uncontrollable eruption of tensions that have escalated during the first phase. Finally, there is 'kindness and contrite loving behaviour' or the 'honeymoon period' which is a period of calm because the abuser knows he has gone too far.

Although, the notion of learned helplessness itself has little contemporary credibility, Bernstein (1993) has usefully extended the theory to include women who separate from their abusive partners. This fourth phase is characterised by the harassment, intimidation and shadowing of the woman, and is seen to constitute another stage of the domestic violence cycle. It is when the woman tries to break the cycle by terminating the relationship and leaving her partner, that the reaction is often met with increased violence, which often takes the shape of stalking:

> If the wife does manage to escape [the abuse], her husband often stalks her like a hunted animal. He scours the neighbourhood, contacts friends and relatives, goes to all the likely places where she might have sought refuge, and checks with public agencies to track her down ... Unless she can afford to leave town and effectively disappear, a woman is never quite safe from a stalking husband. (Martin, 1996)

Those who do leave their violent partners spend their lives 'trying to avoid men fanatically dedicated to pursuing them, harassing them, or even killing them' (Pagelow, 1992: 307) and studies show that separation is a very dangerous period for the escaping partner (Salame, 1993; Coleman, 1997). Mechanic et al. (2000) found that stalking behaviours occur with 'alarming frequency' among physically abused women, while they are in the relationship and after they leave.

Policing stalking and domestic violence

It is evident that there are close links between domestic violence and stalking behaviour and it therefore follows that similar methods of policing can be utilised initially to deal with these offences. The history of the political response to domestic violence has been well documented and criticised by numerous authors. Stanko (1992, cited in Walklate, 2001) noted that the police had never responded appropriately to domestic violence, a pertinent example of political disinterest highlighted by Radford and Stanko (1991: 192):

> In 1984 Sir Kenneth Newman [the then Commissioner of the Metropolitan Police] attempted to shed police responsibility for what he considered to be 'rubbish work', or non-police matters, namely domestic violence and stray dogs are two such examples.

Domestic violence was brought to wider political attention mainly by feminists until 'by 1990 police forces compete with each other to find the most creative policy to deal with domestic violence' (Radford and Stanko, 1991: 192). Domestic violence policing policy and practice had edged in the direction of establishing specific domestic violence units or having named domestic violence officers, or the equivalent based in community safety units (Home Office Circular 60/1990). These specialised units have proven to positively address the problems of domestic violence and its related counterpart, stalking (Morris et al., 2002). However, referral to such units is not automatic and dependent on the often problematic attitude and responsiveness of the police in general to complaints of stalking.

Kelly (1999) found that although most women in her study rated the police response as sympathetic and supportive, three significant issues – being made to feel like time-wasters, police hostility, late or non-arrival and the minimalisation of serious violence – did arise. Similar dissatisfaction with police response and attitude in domestic violence is highlighted in studies of stalking victims. Sheridan et al. (2001) found that 41 per cent of their respondents were unhappy with the way the police had handled their case, citing frustration at their inability or disinclination to act. Finch (2001: 269) found that victims felt marginalised, frustrated and undermined by the police response with one victim saying she had been told 'just ignore him, I'm sure he'll get fed up with it soon' which was seen to trivialise the feelings of the victim.

The disinclination of the police to intervene in a 'private dispute' was a common complaint and is again reminiscent of the notion of a 'domestic' and the associated reluctance to intervene. Stalking victims felt that their situation was not being taken seriously and they were left feeling isolated and unprotected (Morris et al., 2002). Moreover, victims disliked having to recount their history of victimisation each time a new incident occurred but when continuity did occur, they were more positive about the overall response.

A further factor to emerge from Finch's research was the unwillingness of the police to act without corroborating evidence. This is understandable as the activities of many stalkers remain within the law but these are nonetheless perceived as harassment by the victim. Baroness Blatch (1996) notes that stalking is a difficult area in which to legislate

> ... since many of the individual actions in which stalkers engage are, in themselves, quite harmless – walking up and down a street, or standing on a street corner, for example. Much of the activity which can be described as stalking can, in another context, be something entirely innocent done as part of normal activity ... Any legislation in this area must be effective against stalkers and provide victims with adequate security and redress.

There are significant problems gathering evidence because of vague notions of what actually constitutes stalking and many behaviours taken individually seem inoffensive and inconsequential but with intensity and persistence can cause great distress and anxiety. As Sheridan and Davies (2001: 143) observe, stalking is 'an elusive crime, one that is easy to commit, but difficult to define and prosecute'.

Stalking is very much subjectively defined by the victim. What constitutes harassment for one person may be perceived very differently by another. From a policing perspective, this is not an insuperable problem, being able to reassure the victim, recognise the mechanisms of a stalking campaign and provide the victim with security advice and methods of collecting potential evidence where available would make a useful future contribution to the policing of that particular offender. Studies have found nonetheless that police officers are not familiar with the intricacies of the Protection from Harassment Act 1997 (Harris, 2000) and that divergent prosecution and conviction rates within different force areas suggest that not only do the police adopt diverse strategies to address the phenomenon (Von Heussen, 2000) but the criminal justice response itself is problematic.

Police attitudes to stalking negate the credibility of the behaviour at various levels. First, for an incident to be accepted as stalking there needs to be a stranger danger element. Second, there is an expected and accepted pattern – without certain elements being present the incident will not be acknowledged as stalking. This is very much an issue of police officers making value judgements, responding subjectively to incidents based on personal history and principles rather than fact. It seems clear from the studies discussed in this chapter that some decisions about what constitutes a 'true' case of stalking are founded on misinformation and ignorance. Stalking can certainly involve strangers, but the majority of cases emanate from some form of relationship, be it intimate, work-based or neighbourly. As we have seen, it is those cases that originate from severed relationships that tend to escalate in terms of violence, and as such police awareness and support for such victims is imperative and essential.

Some of the problems highlighted in the policing of stalking are not universal and some of the aforementioned specialised units have successfully addressed the needs of victims and supported them through their ordeal. As Sheptycki (1991) notes, community policing-style domestic violence units are successful because they afford the victims an opportunity to explain their individual needs and officers have been afforded the necessary discretion to address the intricacies of each case. It follows from this that more targeted anti-stalking policing strategies are appropriate.

Targeted anti-stalking police initiatives

Positive developments in the policing of stalking behaviour have been linked to the production of a guide written by Brown (2000) that takes police officers through the diverse processes of acknowledging and addressing stalking and which outlines the usefulness and importance of the Protection from Harassment Act 1997. For example, the use of warnings as a possible intervention mechanism are advocated – and hopefully deter any further harassment – but also, if written and the conduct continues, these can serve as evidence in any future proceedings. The First Contact scheme in Flintshire follows these principles and is an example of good practice in dealing with the complexities of stalking. Finch (2001) observes a proactive approach where an officer observing a contravention of the Protection from Harassment Act 1997 issues a written final warning to the offender with the following twofold impact. First, the victim is reassured that their complaint is being taken seriously. Second, the offender has been made aware that the behaviour is causing harassment and that to continue will lead to arrest and prosecution.

Following the above discussion of broader policing strategies, a more specific, crime reduction approach will be considered as a means of minimising, avoiding or preventing stalking. The notion of situational crime prevention provides a different but invariably complementary perspective from which to manage crime – and police resources – whereupon there is a manipulation of the environment to deter the occurrence of crime. As two of its leading proponents Felson and Clarke (1997: 197) note, 'it seeks to forestall the occurrence of crime, rather than to detect and sanction offenders. It seeks, not to eliminate criminal or delinquent tendencies, but merely to reduce opportunities for crime.'

Perspectives such as rational choice, routine activity theory and environmental criminology that underpin this approach can be applied to ascertain any emergent themes or patterns relating to the crime being studied. In accordance with the focus of this chapter, the rational, routine activity of stalking can be examined to elicit whether the dynamics of the activity can be identified and isolated in terms of temporal, spatial and/or domain patterns, thus deterring or reducing further behaviour. It is a focus where the prevention of crime becomes the responsibility of the individual as well as the state.

Few studies have considered the routine patterns of stalking, and those that have, have tended to concentrate on specific sub-groups of the female population, notably college students. The conclusions of these studies should not be disregarded nonetheless because they usefully illustrate the importance of context in the management of stalking. Mustaine and Tewksbury (1999: 57) note that their research 'provides strong support for the notion that it is not who the persons are that determines their chances for victimisation but rather what they do, where they are, and with whom they come in contact'. The researchers found that residential location – specifically not living in halls of residence where there are numerous guardians – employment status such as having a part-time job, drinking alcohol and drug use, and the measures of self-protection employed are evident markers of victimisation. Fisher et al. (2002) similarly establish that victimisation is likely when an individual lives alone (isolation can equate to vulnerability and similarly living alone means that capable guardians are minimal), is involved in dating relationships and frequents places where alcohol is available. This theory works on the premise that for a crime to be committed there needs to be a motivated offender, a suitable target and a lack of capable guardianship. Student victimisation seems to be more heightened, possibly because their routines and schedules are more predictable (for example, lecture timetables and library closing times) and the culture and lifestyle encourages women to put themselves in diverse social situations that increase their exposure to individuals who sexually prey on women, and which also predominantly involves access to – or the availability of – alcohol and drugs. As Roth (1994) infers, alcohol may increase aggression in those individuals already susceptible to aggressive conduct, and as such women who drink out more often may be doing so in the presence of aggression-prone men whose emotional outlet or cathartic release is stalking.

These potential markers of possible victimisation are useful when attempting to avoid the different types of stalking – particularly the sadistic and delusional variations – but they do not explicitly indicate the victimisation risks for those who are stalked by ex-partners. The crux of routine activity theory is that of being out in public and the consequential increasing exposure to motivated offenders; however, the majority of stalking cases are perpetrated by estranged partners, and as Mustaine and Tewsbury (1999: 54) acknowledge 'the division between the safety of one's home and the risks of public activity is blurred for this type of offence'. These researchers refer to a more feminist interpretation of routine activities relating to the lifestyle behaviours of women that may increase the risk of victimisation. Women who either assume a less traditional female role or attempt to challenge the status quo subsequently threatening the innate masculinity of their partner tend to be more at risk of stalking as a means of subordination and oppression (Mustaine and Tewksbury, 1999).

Fisher et al. (2002) also refer to victimisation off campus and propose increasing the number of guardians who would discourage stalkers (which is very similar to the cocoon system detailed below). Felson (1998) discusses increasing the effort it takes for offenders to commit a crime, or in this case pursue a victim, and proposes the use of 'handlers', people whose bond with the offender allows the exertion of some form of social control. On campus, this could be done through peer pressure and education regarding inappropriate and unwanted pursuit behaviours; within the home, it could be friends and family who dissuade the offender or shame him into ceasing the behaviour (Fisher et al., 1999). Target hardening such as blocking or screening calls or redirecting e-mails on the Internet may also be effective in minimising the impact of the stalking.

Kropp et al. (2002) identify eight principles in managing stalking behaviours of which two are relevant for policing, namely supervision through monitoring and victim safety planning. The former refers to monitoring the offender, knowing their routines, patterns and day-to-day activities, and stipulating that offenders meet with healthcare or social service professionals. The latter focuses upon safety planning and improving the victim's 'dynamic and static security resources' as a means of negating further intrusion into their life if the stalking continues. Dynamic security relates to the social environment, more specifically people who can respond to the varying conditions and who have the requisite knowledge of the victim regarding risk. Static security relates to the physical environment and is at its most effective when 'it improves the ability of victims to monitor their environment and impedes stalkers from engaging in stalking behaviour. The case management team should consider whether it is possible to improve the static security where victims live, work and travel' (ibid.: 155–6). Changes to the physical environment include improving visibility through better or extra lighting, modifying gardens or landscapes to make entry more difficult and reducing potential hiding places. Video cameras could also be installed as well as extra security provisions on windows and doors.

Morris et al. (2002) refer to the 'cocoon' scheme developed in South

West Yorkshire whereby the victim is submerged in the social fabric of the community as a means of protection. A community police officer liaises with the victim in their home (target hardening) while also informing people within the locale of the harassment. Thus neighbours, friends, shopkeepers and so forth become potential 'guardians' (in the routine activity sense) informing the police of any suspicious activities and incidents while making the stalking more difficult for the stalker:

> You could say that what we do need to do is wrap the [victim] in cotton wool for the next six months. Well it's the closest thing to that. There are a lot of things we can do. We get full intelligence on the offender, everything from the cars he uses, pubs he drinks in, his routine, habits, where he goes, what he does, who with and all the rest of it. We do the same for the victim and try to identify vulnerability, you know, opportunities that a classic stalker or ex partner could get in to. (Morris et al., 2002: 79)

Stalking is regarded as a by-product of the routine activities of [college] women in these studies, and Fisher et al. (2002: 21) debate the recommendation that women as potential victims should be 'more aware of the risks they face and adopt more cautious lifestyles'. The promotion of awareness and education of possible risks is non-contentiously beneficial (to anyone) but the notion that women should change their lifestyles to avoid men who may stalk them is more contentious, as men are not compelled to alter or modify their routines to assuage potential criminal activities Nonetheless, routine activities which indicate increased risk of victimisation are useful in providing more detailed information about a relatively marginalised behaviour, and in terms of policing can prove advantageous in helping to protect the victim.

The way forward?

Much of the stalking literature emanates from the USA, primarily because legislation was introduced in that country more than ten years ago (Californian Penal Code, s. 646.9, 1990) and has been amended to deal with the complexities of such behaviour. It is with this knowledge that we look to the USA for possible solutions – or at least ways forward – in dealing with this behaviour, and what becomes immediately apparent is the dedication of the majority of states to legally address stalking. Some have established specific anti-stalking units or some form of dedicated team aware of the inherent issues while other state jurisdictions have organised groups or forums committed to address-ing stalking problems. The first specifically created unit was the Threat Management Unit (TMU); founded by the Los Angeles Police Department in 1990, in collaboration with the entertainment industry after the publicised death of actress Rebecca Schaefer, murdered by a stalker. The TMU comprises detectives of varying experience, is involved in training other police personnel and although initially founded to deal with stranger danger associated with celebrity and fame, only about 30 per cent of current cases come from the entertain-ment industry. Complaints from ordinary citizens constitute the great majority of cases, most of which are related to domestic violence (Boles, 2001).

The TMU has a referral process for cases, but regardless of whether they are accepted or not, victims will be provided with safety information and encouraged to keep a log detailing the stalking behaviour. This has the affect of reassuring victims that their situation has been acknowledged or recognised. Boles (2001: 342) details the thorough investigatory techniques utilised by the unit and the procedures in place to ensure that victims of stalking are protected:

> Each stalking case is placed in a separate 'stalking book'. The stalking book is kept by the detective assigned to the case until the case is completed, whereupon the stalking book is placed in the TMU files. The stalking book contains a chronological record of all case activities and all paperwork associated with the case.

Other units which complement the TMU – and emphasise the acknowledgement of the state as to the seriousness of stalking – are the Major Assaults Crime Unit whose duties comprise investigating less serious stalking cases and domestic violence assaults, and the SMART (System-wide Mental Assessment Response Team) team which combines a mental health assessor with a police officer whose remit is to assess suspects who present with psychiatric disorders. Officers can call the Mental Evaluation Unit who will send out a SMART team, an assistance which the Threat Management Unit considers a 'very important resource'. Boles (2001: 348) notes that:

> … the TMU has been and continues to be a leader in responding to stalking crimes on a daily basis, while at the same time improving methods for responding to these crimes that can have devastating

consequences for the victims unless promptly and effectively responded to by the justice system.

Maxey (2001) also addresses policing issues from a practical perspective and alludes to the San Diego Strike Force and SCAT (Stalking Case Assessment Team) approach as means for tackling stalking. These multi-jurisdictional and multi-disciplinary groups develop training manuals, organise forums to discuss training and management issues and, although not traditional policing, it impacts upon training and awareness and as such is a valuable resource 'recognizing that our criminal justice system … was not recognizing the stalking activity or taking action in these cases' (Maxey, 2001: 368).

Conclusion

From the studies discussed, it is evident that certain issues need to be addressed by the police. Importantly, there needs to be more awareness about the intricacies of stalking and the appropriate operational and legal responses to it. As Walklate (2001: 136) observes, there are 'still difficulties in ensuring that women are responded to appropriately by all officers called to the scene' and *all* is the operative word, in that awareness about both domestic violence and stalking has to be consistent and widespread. As Kelly (1999: 59) pertinently note, there is

> … no shared knowledge base amongst the police … these fundamental issues need to be addressed in detail through training. Unless and until this happens women calling the police are entering a lottery, in which one officer will define her experience as a crime, whilst another will not.

This should be supported by central systems that allow more effective flagging of repeat victimisation and previous incidents. It seems that officers need to be more sensitive to and aware of significant issues, that stalking per se is identified and that advice is given to the victim about coping strategies (providing security and protection advice) and the necessary requisites which support the case such as keeping relevant evidence and keeping a diary or log book of incidents. Providing the victim with a point of contact, or some form of continuity, is vital, particularly in ongoing cases, an approach which Morris et al. (2002: 89) found to be 'a source of considerable reassurance and satisfaction'.

It seems that setting up a specific unit to address stalking behaviours is probably the only way forward, a move strongly advocated by Brown (2002). However, resources and training are significant issues. It is not sufficient merely to refer cases to a unit because it is essential that there are properly trained officers in place who are fully aware what they are dealing with. The unique case elements of stalking can make recognition difficult to ascertain without the requisite awareness and training. For example, different types of stalkers react to police intervention in different ways; some offenders become incensed by being confronted by the police and consequently intensify and escalate the campaign, while others when challenged about their behaviour will cease their activities (see Mullen et al., 2001; Boon and Sheridan, 2002 for a more detailed discussion of stalker responses). In terms of policing ex-partner stalking, Sheridan and Boon (2002: 80) highlight the high risk of violence and note that any threats made to the victim should be taken seriously: 'it is not sufficient just to examine the actual behaviour of a stalker. Rather, any stalking investigation should aim to look beyond the physical evidence and into the context for the individual offender's behaviour.'

In relation to the specific issue of stalking, several areas of concern have been highlighted regarding the response of the police to this behaviour, namely the recognition of seriousness and the appropriate actions that need to be taken. Several solutions have been proposed. The most radical in structural and resources terms is the introduction of specific stalking units, although these impact on other problematic aspects such as training, improved awareness and resources, the latter being more of an insurmountable obstacle.

In relation to the wider political and policy sphere, there needs to be a proliferation of proactive not reactive initiatives. These are now beginning to evolve and assume a structured format; however, more thought needs to be focused upon incorporating the knowledge learned about stalking such as the case management schema provided by Sheridan and Boon (2002: 69) who maintain:

> Once law enforcement officers are aware of these differing motivations, they will be equipped with relevant information pertaining to the context for the behaviour, the degree and nature of the threat (if any) faced by the victim, and the criteria for selecting and adopting case management strategies.

To conclude, although typologies such as Boon and Sheridan's provide management implications for the varying types of stalker, it is important to reiterate the fact that most offenders are acquainted with their victim and that, according to Coleman (1997: 430), fostering awareness of the symbiosis between domestic violence abusers and stalkers is an imperative aim of both future research and policing strategies: 'Approaching stalking as a stage in the cycle of violence provides a valuable avenue for understanding who is at risk of becoming a victim or a perpetrator of stalking.' In summary, the closely linked issues of domestic violence and stalking both need to be given social, political and legal credibility.

Note

1   The author acknowledges that there are cases of male victims, female offenders and same-gender stalking (males stalking males and females stalking other women); however, the majority of cases involve a male offender and a female victim, and for the purpose of this chapter, this is taken to be the more prevalent scenario and as such is the main frame of reference.

Chapter 11

Policing financial crime: the Financial Services Authority and the myth of the 'duped investor'

Basia Spalek

Introduction

This chapter is written as two major financial scandals have hit the US, sending share prices falling across stock markets around the world. The US energy firm, Enron, was declared bankrupt in December 2001, while in June 2002 WorldCom, the second biggest long-distance telephone company in the US, admitted a $4 bn hole in its accounts. These scandals have caused politicians, accountants, regulators and the media to question whether similar cases could occur in Britain. Some commentators have argued that the British regulatory framework is more robust and as such there is less likelihood of the US type and scale of financial crime occurring. Others, however, have questioned this position, maintaining that wherever greed and a lack of business ethics dominate then financial crime is likely to occur.

In Britain, individualised risk assessment has increasingly replaced socialised forms of actuarialism (O'Malley, 1992). As a result, the number of private insurance schemes, pension schemes and privately owned stocks and shares has dramatically increased as people find ways of offsetting the financial insecurity that can be brought on by negative events such as illness or unemployment (Burton, 1994). With the creation of a new regulatory structure introduced by the Labour government in 2001 – together with the scandals occurring in the USA – it is an appropriate time to consider the way in which the financial system is policed and the impact of this upon investors and the victims of financial crime. This chapter presents an account of financial regulation in Britain and highlights the predominant strategies used by the Financial Services Authority (FSA), the new body established to police the financial system. It is argued that an actuarial regime dominates the regulatory framework, echoing the rise of 'the new criminologies' in western liberal democracies (O'Malley, 1992; Garland, 1994: 458).

A brief history of regulation

Until the 1960s, the financial system in Britain was largely run by aristocratic or upper-middle-class individuals, connected by similar education, experiences and worldview. Regulation was conducted on a non-statutory basis, operating upon trust whereby a 'gentleman's word was his bond'. The Governor of the Bank of England was able to summon the leading bankers to his office for discussion within half an hour (Clarke, 1986), and methods of controlling behaviour included 'moral persuasion, raised eyebrows, the stern rebuff over drinks and the prospect of the cold shoulder' (Stanley: 1992: 48). Knowledge of members' careers, family backgrounds and friends provided bases from which to evaluate individual agents, and the threat of exclusion from the City was regarded as being a sufficient deterrent against unethical behaviour and law-breaking.

The 1970s and 1980s witnessed a movement in the City away from informal regulation to regulation based around legislation. A series of banking scandals, together with the increasing presence of foreign institutions, agents and investors, led to the adoption of a statutory framework, the most significant piece of legislation being the creation of the Financial Services Act 1986. This gave the Secretary of State for Trade and Industry statutory powers to regulate financial services. Many of these powers were handed down to the Securities and Investment Board (SIB), a private company which authorised a number of self-regulatory organisations (SROs). These included: the Personal Investment Authority (PIA), with responsibility for the retail sector and the supervision of independent financial advisers; the Investment Managers Regulatory Organisation (IMRO), with responsibility for fund managers and conduct of business regulation; and the Securities and Futures Association (SFA), with responsibility for securities houses and conduct of business regulation. SROs issued licences to agents who dealt in the investment instruments of their particular jurisdictions. Failure to abide by the rules could now result in the imposition of a range of disciplinary measures being imposed, including the revocation of an individual's licence to trade, or their being charged with a criminal offence and taken to court (Rider, 1987). It can be argued that this system of regulation reflected a 'disciplinary regime' where control and punishment take the form of impersonal agencies of surveillance and correction and individual deviance is managed by 'coercion, exclusion and correction' (O'Malley, 1992: 254).

In reality, however, the disciplinary regime was only of a symbolic nature, since there was an array of loopholes that potential offenders could exploit. It is clear that the agencies policing the financial system operated on a system of trust, reacting to financial crime after it had taken place rather than effectively policing agents before any crimes took place. As a result, a series of high-profile financial scandals occurred in the 1980s and 1990s, including Lloyd's, Barings, Maxwell, BCCI, Morgan Grenfell and Daiwa Bank, to name only a few. In 1997 the newly elected Labour government renamed the SIB the Financial Services Authority (FSA). Over the next few years the self-regulatory organisations were merged into this new body, so that on 1 December 2001 – following the implementation of the Financial Services Market Act 2000 – the FSA became the single regulator with powers over the entire financial system, including the banking sector (which had been previously supervised by the Bank of England). The FSA regulates approximately 11,000 firms, its regulatory activity costing £167.4 m between 2001 and 2002 (FSA, 2001/02: 41). Upon examining the literature and policy documents issued by the FSA, a number of themes can be identified as underpinning the present financial regulatory structure. These are discussed below.

The Financial Services Authority as operating an actuarial regime

The term 'actuarialism' refers to a form of governance of populations through statistical analysis of risks (Simon, 1988; Ewald, 1991; O'Malley, 1992). The notion of risk features significantly in the approach taken by the FSA, and there are many strands to the actuarial approach adopted. Risk assessment methods are used as the basis upon which to decide the form and intensity of supervision. All firms operating within the financial system are risk assessed in terms of probability and impact factors. Probability relates to the likelihood of the event occurring and factors considered include the composition of the firm's board, management and staff, and the controls culture. Impact refers to the potential scale and significance of the problem in terms of, for example, the impact on and number of retail customers and the availability of compensation for consumer loss. At a superficial level, this actuarial approach appears to signal a major shift from the previous regulatory structure that was in operation under the SIB. The FSA can adopt a more proactive approach to regulation and target its resources at firms identified as being at 'high risk'. Policy documents show that resources are being purposefully switched from 'reactive post-event action towards front-end intervention' (FSA, 2002: 4). Through actively assessing the risk of every firm and determining the level of supervision required on that basis, the FSA is thereby trying to adopt a proactive rather than reactive approach which will prevent financial scandals occurring.

This is nonetheless a problematic approach. There is an assumption that the danger posed by financial crime and mismanagement can be reduced by mathematical assessment tools. It could be argued that the figures supplied by companies to the FSA to assess their level of risk are not 'solid facts' but social constructions that can be manipulated and used creatively in order to give certain results. It would be quite dangerous therefore to place too much faith in the results of risk analysis. Rather, the kind of business culture prevalent in the firms operating in the financial system should be given greater attention. The financial system essentially consists of a plethora of agent–principle relationships, principles being 'individuals who invest resources, authority or responsibility in an agent to act on their behalf for some uncertain future' (Shapiro, 1987: 625). Although agents are policed by the regulatory structure, opportunities for abuse arise, largely due to the asymmetrical and unbalanced nature of agent–principle relationships. So while mathematical formulas and procedures may prevent some crimes and financial losses from occurring, there remains a large potential for the abuse of trust since there continue to be a large number of 'sites of trust' that can be exploited. Certain key individuals will continue to have privileged access to knowledge over consumers of the system, and will therefore continue to be able to exploit this knowledge to the detriment of others.

One of the recent financial scandals to occur in the USA clearly illustrates this point. Enron, a US energy firm, was declared bankrupt on 2 December 2001. Securities fraud, illegal insider trading and filing false financial reports are some of the practices that occurred there. The financial manipulation of Enron's profitability meant that its earnings had been overstated during the previous four years, leading to the largest bankruptcy in history. While top executives were able to sell Enron shares for large amounts of money, lower-level employees were locked into retirement plans with company stock. This means that at the same time as a group of 29 Enron executives and directors received around $1.1 bn by selling shares between 1999 and 2001, the employees lost around $1.2 bn from their pensions (*The Guardian*, 18 January 2002). Ordinary employees had not been allowed to sell their share options. City analysts have criticised the business culture at Enron, which some claim led to its bankruptcy (*The Guardian*, 18 June 2002). This case illustrates the financial manipulation that can occur within a company when an atmosphere of greed pervades. It suggests that financial regulators need to be acutely aware of the business culture that operates within a particular firm and within the wider industry in general, rather than overly relying on statistical analysis to convey the risk level of a firm. An 'enterprise culture' that views profits to be more important than ethics can be detrimental to individual investors.

Another, potentially problematic, aspect of the actuarial approach pursued by the FSA is the contradictory attempt to construct an image of the financial consumer as an informed individual who has choice, while the victim of a financial crime is conversely seen to be an un-informed person who made the wrong decision, thereby perpetuating the myth of the 'duped investor'. This has important implications for how the financial system is policed and in terms of the consequences for users of the system. This contradictory myth is discussed below.

Individual responsibility and the notion of individual choice

Under the new regulatory regime, the FSA is giving the voice of the consumer a much more significant role. It is planning to assess probability factors for consumer and industry-wide risks, taking into account factors such as the mismatch between the complexity of the product being sold and the knowledge of the consumers being targeted, the volume of consumer complaints and external comments from, for example, the industry, consumer groups and the media. Actively listening to investors and consumer groups appears to be beneficial to regulation, since in the past regulators had often ignored the voices of individual consumers of the financial system, even when they had raised concerns over particular financial agents and insti-tutions for their involvement in crime and financial impropriety (Spalek, 1999). At the same time, the FSA intends to increase the knowledge that consumers have of financial institutions and products through education – for example, in schools and the workplace – and also through the wider provision of information. Thus two aims of the FSA are 'to improve general financial literacy and to improve the information and advice available to consumers' (FSA, 2002: 7). It is keen to create informed consumers who are knowledgeable of the risks that are evident in the financial system so that investors take responsibility for avoiding financial crime.

The FSA – in line with the previous regulatory structures operating in the financial system – functions in accordance with the claim that there is a role for the principle of 'caveat emptor'. Investors and depositors are deemed accountable for the transactions that they make, and should not therefore be given complete protection by regulators (Davies, 1998). In short, if financial institutions were to be rescued every time they collapsed, this would provide a disincentive through-out the market to take precautions against risk. More cautious institutions would be further penalised since these would be asked to help rescue failed institutions while being less competitive than these more cavalier risk-taking institutions. Thus it is argued by regulators and economists that too much regulation could create a disincentive to be prudent. Similarly, if depositors were to be compensated fully for their losses, then this would act as a disincentive for them to be cautious about where they place their money, thereby making it easier for dubious institutions to obtain deposits (Gowland, 1990). Underpinning this approach to regulation is a belief that economic prosperity arises from liberalisation and free market competition (Hutton, 1996).

Financial regulators argue that although people might yearn for a risk-free environment, this would conflict with the financial prosperity that arises from free competition and deregulation (Leigh-Pemberton, 1992: 210). Thus the FSA (2002: 3) 'recognises the proper responsibilities of consumers themselves ... and the impossibility and undesirability of removing all risk and failure from the financial system'. It is an ideology that echoes the rise of the new criminologies, whereby responsibility for crime is placed squarely onto victims and offenders, as exemplified by the popularity of, for example, situational crime prevention initiatives. In this context, the FSA issues a myriad of advice as to how a consumer of the financial system can protect him/herself:

> Protect yourself when you shop around
> DO check that any investment firm you deal with is authorised.
> DO have a clear idea of what you are looking for.
> DO read the product details before you commit yourself.
> DO check all paperwork and keep it safe.
> DO remember: if a deal sounds too good to be true it probably is!

<u>Tips on shopping by Internet</u>
DO check out a number of companies, not just one.
DO be wary of dealing with companies you've never heard of.
DO check the paperwork when it arrives.
DO print off the contract terms – they may have changed if you go back to the site later.
DO check that the website gives a real address and telephone number. Check these details against the phone book.

This advice suggests that individual consumers have some degree of choice over the risks that they are exposed to and that, moreover, they can act to avoid becoming the victims of financial crime. The FSA clearly does not acknowledge the constraints on individual choice, but rather views consumers as individuals who can make an informed, free choice. However, it can be argued that we need to view 'individual choice' within the structural constraints placed on individual action. In a political climate that promotes self-sufficiency and self-protection, where the state has sought to impose the costs of welfare upon individual citizens, it might be argued that notions of 'free choice' are problematic. Put simply, government policy influences the choices available to people: 'technologies, although they have their own dynamics, nevertheless develop primarily in terms of their role in relation to specific political programs' (O'Malley, 1992: 258).

In Britain during the 1980s and 1990s, successive governments have pursued a policy of 'popular capitalism' that has encouraged people to become homeowners, shareholders and portable pension owners (Jessop and Stones, 1992). Social welfare has become regarded as costly and inefficient with individuals encouraged to protect themselves from unwanted future events such as illness and unemployment by providing themselves with private insurance schemes and other technologies offering protection. Personal pensions have been created which – while providing people with greater flexibility – do not offer a final sum as a percentage of salary but depend upon the investment performance of the pension plan. Trade unions are outraged that many employers have ended final salary pension schemes. The number of employees covered by such schemes has been estimated to have declined by an excess of two million during the last ten years. As a result, many workers face poverty upon retirement (*The Guardian*, 17 June 2002).

The notion of individual choice and responsibility is also problematic when we consider actual cases of financial crime that have occurred. There is little that the individuals who were caught up in financial scandals such as Barings, Maxwell, Lloyd's, BCCI and, most recently, Enron and WorldCom could have done to prevent being victimised. These cases illustrate how fraudulent agents can hide information and carry out illegal operations without the knowledge or consent of investors. Moreover, in the case of Maxwell, BCCI and Enron, the individuals who were victimised largely consisted of employees who worked for these institutions (see Spalek, 1999, 2001a). As a result, they did not conform to the imagery of free consumer choice as espoused by the FSA. These cases draw attention to what Walklate (1989: 104) refers to as victimisation that is structurally based. The structural framework is capitalism, which encourages corporations, employers and managers to maximise profits at the expense of the individuals who vest their trust in them. Indeed, white-collar crime is invariably an ordinary part of business, since this is normally the outcome of the struggle to maximise profit and efficiency (Clarke, 1990). Employees are structurally less powerful than their employers. While fraudulent employees can be sacked or demoted, there is little that employees can do to a fraudulent employer. 'Where the employer engages in abuses, his staff have to organise strongly if their interests are affected, and may still find it hard to gain access to information essential to proof of misconduct and to resist selective or collective dismissal' (Clarke, 1990: 24).

In the global world of finance, where money can be shuffled around from country to country at the press of a computer button in a virtual space economic system, it is difficult to see how investors can protect themselves. The offender may be unknown to the victim and may carry out the crime thousands of miles away. At the same time, individual investors may belong to collectivities – as in the case of pension or insurance schemes – and as a result there may be little that an individual investor can do if they suspect that something is wrong.

The myth of the 'duped investor'

Alongside the myth of individual free choice is that of the 'duped investor'. The FSA functions according to a belief that individuals are the victims of financial crime that have somehow been conned into investing in the wrong products. This is perhaps unsurprising, since in criminological accounts, as well as in the media, victims of white-collar crime have often been portrayed as individuals who have been tricked into buying or investing in fraudulent goods (Croall, 1992; Levi and

Pithouse, 1992). This is why the FSA views 'consumer education' as being 'a key part of consumer protection' (FSA, 2002) and why the agency is keen to inform consumers about the various financial products that are available and the risks they carry, in order to create an informed investor who can avoid becoming the victim of financial crime.

Not only does the image of a 'duped investor' over-simplify and over-generalise the victims of financial crime, it also fails to appreciate the nature of trust in the financial system. Investors may be more knowledgeable about the risks that they carry than the regulator would accept. Interviews with people who have been the victims of financial crime suggest that prior to their victimisation, many of these individuals engaged in risk-avoidance strategies. They were nonetheless required to have a generalised trust in the financial system itself which carried an inevitable element of risk. Trust involves placing faith in a person or institution where something serious is at stake if such reliance turns out to be misplaced (Nelken, 1994: 4). It necessarily contains an element of risk and uncertainty, since in conditions of absolute certainty there is no need for trust at all. As such, experience of victimisation may simply re-affirm individuals' understandings that when using 'expert systems of knowledge' (Giddens, 1990) they are taking risks. Therefore, in the aftermath of a crime, individuals may continue to display a generalised systemic trust of the financial system, although their risk minimisation strategies may be reassessed and adjusted. System trust thus does not consist of blind faith; rather, systems are questioned and regarded with a degree of cynicism (Giddens, 1990).

Following a financial scandal, share prices may dramatically fall; however, this tends to be a short-lived situation, with investors soon returning to the stock markets. Following the discovery of a major financial crime, regulators tend to place blame on a deviant institution or a deviant person. Barings, Morgan Grenfell and Maxwell are all examples where the regulatory authorities sought out a particular person to blame even though various banks, accountants and lawyers were involved (Spalek, 2001b). This process has the consequence of absolving the financial system of any blame thereby helping to maintain trust in that system. Shapiro (1990) criticises this emphasis on offender characteristics, since this does not inform us about the wider context in which such crimes occur, the characteristics of such acts or the norms that they break. However, dominant players such as financial regulators and politicians are strongly committed to the perpetuation of the dominant capitalist system, and as such largely uncritically accept the global system of financial operations. Through absolving the system of any crime, the financial industry is thereby protected and legitimised.

The image of the 'duped investor' is unhelpful as it perpetuates the (false) claim that investors can act to prevent becoming the victims of a financial crime. In this way, crimes that occur within the financial system are normalised and viewed as being potentially avoidable to astute investors. Victims may then be blamed for the crimes that have been committed against them, since they have not acted to become knowledgeable investors who can avoid white-collar crime. In some cases victims have successfully contested the assumption that they have been 'duped' into investing in corrupt products and institutions. They have argued that there is nothing that they could have done to avoid becoming victims. This was clearly the situation with the Maxwell pensioners – many of whom claimed that they had always distrusted Robert Maxwell – who had no choice in contributing to the company pension schemes (Spalek, 1999). It is likely that these individuals were successful in gaining sympathy and support from the general public and the government because they fitted closely to 'ideal victim' status (Christie, 1986: 52), that is they were viewed to be 'weak' in comparison to Robert Maxwell and many were elderly people. However, in other cases of financial scandal, such as BCCI for example, the victims did not fit 'ideal victim status' and so were vilified by the financial regulators and the media (Spalek, 2001a).

White-collar victimisation

The FSA also lacks an accurate appreciation of the nature of financial crime and its significant impact on victims. Its policy documents refer solely to financial compensation, as though this were the only effect on individuals caught up in financial scandal. Research that has looked at the consequences of a wide range of white-collar crimes, including fraud, embezzlement, financial crime and so forth, indicates that as well as financial costs, there are also psychological, emotional and physical costs (Moore and Mills, 1990; Shover et al., 1994; Titus et al., 1995; Spalek, 1999). This would suggest that victims not only require financial compensation, but also emotional and psychological help. The regulatory response itself can victimise people further, as demonstrated by a study looking at BCCI, where the entire bank was labelled as being corrupt, thereby stigmatising the employees who had worked there (Spalek, 2001a). Currently no consideration is being paid to the potential of an adverse regulatory approach to harm victims further. This is in stark contrast to the extent of attention paid to the secondary victimisation of victims of 'street crime'. A whole range of policy initiatives have been developed in order to try to reduce the harmful impact of the actions of criminal justice agencies upon the victims of burglary, theft, physical and sexual assault and so forth (Zedner, 1994). It would appear that the ambiguous nature of white-collar crime, whereby many instances of deviance may not be viewed as criminal, has meant that many are often not viewed as 'real victims' (Nelken, 1994).

At the same time, in many cases the victims of white-collar crime are not required in the process of investigation and prosecution and so the agencies policing white-collar deviance are not so concerned about the plight of victims. Perhaps this is why victims' voices have been unheard or marginalised by the regulatory structures in place for policing white-collar offences. Despite the victims of financial crime – and indeed health and safety law violations – arguing for a 'zero tolerance' approach to the policing of white-collar offences, a compliance-based approach, whereby prosecution is regarded as being a 'last resort', continues to be adopted. Many victims of white-collar crime have no 'bargaining tool' with which to attract the attention of policy-makers. This is in contrast to the victims of 'street crime'. Researchers have argued that the recognition by criminal justice agencies that the reporting and prosecution of physical and sexual violence and burglary often requires the victim to be actively involved (Zedner, 1994) has enabled them to get their voices heard. This is not the case for the victims of many white-collar offences and so their concerns have largely been bypassed.

Conclusion

This chapter has raised some important concerns about the nature of financial regulation in Britain and its impact on investors and the victims of financial crime. Essentially, an actuarial regime operates whereby the risks associated with financial crime and mismanagement are foisted onto the shoulders of individual consumers. The notion of 'free choice' and the myth of the victim as 'duped investor' are perpetuated by the Financial Services Authority. This means that the regulatory framework views investors as being able to freely choose whether or not to invest in a particular product and institution, and that, moreover, individuals who become the victims of a financial crime have been conned as a result of them having insufficient knowledge about the financial system and the risks that it carries.

It has been argued in this chapter that both of these positions are inaccurate as they fail to consider the many constraints on individual choice. Moreover, in many cases of financial crime the victims may be knowledgeable about the risks that they carry, yet there is little, if anything, that they can do to avoid being victimised. The perpetuation of the notion of 'free choice' and that financial crime is avoidable to the astute investor means that in some cases victims may be directly blamed for their plight. At the same time they have little bargaining power to enable a full and adequate response to their situation, since they are not often a part of the subsequent investigation and prosecution of offenders. As a consequence, their emotional, psychological and, indeed, financial needs are rarely adequately addressed, and they are largely left to themselves to cope with the crimes that have been committed against them. It is imperative that the Financial Services Authority reconsiders its understanding of the relationship between financial crime and its victims, as only then might the individuals who are caught up in a financial scandal gain proper support.

Chapter 12

Hard coating, soft centre? The role of the police in Dordrecht offender rehabilitation programmes

Mandy Shaw

Introduction

Taken from a successful first programme in Holland in 1992, in a town of the same name, the Dordrecht approach offers offenders an alternative to a custodial prison sentence when found guilty in a criminal court of the offence of burglary.[1] Aimed at tackling the root causes of persistent offending practices, the individual offender agrees to cooperate within an intensive supervision and rehabilitation regime instead of serving a prison sentence. Typically, two programme personnel – one from the police service and one from the probation service – are involved in addressing both these elements.

The Dordrecht programme aims to address a number of factors known to affect persistent criminality, including drug addiction, poor educational attainment and limited social skills. There is recent research evidence to show that addressing these factors is an effective offending/crime reduction tool, and more effective than punitive measures on their own (see Raynor, 2002). To this end, a small number of Dordrecht schemes have been operating in different police force areas in the United Kingdom (UK) since the late 1990s, many of which have been wholly or partially funded by the UK Home Office. The first programme in the UK started in Burnley in 1997, within the Lancashire Constabulary area. At the time the initial results were published there were three people on the scheme who had not reoffended up to that point. That was considered a considerable achievement as two of them were in the top thirty offenders in the area (Home Office, 1997a: 3).

Some offenders may initially perceive the programme as being a 'soft' alternative to prison, despite the 'hard' and 'soft' elements of the project explained to them before they are selected for involvement in Dordrecht. The presence of a police officer in a supportive role – which tends to be contrary to the usual role they perceive – may well contribute to that perception. Nonetheless, while these acquired roles might challenge the traditional functions of both the police and probation service in their equal rehabilitative and punitive elements, if at any stage the offender ceases to cooperate or commits an additional criminal offence they are immediately brought before a judge and imprisoned. Thus police officers working on Dordrecht programmes have to tread a fine line between 'hard' and 'soft' roles.

This chapter reflects on the role of the police in the complex interplay between the 'hard' and 'soft' elements of Dordrecht and asks whether, ultimately, this is a soft option for the offender or whether real improvements in offending risk indicators are reduced, particularly with regard to drug addiction and offending while on the programme. There is a consideration of a variety of different sources of data: first, evaluation documents on individual Dordrecht programmes, and second, the author's reflections on the UK Home Office's Burglary Reduction Programme where some of the Strategic Development Projects (SDPs) incorporated Dordrecht in the period 1999–2001.[2] Jointly managed by two personnel in each SDP – one a probation officer and the second a police officer – they were the first such programmes to be implemented in the UK. In exploring the role of the police, this chapter will also explore the following (linked) reasons why this strategy addresses a range of challenges facing the contemporary police service. First, it is widely recognised that crime is concentrated on a small proportion of the population who suffer a high proportion of all crime (repeat victimisation) and these repeat crimes are committed by a small proportion of offenders. Second, over the past decade policing has moved from a predominantly reactive to a more proactive approach and the manifestation of that is the introduction of Problem Oriented Policing (POP). Third, it is recognised that punitive measures alone do not address the root causes of prolific offending, for example drug addiction, poor educational attainment and lack of social skills. Fourth, it is apparent that these issues cannot be solved by a 'hard' policing approach alone. A changing relationship has to occur between the police and prolific offenders in order for the problem of persistent criminal activity to be addressed successfully. Conceptually this chapter argues that this is an extension of the restorative justice approach recently adopted between victims and offenders. Just as the latter represents a change in offender–victim interaction after a crime event, from that of retribution to one of restitution, the Dordrecht approach represents a new interaction between the offender and the police.

The Dordrecht approach

The aims of Dordrecht

It is the aim of Dordrecht to stimulate a sustainable long-term approach to tackling persistent offending in local areas by tackling the root causes of offending behaviour. This aim is facilitated by a two-pronged approach: targeted policing of prolific offenders to crack down on criminal activity; and intensive supervision by dedicated personnel to change the motivation for committing crime. These two aspects, which might be perceived as 'hard' and 'soft', represent two traditional (and traditionally opposing) approaches to the 'treatment' of offenders. However, as the chapter unfolds, it will be seen that this distinction between 'hard' and 'soft', traditionally police and probation, is not clear-cut. Both agencies are active in roles which challenge the traditional assumptions about the police and probation, and the respective purpose in relation to persistent criminals. The focus will be on the role of the police in Dordrecht.

The participation of an offender in a Dordrecht programme is entirely voluntary. If consent is given by the convicted offender to participate, after consultation with a representative from the police and probation, and the two partner agencies formally recommend the suitability of the individual, participation becomes a condition of an Order or Licence.

Selection criteria

Offenders have to be a minimum of 16 years of age and not all are suitable for selection. Typically, the criteria upon which offenders are chosen to participate in Dordrecht include a prolific criminal career with at least six convictions including at least one burglary and a concentration of their criminal activity in one police area. While the initial intention of Dordrecht strategies was to address persistent local burglary problems this is no longer the case and access to some programmes has been widened to include offenders convicted of other acquisitive crimes.

Offenders are chosen primarily because of their criminality rather than their drug use although it is recognised that the two are not mutually exclusive. Once selected, they are interviewed in depth regarding their criminal motivation by a representative from the police and the probation service. Indicators of criminality such as drug use, educational attainment and social skills are assessed and whether the criminal acts were committed alone or in a group. Place and nature of residence are investigated (for example, if the offender is living with a co-offender they are encouraged to leave that situation).

Participants agree to engage in an intensive supervision programme instead of a custodial sentence. This includes formulating individually oriented objectives to address the individual's personal welfare issues, for example housing and employment, lifestyle issues and any drug addiction. Offenders are given access to specialists in each of these areas. Intensive home visits by the police and probation representatives are crucial, particularly in the early stages, and offenders also agree to attend regular meetings at the local probation office. In return, the offender agrees not to commit further crimes. He or she acknowledges that they will be legitimately open to police scrutiny in the form of surveillance. For many such offenders, this proactive policing response is not new. In the event of offending while on the programme, the offender is immediately brought before a judge and will inevitably receive a custodial sentence. The following section addresses the nature of repeat offending typically addressed in Dordrecht.

Addressing repeat offending

The nature of repeat offending

For more than a decade, the notion that a small proportion of the population suffer from most crime has been propounded in varying circles (academic, police, policy-making) in the UK:

> The basic facts of repeat victimisation are well known. Substantial proportions of differences in rates of crime are attributable to differences in their concentration on particular targets, where those targets are defined in terms of people, organisations or households. (Farrell and Pease, 2001: 1)

Crime is concentrated in certain areas and, even in these 'hot spots' at the local level, crime is experienced by a small proportion of people. These themes have been found to be true both in the UK and overseas.

Analysis of three sweeps of the International Crime Victims Survey (1989, 1992, 1996) found that 'repeat victimisation ... [was] widespread in the industrialised countries surveyed' (Farrell and Bouloukos, 2001: 5).

Themes apparent in the study of repeat victimisation are consistent when applied in the area of repeat offending. Just as a large proportion of crimes are experienced by a relatively small number of victims, a small core of persistent offenders commit a high proportion of all crimes, and against the same target (Farrell, 1995; Shaw and Pease, 2000). This is significant because it is now known that 'offenders known to commit crimes against the same target are found to be more prolific' (Everson and Pease, 2001: 199). In local areas, a small number of persistent offenders are likely to be responsible for most high-volume, priority crimes including burglary. Everson and Pease draw parallels with a well-known nursery story which, albeit lengthy, is worth referring to at this point:

> It is an immoral tale, whose message seems to be that crime does pay. Jack, son in a lone-parent household, sold his mother's cow for a handful of beans. While the deal reflects the going rate for cows in a U.K. plagued by Bovine Spongiform Encephalopathy, it did not do so in the age inhabited by Jack and his mother. The claim of the cow's purchaser that the beans were magic did not impress Jack's mother who threw them from the house. They grew quickly and Jack climbed the resulting beanstalk. In the land at its top, he persuaded a kind woman (wife to giant) to let him into the castle. She fed him soup. He repaid her hospitality by stealing the giant's hen, which laid golden eggs. Later, he returned to the scene of his crime to steal the giant's bag of golden coins. He retuned yet again to steal the giant's talking harp. Despite the giant's well-justified cry of 'Stop, thief', Jack got safely home and chopped down the beanstalk, causing the pursuing giant to fall to his death ... Let us review Jack's actions. While the first visit to the giant's castle was simply theft in a dwelling, his second and third could certainly be charged as burglary by deception. His action in causing the giant's death would be charged as murder ... Jack has committed one theft, two burglaries and one murder against the giant. The giant and his wife were repeat victims. The perpetrator of crimes against them was one person, the repeat offender, a.k.a. Jack. (Everson and Pease, 2001: 200)

The perpetrator in the above tale is 'versatile' in that he is not only a burglar but he also commits other types of offences. By addressing the reasons for the index crime of burglary, and putting Jack under surveillance to show that the authorities were taking this seriously, there would be a reduction in other types of crimes committed by Jack (set aside the fact that chopping down the beanstalk represents a significant loss in opportunity for the offender). There would be a reduction, for this repeat offender, of the crimes of burglary by deception and murder. Moreover, Jack's offending activity was perpetrated against the same target. By targeting this one offender, a significant reduction in overall crime levels for that area would be achieved. Thus it is argued that any crime control activity which addresses prolific offenders will effectively, and in a sustainable way, reduce crime.

The role of police in crime control

The UK Labour Party came into power with the promise of being 'tough on crime, tough on the causes of crime'. Essentially, the police's traditional role has been to be 'tough on crime', with the 'causes of crime' being dealt with by other agencies. Of course, this is now less so the case. We are now in a crime reduction age which is focused on inter-agency partnerships and where the police are now under a statutory obligation to be in partnership with other criminal justice agencies. Since the Crime and Disorder Act 1998, the role of the police has had to become more integrated with other agencies in the criminal justice system. Furthermore, the emphasis on a proactive approach to policing, evidenced in the increasing use of the Problem Oriented Policing (POP) approach, has meant that the role of the police has changed to address the underlying causes of crime. Increasingly, intelligence-led and proactive approaches to crime problems in local areas are being taken up. Both 'hard' and 'soft' approaches are increasingly being adopted by the police in crime control. Inevitably, this has been fuelled by the existence of national performance indicators.

This practical change in approach in recent years has partly been a result of a theoretical realignment of crime reduction policy. In essence, the approach debated here represents a merging of 'zero-tolerance' and more liberal approaches to crime control (police and probation, respectively):

Supporters of zero tolerance-style policing point to large reductions in the recorded crime figures as incontestable evidence of its success. Opponents observe the failure to establish a causal link between implementation and outcomes ... The positions of supporters and opponents seem incompatible. (Hopkins-Burke, 1998: 7)

Problem Oriented Policing

The crime prevention implications of focusing on repeat victims, and implicitly those who carry out repeat crimes, has been documented increasingly widely in the UK since 1988 (Forrester et al., 1988; Anderson et al., 1995; Shaw and Pease, 2000). Since the mid-1990s (Leigh et al., 1996) POP has increasingly been incorporated into UK policing. Because POP '... is about examining patterns of incident clusters to identify and tackle underlying problems within the community' (Leigh et al., 1996: v) common themes occur between this policing approach, repeat victimisation and repeat offending. As stated earlier, most crime is experienced (victims) and perpetrated (offenders) by a small proportion of people and crime problems are therefore focused on specific locations. In either rural or urban areas, crime is concentrated in 'hot spots'. Pease and Laycock (1996) define the repeat victim as the most precise 'hot dot' in a crime 'hot spot' while these crimes will be committed by a small proportion of active offenders. Therefore, by implication, by attending to repeat offending one is addressing the problem of repeat victimisation.

POP was first developed by Herman Goldstein in the United States in 1979, although it is only recently that it has been adopted in UK policing. The first report on UK POP observed:

The idea behind POP is disarmingly simple. It suggests that policing should, at heart, be about solving underlying problems within the community ... (this is because) the incidents that come to the attention of the police are by no means random. Police officers find that they return repeatedly to the same place or they are dealing with the consequences of behaviour by the same individual or group. (Leigh et al., 1996: 2)

The Dordrecht offender programmes present an opportunity for the police to solve underlying repeat offending behaviour by known criminals by being 'tough on criminals' and 'tough on the causes of *repeat* criminal behaviour'.

Zero tolerance policing and the problem of persistent offenders

Being 'tough on criminals' had previously meant adopting a 'zero tolerance' approach to the problem criminal. Influenced by the 'three strikes and you're out' principle (Kelling and Coles, 1996: 1) tried and tested in New York, some British police forces (e.g. Cleveland Constabulary) became obsessed with clamping down on minor disorder to prevent more serious crime. The link between disorder and, if left unchecked, more serious crimes is proven:

> In the words of Wilson and Kelling: serious street crime flourishes in areas in which disorderly behavior (*sic*) goes unchecked. The unchecked panhandler is, in effect, the first broken window. Muggers and robbers, whether opportunistic or professional, believe they reduce their chances of being caught or even identified if they operate on streets where potential victims are already intimidated by prevailing conditions. If the neighbourhood cannot keep a bothersome panhandler from annoying passers by, the thief may reason, it is even less likely to call the police to identify a potential mugger or to interfere if the mugging actually takes places. (Kelling and Coles, 1996: 20)

This philosophy was adapted to different crime types in what, some would argue, was a POP approach (the underlying causes of crime problems were not solved, but on the face of it the crime problem reduced or even disappeared). Representatives from British police forces were impressed with the results seen in the United States. Dennis and Mallon (1998) report that:

> According to police figures, in New York serious crime dropped by 27 per cent from 1993 to 1995. In 1995 there were 35,400 street robberies; in 1996 there were 30,400. The record of 2,200 murders was set in 1990. In 1996 the total was under 1,000 for the first time since 1968. (Dennis and Mallon, 1997: 62)

The then Head of CID at Middlesbrough, Ray Mallon, began to target prolific burglars within a zero tolerance approach as 'targeting the burglar could be effective in the short term, by putting him out of business' (Dennis and Mallon, 1997: 70). This was facilitated by the increasing, and targeted, use of police stop and search powers to apprehend criminals and – as soon as possible – imprison them.

There is little doubt that cracking down on persistent offenders does reduce crime in the short term. Given what we know about the likelihood of reoffending after release from prison (Raynor, 2000), though, there is an increasing recognition that 'zero tolerance' does not solve the problem of persistent offending long term.

So what does solve persistent offending long term? It is argued here that programmes similar to Dordrecht are the way forward. It is suggested that the 'hard' zero tolerance approach alone does not solve the problem completely. Similarly, the police cannot solve the problem alone. Similarly, more liberal models of rehabilitation are not the sole answer. However, where both elements are represented, possibly by different partners as in Dordrecht, the likelihood is that success will be met.

Restorative justice revisited

In recent years in the UK, there has been a growth in the restorative justice approach to crime control. It has been defined by the United Nations as '... a process in which the victim, the offender and/or any other individuals or community members affected by a crime participate actively together in the resolution of matters arising from the crime' (UN, 1999, cited by Zedner, 2002: 445).

There has been a move – linked with victim rights – towards the empowerment of victims and from a retaliation approach towards restitution and reparation. Reparation Orders were introduced by the Crime and Disorder Act 1998 and for the first time there was a provision for restorative conferences under the auspices of Youth Offending Teams. More recently, restorative justice has been strongly influenced by models of community justice in non-western cultures, for example indigenous populations of North America and New Zealand. These inspired family-group conferencing in New Zealand, Australia, the United States and Britain. The approach is greatly influenced by John Braithwaite, among others.

In practice, restorative justice is intended to involve offenders, their families, victims and other interested members of the community, and a facilitator. The facilitator may be a youth justice coordinator, social worker or police officer. The police are therefore becoming more involved in the process of offender rehabilitation, a shift in their role.

The aim of restorative justice is to evoke a change in attitude by offenders to crime by encouraging recognition of the victim and the harm caused, and in the UK this has been mainly directed at young people through Youth Offending Teams (YOTs). Some victims wish to participate in the restorative justice process because they consider that facing the offender will help them recover from the trauma of being victimised. However, if it is true that punishment alone does not work, and there is research evidence to support that supposition, the case for management of individuals through crime desistance objectives through community reintegration is strong. Dordrecht complements such an approach.

There are two reasons why restorative justice has been discussed here. First, there has been transition from within the criminal justice system away from retribution and towards restitution. Second, there has been the influence of zero tolerance in policing acknowledged above. Dordrecht reflects both these two influences from pure zero tolerance (retribution) towards addressing the causes of crime for individual offenders. Building relationships with offenders is crucial in order for this to happen successfully.

It has been increasingly recognised, in recent years, that purely punitive sanctions against persistent offenders does not work. Restorative justice has played its part, in particular in relation to young offenders, in mending broken 'relationships' between offenders and victims. However, if there is evidence to suggest that offenders also suffer from broken relationships – and the evidence is reviewed below – and these can be proven to be one of the predictors for the onset of criminality, then there is an argument for the restoring of traditional relationships between offenders and criminal justice agencies. This includes the police. One intensive supervision programme similar to the original Dordrecht programme in Burnley quoted one client as saying 'I know the police officer quite well ... he has locked me up before. For years he has been locking me up ... I've seen a different side of him now ...' (Home Office, 2002d: 2).

Does Dordrecht solve the *problem* of persistent offending?

Anecdotal evidence suggests that around two-thirds of Dordrecht clients succeed without return to court for breaching conditions of the Order or Licence and around one half of offenders have no recorded offences for the period they are on Dordrecht. These figures reflect some success in the programme. The fact that some offenders are returned to court reflects the intention, and the practice, of the police to apply the penalties which offenders agreed to when signing up for the programme. An evaluation of a scheme in Staffordshire noted the following:

> We are very heartened by the research findings as these hard core offenders are usually extremely difficult to work with on a constructive and socially inclusive basis. But 'success' for prolific offenders' projects can be double-edged as offenders can opt for positive change if they are prepared to make the commitment and stop offending. If not, then they run the risk of detection at a much earlier stage than they have previously experienced, and either way crimes will have been prevented. (Home Office, 2002g: 1)

The character of persistent offenders is just that: they are persistent in their offending. Dordrecht is not a soft option, in policing terms. Any team working on Dordrecht faces an uphill struggle in maintaining the motivation of offenders to adhere to their individual objectives and, ultimately of course, to desist from drug use and offending.

Dordrecht is the start of a process in which offending behaviour is challenged. It does not necessarily imply a complete change of approach by the offender, at least in the first instance. It is here, given that some offenders do not desist from offending, that problems begin for the police. It is here that the 'hard' side of the police's role in Dordrecht is tested.

At the outset, offenders have to agree not to offend while they are on the programme. They know that the police can legitimately place them under surveillance, and they agree to 'allow'[3] this when they sign up to the conditions of the programme. The knowledge of the dual roles of the police is apparent for every offender. As relationships between the police and offender 'soften' and trust begins to develop between two parties who are traditionally on opposing sides, offenders are encouraged to confess if they commit any additional crimes. Swift action is taken against offenders who continue to offend at high rates.

Although the police can implement surveillance techniques, the reality is that offenders on Dordrecht cannot be tracked constantly. Although most offenders on Dordrecht would be likely to say that they have not committed offences while on the programme, how confident can the police be that this is the truth? It is possible that a proportion of offenders on Dordrecht will still be participating in criminal activity contrary to the knowledge of the police officer. In some cases the police may not be in possession of the full facts. This might lead the offender to conclude that the 'soft' side of the police on Dordrecht outweighs the 'hard' side. Offenders are set to gain if this issue is taken in isolation.

However, the home visit by Dordrecht personnel is viewed as a positive factor in preventing the onset of offending for longer. The visits are an incentive not to get involved in crime, at least not as soon as might otherwise have been the case. Offenders who really want to change their behaviour – and offenders are selected who appear to want to do this – benefit from the high level of supervision. The probation service and the police work together. There is the formal knowledge that formal and informal surveillance is taking place and the penalties for being caught offending are serious.

Does Dordrecht address the *causes* of persistent offending?

Because it is still difficult for participants in Dordrecht to find legitimate employment, it is uncertain as to whether the approach offered gives a credible alternative to crime. This is still one of the major challenges for the field of offender rehabilitation. Nonetheless, clients who have reduced or eliminated drug use are more likely to be able to gain, and sustain, employment than those who do not.

Anecdotal evidence suggests that Dordrecht is perceived favourably by participants. In particular, benefits are seen in relation to learning new skills and decreasing drug involvement. Decreases in individual levels of criminal activity, albeit in some cases perhaps not eliminated altogether, are also evident. Therefore, although for some offenders long-term habits are hard to break completely, the likelihood of being caught is an incentive at least to reduce levels of criminal activity. Research has suggested that intensive supervision schemes do address the causes of prolific criminal activity. One such scheme run by the police and probation officers showed that 53 per cent on average are less likely to be reconvicted when compared with a control group (Home Office, 2002g: 1).

Anecdotal evidence suggests that the kind of rehabilitation offered in Dordrecht programmes is viewed positively by offenders. Some of the success is related to the appropriate targeting of offenders, all of whom are vetted prior to being taken onto such schemes. Perhaps some of the success is related to the selection of those who have recognised that they have problems, including the fact that they are heavily influenced by their criminal networks, a large proportion of which are long-standing friends. Many participants in the programme see improvements in their home circumstances. Either relationships between family members or partners improve to enable them to stay at home, or other better quality accommodation is found for them.

Improvements have also been reported in the following areas: employment prospects, self-esteem, overall feeling of well-being and new interests or hobbies.

Important success factors in Dordrecht

A number of factors can be identified as important in Dordrecht programmes. First, it is important to have *clear definitions* of the types of offenders to be targeted and a clear notion of the type of character suited to this approach. This may come from knowledge of previous prolific offenders. Second, *procedures for referral* through the courts should be set up prior to the start of the programme. Third, there needs to be an awareness of the way in which a *police and probation partnership* might be perceived by offenders, as the Dordrecht approach challenges the traditional roles of both agencies, and in particular an acknowledgement of likely initial scepticism on behalf of offenders towards the former. Fourth, there is a need for a *realistic approach* because a simple progression through such an intensive rehabilitative approach may not occur. It might therefore be necessary for offenders to be taken off the programme and then reinstated at a later date when they are more receptive and willing to fulfil their side of the agreement, in particular in the area of reoffending and drug use. Fifth, there is the recognition that *intensity increases success*. In the first weeks after starting on the programme, offenders are visited in their homes numerous times, as well as receiving advice and help in relation to drug use and lifestyle issues, among other matters. Sixth, *resource input* is important. Costs should include the full-time employment of two people (one high-ranking police officer and one experienced probation officer). Seventh, the existence of *proper planning* is apparent in successful programmes, including research on the background of the offender and processes for evaluating the success of the individual on the programme. Eighth, it is appropriate to have a *pre-agreed strategic framework*, with advice taken from people familiar with Dordrecht and this requirement is closely linked to nine, the need for rigorous *internal scheme monitoring* established at the outset of the programme. Indeed, the latter is invariably a condition of receiving funding. Tenth, there is a need for *inter-agency collaboration* outside the police–probation partnership. For example, collaboration is essential between Dordrecht staff and representatives of local medical centres, who may be called upon to provide methadone prescriptions for participating offenders. This needs to be established from the start. Although methadone is known to have its own side effects, it is still used widely by practitioners as a substitute for illegal Class A drugs. Heroin use has been proved to decrease through using methadone, as has theft. Furthermore, methadone treatment has been shown to be most effective for those prolific offenders who are also prolific drug users (Coid et al., 2000: 1). Finally, the *character of the staff* involved in implementing the interventions is, finally though not least, crucial. Successful programmes have people who are dedicated full-time to the programme and who have excellent social skills in order to develop a working relationship with the participating offenders.

Conclusions

The above account suggests that Dordrecht offender rehabilitation programmes complement recent, apparently diverse, approaches to policing. On the one hand, there is a 'hard' zero tolerance element. On the other hand, there is a 'softer' emphasis on solving the root causes of criminal activity for individual offenders. Given the nationwide structural emphasis on defining crime as a problem (POP)[4] these two, apparently contradictory, approaches begin to become complementary. There is a strong body of research which has identified what works in terms of tackling the root causes of offending. Raynor (2002: 1186) summarises the characteristics of the programmes which are most effective:

1 The targeting of high-risk offenders who are otherwise likely to continue to offend, rather than low-risk offenders who may gain little benefit or be harmed.

2 A focus on criminogenic need, that is those characteristics or circumstances of offenders which have contributed to their offending.

3 Those which are highly structured, making clear and explicit demands and following a logical sequence determined by their learning goals.

4 Those that use a directive working approach, so that participants know what they are meant to be doing.

5 The use of broadly cognitive-behavioural methods, to provide opportunities to learn new thinking and behaviour.

6 They are best located in the community.

7 They have programme integrity, that is, they are delivered as intended, with procedures to ensure this.

8 There is a committed and effective management team.

9 There is appropriately trained staff who believe they can be effective

10 There are adequate resources for continuity.

11 There are integral evaluation and feedback ideally involving external researchers.

Anecdotal evidence and reflections presented here suggest that many of these criteria can be applied to Dordrecht and therefore provide a strong endorsement of such programmes, albeit the task is difficult:

> The complexities of holding in balance genuine concern for individual offenders and commitment to community safety and public protection result in difficult professional deliberations on a daily basis, requiring skill and integrity from all those working on the project. (Home Office, 2002: 4)

Notes

1 Burglary was the original crime focus of Dordrecht, although this has now expanded in some places to include vehicle crime. In addition, it is recognised that prolific offenders are versatile in that they are likely to be involved in other crimes. Nevertheless, burglary is the index crime used for the identification of prolific offenders for consideration for involvement in Dordrecht.
2 The author was a member of the evaluation teams on that programme.
3 Of course, the police have this right anyway.
4 Problem Oriented *Partnerships* is increasingly the preferred term.

Part 3
Democracy, Accountability and Human Rights

Chapter 13

What's law got to do with it? Some reflections on the police in light of developments in New York City

Graham Smith

Introduction

Since the formation of the first modern police force in 1829, the Metropolitan Police Service (MPS), the social cost of crime control has been a constant feature of the debate on policing. The mere existence of a public body responsible for order maintenance and law enforcement, and entrusted by Parliament with coercive powers for these purposes, has proved to be problematic. Although the structures and methods of the police services of England and Wales[1] have been admired, and adopted, throughout the world, their constitutional status is peculiar to English common law. During the course of history the doctrine of constabulary independence has developed to grant modern police services, under the leadership of a chief officer (normally a chief constable but a commissioner for both the MPS and City of London Police), a wide degree of discretion when performing their law enforcement responsibilities. This discretion in operational policing matters is predicated on the independence and impartiality of every police officer that serves in the office of constable. A practical consequence of the doctrine is that responsibility for strategic and tactical policing matters rests with chief officers. Much criticised for the excessive autonomy it allows the police (Brogden, 1982; Dixon and Smith, 1998; Jefferson and Grimshaw, 1984; Lustgarten, 1986; Marshall, 1965) chief officers have argued that constabulary independence ensures the police services operate as accountable organisations which take public opinion into account rather than follow political orders (Alderson, 1973; Mark, 1978; Oliver, 1997). Hypothetically, the doctrine also places the police on permanent standby in defence of democracy against unlawful rule by tyrannical government (Marshall, 1978).

In this chapter, recent arguments and reforms surrounding police strategies are considered in the changing constitutional context of the twenty-first century. A critique is first presented of the development of the doctrine of constabulary independence and the process by which increasingly remote police services became separated and isolated from the public. Then, with the introduction of measures to rein in police autonomy in the last decade, concerns are raised with the absence of checks and balances in the emerging arrangements for police governance and the onward march to centralised state power. Although it is possible to distinguish between hard and soft strategies, strict adherence to either philosophy can be disastrous, and pro-nouncements by Labour ministers in favour of 'zero tolerance policing' have contributed to the politicisation of policing. Direct comparison is made between the offensive in New York City against 'quality of life' crimes and the anti-social behaviour strategy, which is about to be extended, in the UK. Finally, a brief sketch is presented of some of the excesses committed by New York Police Department (NYPD) officers along with former Mayor Rudolph Giuliani's responses.

Constabulary independence

That the MPS made the statute book at all is attributed to Sir Robert Peel's political acumen (Ascoli, 1979; Critchley, 1978; Radzinowicz, 1968). He astutely avoided the controversy which greeted Patrick Colquhoun's (1796) call for a new force and which had caused two previous legislative attempts to fall by the wayside in 1785 and 1812. In his speech to move the first reading of the Metropolitan Police Bill in the House of Commons,[2] Peel concentrated on criminal statistics and variations in police provision in London's parishes (furnished by the Select Committee on the Police of the Metropolis, 1828). In this manner he outmanoeuvred libertarian opponents and sidestepped concerns with the expansion of state power and the threat to citizens' consti-tutional rights. However, in recognition of widespread public concern, the first modern police officers were provided with few powers which separated them from the citizen and the first commissioners went to great lengths to secure public support by focusing on crime prevention (Dixon, 1997; Emsley, 1996). Despite this cautious approach – the visibility of the blue serge uniform, with black top hat, was intended to deter crime – there was widespread opposition to what was considered an oppressive institution.

It was not until the County and Borough Police Act 1856 that all local and county administrations in England and Wales were required to establish and maintain police forces. In order to more effectively perform their statutory duties, the independent forces relied on the permissiveness of the common law to extend their powers into criminal investigation and the conduct of prosecutions (Stephen, 1883). Police governance during the second half of the nineteenth century, and well into the twentieth, was by a mixture of arrangements. Under the Metropolitan Police Act 1829, MPS commissioners reported directly to the Home Secretary until the creation of a Metropolitan Police Authority under the Greater London Authority Act 1999. Borough police forces came under the responsibility of watch committees, precursors of local police authorities, under the Municipal Corporation Act 1835 (reformed in 1882) and county forces were governed by standing committees consisting of councillors and magistrates as provided by the County Police Act 1939. Historical research has revealed that during this period police officers were considered the servants of local ratepayers, despite the delegation of most policing responsibilities by elected representatives to chief officers (Brogden, 1982; Steedman, 1984). As police professionalism developed around the turn of the century, amid some confusion as to where the powers of the police ceased and those of magistrates commenced,[3] the doctrine of constabulary independence evolved in the mid-twentieth century.[4] The doctrine materialised under dubious circumstances, partly as a consequence of failure by government ministers and local councillors to account for the actions of local police forces even when requested to do so (Keith-Lucas, 1960; Marshall, 1965).

Following a series of scandals in the 1950s (Marshall, 1965) a Royal Commission on the Police (RCP) was appointed in 1960 to consider, *inter alia*, the constitutional status of the police and the condition of police–public relations in the UK with particular reference to the handling of complaints. The RCP's *Final Report* (1962) survives as one of the most authoritative documents on the police and which has set the terms of debate on police accountability for four decades.

The RCP's deliberations on police governance were underpinned by theoretical definition of police powers as 'quasi-judicial', consistent with the need for independent and impartial law enforcement. For this reason: 'We entirely accept that it is in the public interest that a chief constable, in dealing with these quasi-judicial matters, should be free from the conventional processes of democratic control and influence' (RCP, 1962: 30).

It is contended that the commissioners' adherence to this 'quasi-judicial' notion served to excuse the police from external control and accorded chief officers an independent status not dissimilar to that enjoyed by members of the judiciary.

Since the RCP's attempt to define police powers, the House of Lords decided that the police officer exercises an executive discretion when performing his or her law enforcement duties (*Holgate-Mohammed* v. *Duke* [1984] 1 AC 437). This definition is consistent with the police serving as an independent part of the executive with responsibilities for the pre-trial, or pre-judicial rather than quasi-judicial, stages of the criminal justice process. On this point it may be helpful to go back in history, prior to the formation of modern police forces, when the justices of the peace wielded both executive and judicial powers, which provided trading justices with ample opportunities to engage in corrupt practices (Critchley, 1978). In these circumstances, it would seem that the fears expressed for civil liberties at the prospect of a police force were more in opposition to the existence of an organised body holding excessive powers rather than an individual's possession of the same. The importance of police impartiality in law enforcement can be traced back to this moment in history and was responsible for the separation of powers insisted on when the police eventually entered the statute book. Retention of the common law office of constable, with the new police continuing to serve under the legal authority of the justice,[5] gave some semblance of a separation of powers and the police were restricted to largely administrative tasks. However, concurrent with the police's replacement of the magistracy as the institution responsible for pre-trial criminal procedure, the watch committee assumed many of the justice's responsibilities for police administration. The RCP attributed the confusion regarding the constitutional status of the police to these parallel developments, and hoped to resolve this problem by identifying the police as a branch of the executive with quasi-judicial law enforcement powers, which made them unsuited for standard administrative controls.

Most of the RCP's recommendations were accepted by the government and implemented by the Police Act 1964. The Act reinforced the common law position by making chief officers responsible for the direction and control of their forces and provided a tripartite arrangement for police governance consisting of the Home Secretary, local police authority and chief officer. The principal effect of the legislation was to increase the powers of chief officers at the expense of locally elected councillors and remove much of the confusion regarding who controls operational police matters. A few years later, Lord Denning unequivocally declared that a chief police officer 'is answerable to the law alone' when performing his or her law enforcement duties (*R v. Metropolitan Commissioner of Police ex parte Blackburn* [1968] 2 QB 118; Lustgarten, 1986). The pinnacle of the doctrine, perhaps, was reached when Lord Donaldson ruled in *R v. Oxford ex parte Levey* (1986) *The Times*, 1 November, that it was not for the courts to review chief officers' policing methods provided they did not exceed the limits of the discretion accorded them by law.

It is apparent that there is a conflict of principle between the office of constable, which provides the individual officer with his or her original authority when responding to particular incidents (*Fisher v. Oldham Corporation*, see note 4), and the chief officer's sole responsibility for general law enforcement. A practical illustration of this dilemma was the furore that arose when PC Joy pursued a private prosecution against an MP for drink driving because his chief constable wished to issue a caution (*The Times*, 6 July 1974). As argued by Lustgarten (1986: 12), the chief constable determined police policy in this case and the ordinary constable was left to his own devices.

The courts were called upon to determine the complexity of the relation between chief and ranking officers after anti-nuclear protestors delayed construction of a power station in *R v. Chief Constable of Devon and Cornwall ex parte Central Electricity Generating Board* [1982] QB 458. Judgment accommodated the office of constable under the doctrine of constabulary independence by establishing that chief officers

> ... command their forces but they cannot give an officer under command an order to do acts which can only be lawfully done if the officer himself with reasonable cause suspects a breach of the peace has occurred or is imminently likely to occur or an arrestable offence has been committed. (Ibid.: 474, per Lawton LJ)

A consequence of the generous latitude afforded the police under the doctrine of constabulary independence was that during the 1980s police autonomy emerged as a political problem which was eventually to cause serious damage to police legitimacy (Baxter and Koffman, 1985; Fine and Millar, 1985; Reiner, 2000a; Sheehy, 1993). Although constabulary independence continues to define the constitutional status of the police (*R v. Chief Constable of Sussex Police ex parte International Traders Ferry* [1999] 1 All ER 129; Dixon and Smith, 1998) the doctrine has been significantly weakened during the course of the last decade.

The Home Office offensive

Disempowerment of local authorities under the Police Act 1964 combined with the reluctance of the courts to interfere with a chief officer's decisions on law enforcement ensures that change can only be imposed on the police through legislative reform. Of course, the Home Secretary may resort to an array of lesser tactics to persuade chief officers to accede to government initiatives, for example by issuing orders or guidelines with the threat of financial penalty for failure to comply. If all else fails there are two options available to the government to circumvent police independence and guarantee that chief officers fall in line with policy. Under its legislative programme a government can either require the police to take action by criminalising behaviour, or it can introduce procedures which impose duties on the police. Both of these types of reform can be identified in the present Labour administration's crime and disorder programme. On the one hand, the criminal justice net has been widened in all but name by lowering the threshold of unlawful conduct to include anti-social behaviour. On the other hand, the Crime and Disorder Act 1998 introduced a range of sanctions designed to regulate such behaviour and requires police services to work in partnership with other public bodies to control crime and disorder.

Another area of reform which undermines constabulary independence and restricts police discretion is performance management (Loveday, 1998; Neyroud and Beckley, 2001). The die was cast by the Police and Magistrates' Courts Act 1994 (PMCA). Hostility to local democratic institutions, a defining feature of Mrs Thatcher's administrations in the 1980s, continued under John Major into the 1990s and, rather than attempt to restore credibility to the ineffective tripartite arrangement by introducing reforms to revitalise the excessively bureaucratic and powerless local police authorities, the PMCA further emasculated the influence of local democracy on the police. The Major government preferred to put its faith in the new public management ideals which Kenneth Clarke pioneered when responsible for health and education prior to his appointment as Home Secretary (McLaughlin and Murji, 2001; Scott, 2000) and appointed Sir Patrick Sheehy (1993) to examine police responsibilities and rewards. In the face of determined opposition from the police, the latter's proposals for fixed-term contracts for all officers and performance-related pay were rejected (Reiner, 2000). However, the PMCA granted powers to the Home Secretary to set key objectives and performance indicators (Baker and English, 1994; Reiner, 1993).

Performance management has thrived under New Labour. Best Value, introduced under the Local Government Act 1999, has firmly established internal markets at the heart of public services and ensures greater central government intervention in police affairs through the offices of the Audit Commission and the Inspectorate of Constabulary. McLaughlin and Murji (2001) have cogently argued that New Labour's adherence to 'third way' fiscal initiatives cannot be simply discarded as part of a neo-liberalist conspiracy against democratic public services. Their suggestion for a multi-layered approach to managerialist trends has to be considered in tandem with developments at common and statute law which have a bearing on police accountability (Dixon and Smith, 1998). Unfortunately, under its police reform programme New Labour has taken a linear approach and has not taken advantage of the opportunity to introduce a comprehensive system of checks and balances and legislatively reconstruct a democratic police institution capable of responding to local concerns. In the White Paper *Policing a New Century: A Blueprint for Reform* (Home Office, 2001b), Home Secretary David Blunkett focused on improvements to police perform-ance, developing the crime and disorder programme and 'extension of the police family'. Although some of the planned reforms were watered down in the House of Lords, the Police Reform Act 2002 has signifi-cantly increased the powers of the Home Secretary. Three initiatives are deserving of mention here. Firstly, the Act allows the Home Secretary to assume a more prescriptive role by providing for publication of annual three-year national policing plans. This is augmented by the creation of a Police Standards Unit, reporting directly to the Home Secretary, which is responsible for disseminating best practice across the 43 police services currently operating in England and Wales. And, thirdly, in addition to the commitment of the government to increase the number of officers serving in England and Wales to 132,500 by April 2004 (Home Office News and Press Release 310/2002, 20 November 2002) police services may supplement the strength of their forces by employing community safety officers (Blair, 2002).

The government announced its intention to introduce an Anti-Social Behaviour White Paper in 2003 (*Guardian*, 14 November 2002) and it may come as no surprise, therefore, to find that tackling anti-social behaviour and disorder is at the top of the list of primary objectives in the first national policing plan (Home Office, 2002e).

Labour's obsession with anti-social behaviour stands direct comparison with crusades by former Republican New York Mayor, Rudolph Giuliani, and his first Commissioner of Police, William Bratton, against 'quality-of-life' crimes (Bratton, 1997; Kelling and Coles, 1996). The targeting of sub-criminal behaviour of this type, based on Wilson and Kelling's (1982) 'broken windows' thesis, has been acknowledged as a core element of 'zero tolerance' policing (ZTP). Although this label has not been embraced by those responsible for policing New York, it has gained common currency among policy-makers, practitioners, researchers and commentators (Hopkins-Burke, 1998a, 2002; Innes, 1999). In particular, since taking office, Labour politicians have spoken out on innumerable occasions in favour of ZTP[6] and it is evident that recent crime control initiatives owe a debt to developments in New York (Broadhurst, 2002; Silverman, 1998). Senior police officers, on the other hand, with a few notable exceptions (Dennis and Mallon, 1997; Romeanes, 1998), have been sceptical of the strategy (Butler, 2000; Knights, 1998; Pollard, 1997).[7]

Home Office research (Bland and Read, 2000) conducted between November 1997 and April 1998 revealed an array of problems with police attempts to control anti-social behaviour. The researchers, after examining nine forces which had developed anti-social behaviour strategies before the introduction of the Crime and Disorder Act 1998, concluded that it was not possible to arrive at a standard definition of anti-social behaviour. As a result, difficulties were created by association of the term with the activities of young people, irrespective of whether their conduct was unlawful or offensive to other members of the public. Deployment of officers to deal with inter-generational disputes, with a tendency noted for complainants to exaggerate or make false allegations against youths, implies that intolerant residents were deviously reporting incidents in the expectation that the police would clear their neighbourhood of unwelcome members of the public. A senior Devon and Cornwall officer expressed his concern that the young people who the police were dealing with should not be 'coming into contact with criminal justice agencies and questioned the value of legislating against such behaviour' (ibid.: 14).

Operational police officers' responses to local anti-social behaviour strategies researched by Bland and Read reflect the practical difficulties with controlling conduct which is not expressly prohibited by law. Moreover, their experiences and views lend considerable support to the argument that the law is a blunt instrument for regulating behaviour, even where this may significantly increase police powers. David Dixon (1997) argues it was as recently as the 1980s and the introduction of

PACE, which managed to simultaneously increase and regulate police powers, that the law started to play a key role in policing. In his comparative studies of policing in England and Wales and Australia he laments the failure of New South Wales Police to follow the UK example of accompanying statutory police powers with formal guidance for officers under the PACE Codes of Practice (1997, 1999). Since the advent of New Labour, the role of the law in policing is galloping ahead at such speed that unforeseen circumstances may lie ahead. Whereas the permissiveness of the common law may leave too much discretion in the hands of the police (Lustgarten, 1986; McBarnet, 1981), the prescriptiveness of statute law can override their professional judgment and limit the options available to them.

The elusive search for balance

Policing is riddled with dilemmas and the need to accommodate conflicting interests. It was shortly after publication of the RCP's *Final Report* (1962) that the police began to attract the attention of academics in both the UK and USA. In general terms, the research challenged traditional images of the police as upholders of the law by detailing how little the law has to do with day-to-day policing. Examination of police activity revealed that police effectiveness largely depends on the officer's ability to avoid invoking the law (Banton, 1964), and where this proves unavoidable the administration of justice is normally effected prior to attendance at court (Skolnick, 1966). The conflict between 'law' and 'order' – the law being more concerned with individual rights whereas maintaining order requires interference with them – was problematicised and analysis commenced on the realities of police force, violence and brutality (Bittner, 1970; Westley, 1970).

It was an academic lawyer, Herbert Packer (1968), who drew many of these strands of early criminological research together in his quest to understand the conflict between the principles of law and the practice of enforcement. His seminal study on the competing values at the heart of criminal justice – crime control and due process – which coexist in a troubled alliance, continues to be of major importance for practice and research, if only to reflect on the obsolescence of these models (Ashworth, 1998; McConville, Sanders and Leng, 1991; Royal Commission on Criminal Procedure, 1981; Sanders and Young, 2000; Smith, 1997).

Following the inner city disturbances of 1981, Lord Scarman (1981) famously pointed to the potential for conflict between the police's peacekeeping and law enforcement functions. His conclusions, which have informed police practice for more than 20 years, deserve quoting at length.

> The successful solution of the conflict lies first in the priority to be given in the last resort to the maintenance of public order, and secondly in the constant and common-sense exercise of police discretion. Indeed the exercise of discretion lies at the heart of the policing function. It is undeniable that there is only one law for all: and it is right that this should be so. But it is equally well recognised that successful policing depends on the exercise of discretion in how the law is enforced. The good reputation of the police as a force depends upon the skill and judgment which policemen display in the particular circumstances of the cases and incidents which they are required to handle. Discretion is the art of suiting action to particular circumstances. It is the policeman's daily task. (Ibid.: para. 4: 58)

It was Scarman's bloodying of the police nose that serves as a dire warning of the inevitability of controversy, and the potential for break-down in police–community relations, where there is over-enforcement of the law, a lesson that has been borne out by events in New York.[8]

Prior to Giuliani's assumption of office, there had been damaging official inquiries into NYPD corruption (Knapp Commission, 1972; Mollen Commission, 1994) and much had been written on police abuses of power (Chevigny, 1969, 1995; Skolnick and Fyfe, 1993). After the Mollen Commission, appointed by Giuliani's predecessor David Dinkins, reorganisation of the Civilian Complaints Review Board (CCRB) as a body independent from the police[9] and Bratton's appointment as Commissioner, it was hoped that these problems had been overcome. However, Bratton only survived in office a few years and reports critical of the NYPD's record on civil liberties were soon to be published (Amnesty International, 1996; Human Rights Watch, 1998).

Three cases of police violence against young black men – the torture of Abner Louima in 1997 and the fatal shootings of Amado Diallo and Patrick Dorismond in 1999 and 2000, respectively – were to cause New Yorkers to question the aggressive methods of the NYPD. Following the brutal sodomisation of Louima with a broken broom handle in a Brooklyn police station, Giuliani appointed a taskforce to enquire into police–public relations and then cynically dismissed its report the following year (*New York Times*, 27 March 1998). One officer received a

30-year prison sentence for the assault and another had his conviction quashed after serving over two years of a 16-year sentence;[10] the victim accepted a damages settlement of $8.75 million (*New York Times*, 1 March 2002).[11] Four members of NYPD's Street Crime Unit (SCU) were acquitted of murder and lesser charges after the unarmed Diallo was killed in a hail of 41 bullets as he attempted to enter his apartment block (*New York Times*, 27 February 2000). The plain-clothed officers stated in evidence that they mistook the wallet Diallo took out of his pocket as a firearm and immediately opened fire, hitting him 19 times. A grand jury declined to lay charges against the undercover officer responsible for the death of Dorismond after his firearm was discharged during a struggle. The officer had been engaged in a drugs operation and Dorsimond apparently took offence when approached (Colb, 2000). Mayor Giuliani caused a furore when he later revealed the NYPD's confidential file on the deceased (*New York Times*, 7 April 2000).

The Louima, Diallo and Dorismond incidents were exceptional cases and should be considered in context; 11 fatal shootings by NYPD officers in 1999 was the lowest annual total since 1973 and during Giuliani's two terms as mayor there was a 50 per cent decline in the number of intentional shootings (*Daily Telegraph*, 11 August 2000). However, closer examination of the elite SCU reveals that it operated as an oppressive and discriminatory force. Its 350 members operated in plain clothes and relied heavily on 'stop and frisk' to confront drugs and firearms offences. Of all persons stopped by the unit 62.7 per cent were black, and the ratio of arrests for black suspects was 1 out of 16 stopped compared with 1 out of 10 for white suspects (*New York Times*, 27 February 2000). Silverman (2000) compares SCU practice with Macpherson's (1999) finding on the police's discriminatory use of stop and search in Part Two of the Stephen Lawrence Inquiry.

Further comparison with Macpherson can be made with regard to adherence to equal opportunities principles in the police services. With only nine black officers at the time of the Diallo shooting, one black member of the SCU, Yvette Walton, was dismissed from the NYPD after she publicly spoke out against the Unit's practice of racial profiling. She contributed to the citywide protests in response to the Diallo shooting by asserting on a television programme and at a council meeting that SCU officers singled out black persons to stop and frisk. Over three years later she received compensation and won reinstatement after the courts ruled she had been dismissed in 'retaliation for her public statements' (New York Civil Liberties Union, 2002).[12]

Despite Giuliani's rejection of the Louima taskforce report after his re-election to office in 1998, reforms were instigated as a consequence of these scandals (Silverman, 2000). Police Commissioner Howard Safir appointed a black commander and assigned black officers to the Street Crime Unit after Diallo's death and its officers were dispersed around the city. Responsibility for the conduct of misconduct prosecutions was transferred to the CCRB and a rule which exempted officers suspected of wrongdoing from being questioned by superiors for 48 hours is being phased out as existing contracts expire (*New York Times*, 14 July 2001).[13]

In response to his critics, Giuliani has defended his policies by reference to the decline in crime while in office and the overwhelming support of New Yorkers. Pollard (1997), Bowling (1999) and Young (1999) have questioned whether alternative explanations may more accurately account for the reduction in the crime rate which commenced prior to his arrival at City Hall. Results of public opinion surveys have been less than unambiguous (Silverman, 2000) and, as one would expect, opinion has fluctuated with major events.[14] A report following an in-depth survey by the Citizen's Crime Commission credited public concern with the Louima, Diallo and Dorismond incidents and declared: 'New Yorkers support police enforcement when it is carried out in a respectful manner but reject it when it is conducted aggressively' (quoted in the *New York Times*, 26 July 2001).

Conclusions

The incidents of police violence in New York have been presented here in order to reveal former Mayor Rudolph Giuliani's responses to scandal and the overt politicisation of policing during his terms of office. It is suggested that a necessary feature of a formal aggressive policing policy is engagement in a constant polemic to secure the support of an ambivalent electorate. History has shown that the social cost of unrestricted crime control is prohibitive, and the need for balance is a pre-requisite for democratic and accountable policing. The police are faced by a myriad of dilemmas, and this chapter has only managed to address some of them. The increase in complaints against the NYPD (Silverman, 2000), and concerns expressed with the effectiveness of the Civilian Complaints Review Board (Human Rights Watch, 1998), for example, have not been mentioned.

Policing in the USA is not governed by convention comparable with the tripartite arrangement and there is no doctrine of constabulary independence. Giuliani did not need to clip the wings of his police commissioner to ensure adherence to his policies – he hired and fired in order to get the job done his way. Concurrent with Giuliani's departure from office, Bernard Kerik resigned as NYPD Police Commissioner and was replaced by Raymond Kelly, Michael Bloomberg's criminal justice advisor during his successful mayoral election campaign.

Just as the doctrine of constabulary independence evolved over time it is apparent that the process has now been reversed at the instigation of central government. A particularly disturbing feature of police reform, as highlighted in a recently published right-of-centre think-tank report (Loveday and Read 2003), is that the powers of local police authorities have been squeezed during the course of the last 40 years. This was initially effected by increasing chief officers' powers at the expense of local police authorities under the Police Act 1964, and now as a consequence of attempts by central government to rein in the powers of independent chief officers. There is much to be said in favour of the doctrine of constabulary independence. However, like the office of constable and the ethos of policing by consent, it is helplessly utopian during an age in which modern executive government dominates the legislature and it has been relied upon as a rhetorical device to bypass calls for accountability. For the doctrine to serve as a foundation for pragmatic and principled policing, the government has to relinquish some control and put legislation before Parliament which establishes a system for police governance that guarantees the existence of checks and balances and protects against the politicisation of policing. Then, perhaps, the courts will be better placed to ensure that all forms of police practice conform with the principles of pro-portionality that have started to take hold of the common law since the incorporation of the European Convention on Human Rights under the Human Rights Act 1998.[15]

Notes

1   Unless stated otherwise all mention of police in this essay is limited to the services in England and Wales in recognition of the different conditions prevailing in other parts of the UK.
2   Hansard, Parl. Deb., 15 April 1829, cols 867–84.
3   The Judges' Rules – replaced by the Police and Criminal Evidence Act 1984 Code of Practice C: *The Detention, Treatment and Questioning of Persons by Police Officers* – were originally drafted following a request for clarification from the Lord Chief Justice by the Chief Constable of Birmingham in 1906 (Royal Commission on Police Powers and Procedure, 1929).

4   Constabulary independence was extrapolated from the ancient office of constable which has been traced back to the thirteenth century (Critchley, 1978; Rawlings, 2002). In *Fisher* v. *Oldham Corporation* [1930] 2 KB 364, the office's modern meaning was established when it was determined that the local authority was not liable for the false imprisonment of the claimant as the police officer exercised an original rather than a delegated authority (Marshall, 1965; Lustgarten, 1986).

5   For the MPS this was contrived as the first commissioners were appointed as 'ex officio' justices, without judicial responsibilities, a status which was not repealed until the Administration of Justice Act 1973.

6   Tony Blair spoke out in support of ZTP before Labour's election victory in May 1997 (*Daily Telegraph*, 11 April 1997), and more recently declared that 'zero tolerance of anti-social behaviour' is government policy (Blair, 2002). On appointment as Home Secretary, Jack Straw (*Daily Telegraph*, 5 May 1997) continued to express his support for ZTP while on the opposition front bench (Bowling, 1999). David Blunkett has been more cautious with his language and stated his interest in Wilson and Kelling's (1982) 'broken windows' thesis (*The Guardian*, 25 January 2002; *The Observer*, 10 February 2002).

7   The Deputy Commissioner of the MPS, Ian Blair (2002), consistent with the views of the Mayor of London, Ken Livingstone (2000; *The Guardian* 14 February 2002), has opted to focus on the increase in NYPD numbers as an important lesson for the MPS.

8   Adoption by Cleveland Constabulary of NYPD methods has also attracted much controversy to the service (Innes, 1999). A Police Complaints Authority (2002) supervised investigation codenamed Operation Lancet concluded with disciplinary proceedings brought against 12 officers, some of which are continuing at the time of writing.

9   Mayoral candidate Giuliani joined with NYPD officers in a protest against reorganisation of the CCRB at New York City Hall (Human Rights Watch, 1998) and as mayor he remained staunchly opposed to the independent body (ibid.; New York Civil Liberties Union, 2002).

10   Judgment in the New York Federal Appeals Court was that there had been a conflict of interest between the co-defendants represented by the same lawyer and ordered a retrial. Two other officers had their convictions for conspiracy to obstruct the course of justice quashed without a retrial ordered (*New York Times*, 1 March 2002).

11   The $7.125 million paid out by New York City was the highest ever paid in a brutality case and $1.625 million of the settlement was paid by the Patrolman's Benevolent Association (*New York Times*, 13 July 2001), believed to be the first occasion that a payment for brutality had been made by a representative staff organisation after evidence at the criminal trial revealed that the Association had advised its members after the incident: 'Sit tight, don't talk about it. Don't talk to anyone unless something official comes down' (ibid.).

12 See also responses of black NYPD officers reported in the *New York Times* (3 March 2002) after the quashed convictions of three officers involved with the Louima assault.

13 In addition to incidents of violence, other police actions have given rise to concern with Giuliani's crime offensive. Before dawn on 19 January 2000, mid-winter, over 100 homeless persons were arrested in a coordinated series of raids on shelters across New York City for failing to answer summonses for 'quality-of-life' offences (*New York Times*, 20 January 2000 and 31 December 2001). A year later the city agreed to settle a mass action involving tens of thousands of claimants who had their rights violated after they had been routinely strip searched following arrest for misdemeanours (minor offences including loitering, disorderly conduct or subway offences) for £50 million (*New York Times*, 10 January 2001; Sebok, 2001).

14 Most important, historically, the upsurge in support for Mayor Giuliani when he captured the mood of the nation after the terrorist outrages of 11 September 2001 (*New York Times* 31 December, 2001)

15 See Wadham and Modi in Chapter 14 of this volume.

Policing and the Human Rights Act 1998

John Wadham and Kavita Modi[1]

Introduction

While the Human Rights Act 1998 (the 'Act') does not promote or prohibit any particular strategy of policing it does impose serious boundaries within which the police must act. In order to catch the perpetrators of criminal offences, and prevent offences from taking place, it is obviously necessary to permit some incursion into the liberties and rights that citizens usually enjoy. However, it is also vitally important that such incursions should be strictly limited and remain within certain parameters, not only to protect the fundamental human rights of all citizens, but to ensure that innocent people are not wrongly convicted. The Act attempts to strike the right balance between these two interests. It has been in force since October 2000 and incorporates the European Convention on Human Rights (the 'Convention') into domestic law.

This chapter selects and examines some of the areas where there might be a conflict between police activities and human rights. For reasons of space this cannot be a comprehensive account of this area of law.

Overview of the Human Rights Act 1998

The Act incorporates into English law most, but not all, of the rights protected by the Convention. The main rights protected are as follows:

Article 2   The right to life and prohibition on arbitrary deprivation of life.
Article 3   The prohibition on torture and inhuman or degrading punishment or treatment.
Article 4   The prohibition of slavery and forced labour.
Article 5   The right to liberty and security.
Article 6   The right to a fair trial.
Article 7   The prohibition on retrospective application of the criminal law.
Article 8   The right to respect for privacy, family life, home and correspondence.
Article 9   Freedom of thought, conscience and religion.
Article 10   Freedom of expression.
Article 11   Freedom of association and assembly.
Article 12   The right to marry and found a family.
Article 14   Freedom from discrimination.
Protocol 1
Article 1   The right to peaceful possession of property.
Article 2   The right to education.
Article 3   The right to participate in elections.

The law recognises that not all of these rights can be absolute and many can be limited in certain defined circumstances. The most important rights are Articles 2, 3, 4(1) and 7 which are *absolute rights* and cannot be limited in any circumstances. Next in importance are *limited rights* such as Articles 5, 6 and 12 which cannot – with certain exceptions – be limited on the basis of public interest. Finally there are the qualified rights such as 8, 9, 10 and 11 that allow restrictions on the basis of public interest.

Rights relevant to policing

The rights most likely to be affected in the policing context are probably 2, 3, 5, 6, 8, 11 and 14. Article 2 protects the right to life and imposes important positive duties on the state, including the duty to hold an effective and independent investigation into the death of any person whose death might be the responsibility of the state. Article 3 protects the right not to be subjected to torture or inhuman or degrading treatment or punishment and infringement cannot be justified for any reason whatsoever.[2] The relevance of the article for policing arises particularly in regard to treatment in custody. Assault, rape, some interrogation techniques and, of course, torture are all actions that may breach Article 3, depending on the circumstances.

Article 5 protects against the deprivation of liberty and is one of the most relevant rights for police practice and has two components. The first lays out the circumstances in which detention is allowed, the second puts in place safeguards to protect the person detained. Once lawfully detained there are certain safeguards to protect the detainee such as being informed of the reasons for arrest and, after being charged, being brought promptly before a judicial authority.

Article 6 sets down the minimum procedural protections and the right to a fair hearing for those charged with a criminal offence. To a large extent this right will come into play after the police investigation but it may be used to exclude evidence unlawfully obtained. This is discussed further below.

Article 8 is a qualified right that gives protection to the individual within their private life and may be interfered where prescribed by law but only in circumstances proportionate to the aim pursued. In a police context, this article is particularly relevant in the area of search or surveillance. This is discussed below.

Article 11 is a qualified right that protects the freedom of peaceful assembly and association in identified circumstances prescribed by law. There are special exceptions for the armed forces, police and administration of the state. The main relevance of Article 11 for the police is in the policing of public demonstrations and marches and in the use of their powers to maintain public order.

Article 14 prevents discrimination in the enjoyment of rights on a wide range of grounds of discrimination – including sex, race and religion – but the list is not finite. The Article is likely to arise in areas such as stop and search where it has been alleged (in conjunction with Articles 5 or 8) that there is a discriminatory practice of stopping black people.

The Act works through placing duties on public authorities, the courts and ministers. In the context of policing the most important duty is that put on public authorities where they are prohibited from acting in a way incompatible with the Convention rights unless required to do so to comply with an Act of Parliament.

Surveillance

The expansion in surveillance techniques and usage appears to have no end in sight. However, fear is a non-objective and unhelpful decision-maker, for not only has it led people to accept increasing incursions on their freedom, but can also serve to blind people to a realistic assessment of how successful various surveillance techniques are in achieving the security that we all desperately crave.

Most surveillance techniques interfere with the right to respect for privacy protected by Article 8. However, interference can be justified under Article 8(2) if in order to prevent crime or protect the rights of others and the intrusion goes no further than necessary. The European Court has also held that both the method of authorisation and use of surveillance must be properly accountable and that there must be legal safeguards against abuse.

The legal basis for the interception of communications has changed several times in recent years after the European Court found existing schemes incompatible with the Convention. The first problem was that no statutory scheme or common law power governed the interception of communications or the right to privacy. The national court in *Malone*[3] decided that where no right had been infringed, the government did not need a positive legal basis for action. The European Court found that such an invasion of privacy could not be justified under Article 8(2) because the interception had not been 'in accordance with the law'.[4] This led to the Interception of Communications Act 1985, which put most interceptions on a statutory footing but was later found to violate Article 8 because it did not cover those transmitted on private systems.[5] Consequently, provisions in the Regulation of Investigatory Powers Act 2000 (RIPA) replaced and extended the remit of the 1985 Act.

The work of the Security Service (MI5) remained unregulated until the Secret Service Act 1989, which provided that the agency must seek prior authorisation before, for instance, conducting intrusive surveillance. It was extended to include the Secret Intelligence Service (MI6) and the government's eavesdropping centre (GCHQ) by the Intelligence Services Act 1994. The European Commission has held that this scheme is compatible with Article 8.[6]

Intrusive surveillance by the police was still governed only by non-statutory guidelines and this was sufficient for the European Court to find a violation of Article 8 in *Khan* v. *United Kingdom*.[7] This prompted Parliament to try to ensure that Part III of the Police Act 1997 was compatible with Article 8. It requires prior approval of an independent Commissioner where the property to be entered is a dwelling, office or hotel bedroom or where the information likely to be revealed is under legal professional privilege, confidential personal information or confidential journalistic material.[8] In other cases, and in all cases where surveillance is a matter of urgency, only the approval of an authorising officer is needed.[9] The criteria for giving authorisation and approval are that the action in question is necessary for the purpose of preventing or detecting serious crime and is proportionate to its objective.

RIPA was largely enacted in order to regulate a whole variety of techniques which would, without this regulation, violate Article 8 of the Convention. Three types of surveillance are defined: directed, intrusive and covert human intelligence sources. Directed surveillance is covert but non-intrusive monitoring, observing or listening which is likely to reveal private information. Covert human intelligence sources are informants or undercover agents. Intrusive surveillance is covert surveillance that is carried out in relation to anything taking place in residential premises or in a private vehicle.

For all surveillance covered by RIPA, authorisation may only be given where the particular type of surveillance would be proportionate to the objective. The placing of all the various types of surveillance on a statutory footing is an important step towards bringing the UK law in line with the Convention. However, there are still areas where existing safeguards are inadequate to prevent abuse (Ferguson and Wadham, 2003). The breadth of reasons for which surveillance may be authorised and the lack of judicial or independent supervision leave the system vulnerable to attack under the Act.

Policing demonstrations and marches

Article 11 protects the right to freedom of peaceful assembly and freedom of association. Incursions into this right can be justified if they are prescribed by law and necessary in a democratic society to further the aims specified in Article 11(2). The case law on Article 11 overlaps with, and is sometimes subsumed within the case law on Article 10, which protects freedom of expression.

Rights of assembly and association have been protected in the United Kingdom as traditional civil liberties, although there is an uneasy balance in English law between a lawful public assembly and the need to maintain public order. The Divisional Court has held that the existing line is compatible with the Convention.[10] However, the burgeoning number of statutory legal provisions, combined with the common law 'breach of the peace' powers, has meant that '... there is no place in which citizens can insist on meeting. They depend at all turns on the "good grace" or "common sense" of the authorities. This represents too fragile a base for such an important political right' (Klug et al., 1996: 2003).

A breach of the peace takes place when there is violence or threat of violence that results in actual or likely harm to a person or his property, or a fear that such harm will occur.[11] To constitute a breach of the peace, the violence or threat of violence must be unlawful.[12] 'Public alarm and excitement', 'noise alone' or 'being a nuisance and keeping one's neighbours awake' are not enough.[13] The breach of the peace must be imminent to enable a police officer to act. A peaceful protest cannot be prevented purely because its occurrence may provoke others into using violence.[14] However, if the natural consequence of the assembly will be to provoke others to violence, then the assembly may be prevented on breach of the peace grounds,[15] particularly if demonstrators act in a way that is intended to provoke others into using violence.[16] To make matters more complicated, it has been held that if the demonstrators are acting lawfully, not interfering with anyone's rights and merely exercising their own rights, then it would be 'wholly unreasonable' as well as unlawful for others to use violence, and so the demonstrators will not have caused a breach of the peace.[17] It is apparent from this that the legal position is thoroughly confused on this point, and this may itself breach the Convention provision that the law must be certain.

The Public Order Act 1986 has added statutory offences of riot, violent disorder and affray, conduct causing fear of violence or that provokes violence or conduct causing harassment, alarm or distress.[18] The last of these offences is particularly broad in its scope, for it requires no threat, use or provocation of violence. Abusive or insulting words or behaviour or abusive, insulting or threatening writing or symbols are enough to constitute the offence.[19] The defendant must have intended the display to be abusive or insulting or at least realise that it might have that effect.[20] Slogans or placards at demonstrations which meet this criterion are therefore criminal, and the criteria themselves are highly subjective.

The Criminal Justice and Public Order Act 1994 created the new statutory offence of aggravated trespass if protestors trespassing on private land do anything intended to deter, obstruct or disrupt persons engaged in a lawful activity. A police officer may ask protestors to disperse because he or she reasonably believes the gathering may lead to a breach of the peace; anyone who refuses will be committing an offence. The police also have a power to reroute a march or move a gathering in order to prevent an imminent breach of the peace. The use of such powers to prevent Orangemen from joining a march in a Nationalist town in Northern Ireland was held to be compatible with

Article 11.[21] There are also statutory powers to prohibit marches or assemblies that wilfully obstruct free passage along the highway, unless they are engaged in reasonable use in the circumstances.[22] This means a moving procession will be lawful, while sitting in front of traffic will not.

Assemblies on the highway can also be controlled or prohibited under Part II of the Public Order Act 1986. Section 11 requires the organisers of a march to give six days' notice, unless not reasonably practicable, so that police may assess whether it is necessary to impose conditions to avoid disorder, property damage, disruption to community life or the intimidation of others. Requirements to give notice are not considered to be interferences with freedom of assembly under the Convention.[23] The vagueness of the power to impose conditions to prevent disruption to community life has been criticised as being incompatible with Article 11, particularly as this provision allows restrictions on freedom of assembly where there is no risk of disorder or property damage (Clayton and Tomlinson, 2000: 1181). Prohibitions on assemblies or criminal penalties for participation will breach Article 11(1) and therefore must be justified under Article 11(2).[24] Banning a particular assembly has been held to be justified in a number of different situations including excessive noise[25] and disruption to passers-by.[26] A complete ban on processions for a certain period was also upheld because it would prevent disorder arising from the actions of one group, despite the fact that this meant that the rights of other groups were infringed.[27] However, this power could conflict with Article 11 if it were used in circumstances where it was disproportionate to the aim. The fact that such bans are difficult to overturn may also be held to be disproportionate.[28]

Article 11 also imposes a positive duty on the state to protect the right of assembly, though there is wide discretion for the state to determine how this is to be done in the particular circumstances.[29] This includes protecting those engaging in peaceful assembly from violence by other groups.[30] Clayton and Tomlinson (2000: 1170) suggest that there may be a positive obligation on states to require individuals to allow peaceful assemblies on their private property. This is particularly pertinent in relation to places such as shopping malls and other communal areas which are increasingly under private ownership.

The police clearly have a certain amount of discretion about how they use the powers described above. Fears of disruption and property damage have led to a huge police presence in May Day protests in London, though such fears were unsubstantiated.

Stop and search

Stop and search powers present several problems in relation to human rights and civil liberties. They may involve unwarranted invasions into the liberty of the individual, particularly where exercised in a discriminatory fashion (Articles 5, 8 and 14). Zero tolerance policing involves an extension of such powers to ensure that the public are aware of the heavy police presence and its ability to detect minor crimes. Such strategies focus on areas with high rates of street crime and correspondingly high levels of poverty. The demography of the area is often non-white, and includes a large proportion of very vulnerable people. Zero tolerance therefore targets (intentionally or not) the vulnerable, leading to increased rates of criminalisation and increased levels of social exclusion (see Wadham, 1998). It also targets ethnic minorities, further damaging police–community relations and sometimes bringing existing tensions to boiling point, as in Brixton (Scarman, 1981). Furthermore, Alderson (1998: 69) points out that zero tolerance '... leaves no room for the ethical exercise of police discretion which may involve tolerance'.

The European Court of Human Rights has not yet examined the compatibility of the stop and search powers under PACE with the Convention. Very quick searches carried out at the place where the suspect is stopped may not engage Article 5 at all. This is because Convention jurisprudence does not regard all restrictions on freedom of movement as deprivations of liberty. However, where a person has been arrested, Article 5 is always engaged. However, where the police have only exercised their powers to stop and search, the length and objective of the detention will be crucial factors in assessing the level of severity. If the objective is to deprive a person of their liberty, Article 5 comes into play. However, this test is clearly subjective as the Commission has held that detention in order to conduct a lawful search does not engage Article 5[31] whereas detention for the purposes of a blood test does.[32]

Where the detention is for a significant period the deprivation of liberty may be justifiable under Article 5(1)(c) which permits detention '... for the purpose of bringing him before the competent legal authority on reasonable suspicion of having committed an offence ...' Arguably, stop and search does not come within this provision because the purpose of the detention is not to bring the person before a court. Another difficulty is that although s.1 of the Police and Criminal Evidence Act 1984 requires reasonable grounds for suspicion before the powers it gives become exercisable, other statutory stop and search powers do not. Section 60 of the Criminal Justice and Public Order Act 1994 merely requires the superintendent to have a reasonable belief that incidents involving serious violence may occur in the area. Similar provisions exist in relation to terrorism.[33] Article 5(1)(c) would not apply to these provisions.

The only other possible justification for stop and search under Article 5 would be 5(1)(b). This permits detention '… in order to secure the fulfilment of any obligation prescribed by law'. However, this has consistently been interpreted as only applying where there is a specific obligation, not to a general obligation to obey the law. However, in *McVeigh, O'Neill and Evans* v. *UK* (1981) 5 EHRR 71 the Commission found that detention pending 'examination' under the Prevention of Terrorism (Temporary Provisions) Act 1976 was justified under Article 5(1)(b). The Commission was careful to distinguish this case on the grounds of the context of terrorism; ordinarily, there must have been a prior opportunity to fulfil the obligation before Article 5(1)(b) applies. It is therefore unlikely that stop and search powers could be justified under this provision, except those under the terrorism legislation.

Figures from the Home Office (2000a) show that black people were eight times more likely to be stopped and searched than white people in 2001/2 and Asians were three times more likely to be stopped and searched than white people in the same period. Discriminatory use of stop and search powers violates Article 14, even if the proper use of such powers might not, because an activity must only come within the ambit of a Convention right for Article 14 to apply. Such discrimination would also now be unlawful apart from the Human Rights Act because s. 1 of the Race Relations (Amendment) Act 2000 has extended the prohibition on direct and indirect racial discrimination to include the police.

Sanders and Young (2000) argue that the concept of 'reasonable suspicion' is too vague to provide any real safeguard against arbitrary exercise of power. This is supported by the case of *Lodwick* v. *Sanders*[34] where the court reversed the first instance decision to hold that a police officer detaining a person on suspicion of theft was acting lawfully, despite the fact that there were no grounds on which a reasonable suspicion could be based. This is in contrast to the European Court's approach in *McLeod* v. *United Kingdom*[35] where, though no violation of the Convention was found, the Court was prepared to examine whether reasonable grounds for apprehending a breach of the peace existed.

However, a more recent United Kingdom case on the issue takes a far more rigorous approach, albeit without mentioning the Convention. In *Samuels* v. *Metropolitan Police Commissioner*,[36] the Court held that the existence of 'reasonable suspicion' has to be decided objectively. Walking slowly, hands in pockets in a high risk burglary area could not be grounds for such suspicion; neither was the plaintiff's legitimate refusal to answer questions[37] sufficient basis on which to found a reasonable suspicion. The court also recognised that poor relations between the police and the public, particularly ethnic minorities, meant that cooperation beyond legal requirements could not be expected, and there was nothing particularly suspicious in a black man being less than forthcoming with police officers. Though it was not explicitly stated, the decision also demonstrates an acknowledgement that poor community relations mean that a more exacting approach to the requirements for a stop and search is desperately needed in order to change police culture.

The government admits that there is an element of racial discrimination within the criminal justice system in general, but argues that some of the statistics which appear to show racial bias can be explained by other factors (Home Office, 2000b) The appalling statistics, combined with the findings of institutional racism in the MacPherson report, do seem to suggest racial discrimination, even allowing for some variation between impact on different racial groups due to age, class and other factors that affect crime.

Although the discriminatory use of police powers could now theoretically be challenged as direct[38] or indirect[39] discrimination, an individual case may be difficult to prove. More importantly, the race relations legislation is ill-suited to providing a remedy in this case because the discrimination causes a serious problem for a group of people rather than for one individual in particular. However, the positive duty imposed on public bodies to eliminate unlawful race discrimination and promote equality of opportunity and good race relations[40] may be more useful in bringing about a cultural shift within the police force. To this end, the draft PACE code will require police to record all stops they make, together with the ethnic origin of the suspect, instead of only recording incidents where the suspect was searched as well as stopped.[41]

Arrest

Many of the human rights issues that arise in relation to arrest are similar to those considered above in regard to stop and search. Article 5 is always applicable where a person is arrested but there is a specific exception to allow for lawful arrest. To fall into this category, the arrest must be 'in accordance with a procedure prescribed by law' and must be lawful. To fall within Article 5(1)(c) the arrest must be for the purpose of bringing the person before the court 'on reasonable suspicion of having committed a offence or when it is reasonably considered necessary to prevent his committing an offence or fleeing after having done so.' However, where the person is released without charge, there will be no violation of the Convention so long as the purpose for their arrest was to bring them before a court.[42]

It is unclear how far informal questioning at a police station is compatible with Article 5.[43] Emmerson and Ashworth (2001: 176) suggest that where a person clearly consents to 'help the police with their enquiries, Article 5 will not apply. However, if the questioning ceases to be consensual at any stage, Article 5 will apply from that time.'[44]

The situation is clearer where a person is arrested simply for questioning purposes. In *Brogan* v. *United Kingdom*,[45] the European Court held that, so long as reasonable grounds for the arrest existed, there was no violation of Article 5.

Article 5(2) requires that any person who is arrested should be promptly informed of the reason why he was arrested and any charges being brought against him. This requirement is mirrored by s.28 of PACE. Article 5(3) puts further requirements on the state, to ensure that the arrested person is brought before a judge or magistrate promptly, and is either tried within a reasonable time or released on bail. In addition, Article 6(3) requires that when a person is charged, he should be told promptly the details of the nature and cause of the accusation against him. This obligation is fulfilled where the similar requirements under PACE are met.[46]

Race discrimination is also a problem in regard to arrest, as Home Office (2000a) statistics show. Black people are four times more likely to be arrested then white people or other minority groups (Home Office, 2000c). As with the discriminatory use of stop and search powers, racial discrimination could be challenged under Articles 5 and 14 using the Act or, alternatively, under the Race Relations Act. Problems of race discrimination are severe throughout the criminal justice system so where racism occurs at the beginning of the chain, it is confirmed by the charging, prosecuting, conviction and sentencing stages (Cheney et al., 1999: 54).

Detention, treatment and protection at the police station

Article 5 places obligations on the state in regard to a person who has been detained. Articles 2 and 3 also place requirements on the state regarding how a detainee is to be treated and the standards of protection that must be in place. Preventative detention may only be used to genuinely prevent the commission of an offence. It cannot be used as a general strategy to maintain order where no offence has been committed or is likely to be committed.[47]

Article 5(3) requires that any person arrested or detained within the provisions of Article 5(1)(c) must be brought promptly in front of a judge or magistrate. The European Court has held that this clause entails a substantive obligation on the judge to review '... the circumstances militating for or against detention ...' and to decide '... whether there are reasons to justify detention ...'.[48] The requirement of promptness has been interpreted quite narrowly,[49] but the Court has not set any time limits. It is likely that the standard procedure established by PACE[50] would meet these requirements.

Prolonged detention under the anti-terrorism legislation, however, has violated the Convention.[51] However, the United Kingdom subsequently derogated from Article 5(3), so far as is inconsistent with powers of extended detention, allowing the practice to continue. This derogation was withdrawn following the revision of these powers by the Terrorism Act 2000.[52] The new scheme allows extended detention for up to seven days but, crucially, requires the police to apply to a 'judicial authority' for a 'warrant of further detention' if the detention is to continue for more than 48 hours. Article 5(3) also includes a right to bail. More recently, the United Kingdom has entered a new derogation[53] in respect of Article 5(1)(f) to allow the government to detain suspected terrorists, who are not British nationals, without charge[54] where it is not possible to deport them because to do so would violate Article 3.[55]

Article 5(4) requires that anyone arrested or detained, under whichever provision, has a right to bring proceedings to determine the lawfulness of their detention, and that such decisions should be made swiftly, providing for the release of the detainee if the detention is unlawful. In English law, the equivalent right of habeas corpus is an ancient and well-established right. The burden for establishing the legality of detention falls on the state. The opportunity to challenge the legality of detention arises automatically when the detainee is first brought before the court. However, both habeas corpus and Article 5(4) give the detainee the right to instigate proceedings before being brought to a court, if he so chooses.

Treatment of detainees and the condition of detention are not covered by Article 5 but may engage Articles 3 or 8. Evidence obtained by ill-treatment severe enough to violate Article 3 cannot be admitted at the trial consistently with Article 6; this is an effective way of protecting the most important rights of defendants and deterring the police from using certain techniques.[56]

Article 6(3) gives a right to legal representation and to have time and facilities to prepare your defence. Correspondingly, PACE gives a right to legal advice and provides for the operation of the duty solicitor scheme.[57] These rights are seen as important by the national courts as well as the European Court, and failure to observe the rules can result in evidence obtained in violation of their rights being excluded from criminal proceedings.[58] English law does allow for access to a solicitor to be delayed if the detainee is suspected of committing a serious arrestable offence and it is feared that granting access may lead to interference with evidence, alerting of accomplices or prevent the recovery of property.[59] This dilution of rights may well be incompatible with Article 6(3) (Cheney et al., 1999: 59). The European Court has held that where the right to silence is no longer protected (as is the case in this country), the right of access to a solicitor becomes 'of paramount importance',[60] and any delay will violate Article 6.

Deaths in custody

Depriving a person of their liberty makes them particularly vulnerable as they have little freedom to escape any harm, including threats to their life. The state's responsibilities therefore increase in respect of those detained. Article 2 places obligations on states to protect people from threats to their lives.[61] In respect of those in custody, the burden of this obligation increases and the European Court has held that the state is liable for any death in custody, unless it can prove that it was not responsible in an individual case. This also relates to suicides in custody which the state could have prevented by instituting the proper safeguards.

The standard of proof is the same as that which applies in a criminal trial: beyond a reasonable doubt. In the recent case of *Edwards* v. *United Kingdom*,[62] the European Court found a violation of Article 2 where a prisoner was killed after being placed in the same cell as a violent and schizophrenic prisoner due to failures in communication between agencies and poor screening on arrival at the prison.

Evidence

The Strasbourg jurisprudence on evidence does not exclude the use of evidence solely because it was obtained unlawfully as these issues are viewed as being primarily matters to be resolved by domestic law. The admissibility of evidence will depend on whether the defendant has received a fair trial.[63] English law has also taken a similar approach.[64] However, where the evidence has been obtained by ill-treatment that infringes Article 3 it will not be admissible,[65] because the use of any such treatment automatically violates Article 6. As mentioned earlier, any unnecessary force against a person who is being detained will violate Article 3.[66]

Where other Convention rights are violated in obtaining evidence, this will not always lead to a violation of Article 6; all the circumstances of the case must be considered before deciding whether or not the trial was fair.[67] In particular, the nature of unlawful activity and the nature of any violation of the Convention should be examined in relation to Article 6.[68]

Civil liberties

Although the Human Rights Act places limitations on what the police might legitimately do, it does not provide any guidance to the best approach to policing within those limits. The tradition of civil liberties has strong roots in this country going back far further than the Act. Civil liberties principles do affect the decision as to the strategy to be taken. The following list shows some of the most important factors to be taken into account:

- avoiding the criminalisation of more people;
- the possibility of backlash/race riots;
- proper use of resources (for example, the diversion of funds from serious violent crime to street crime);
- accountability of decision-making.

Criminal offences

One particular problem, outside the scope of the Human Rights Act, is the circumstances in which it should be possible to create new criminal offences. One of the most important libertarian principles is the principle that the state should not interfere with an individual's freedom of action except where it is absolutely necessary. Unfortunately there is nothing in the Human Rights Act which prevents Parliament from creating criminal offences further reducing liberty even where that criminalisation is an excessive reaction to a situation.

This is sometimes in the form of poorly thought out legislation being rushed through Parliament in order to respond to a public outcry, for example the Dangerous Dogs Act 1991 or the Anti-Terrorism Crime and Security Act 2001. Problems also occur when legislation is drafted in a way that makes what would ordinarily be criminal offences into civil penalties, with the consequence that those who are penalised are denied the usual protections afforded to those charged with criminal offences. This is an issue in relation to Anti-Social Behaviour Orders[69] and has also caused difficulties in regard to hefty fines imposed on lorry drivers who unknowingly bring immigrants into the country.[70]

Conclusion

This chapter has examined a selection of the most pertinent human rights issues affecting policing. The increasing use of surveillance conflicts with the right to respect for privacy, particularly given the breadth of reasons for which certain surveillance techniques can be used and the gaps in the systems of independent authorisation under the Police Act 1997 and RIPA 2000. The proliferation of powers to control public demonstrations and marches has lead to uncertainty and the breadth of certain powers, especially under the Public Order Act 1986, may well be incompatible with Article 11 if used disproportionately.

Stop and search powers allow unjustified interferences with Article 5 and, in the way they are used, breach Article 14 as well. Race discrimination in regard to arrest also conflicts with Article 14, in conjunction with Article 5. The power of internment, though permitted due to the derogation from Article 5, is obviously incompatible with the Convention, and raises concerns about discrimination and civil liberties issues as well. The discretion to delay a detainee's access to a solicitor, combined with limitations of the right to silence, violates the right to a fair trial. The United Kingdom has recently been found in breach of its obligations under Article 2 for failing to adequately protect the lives of those in custody and for failing to conduct a proper investigation into such deaths,[71] so this is a matter in which reform is urgently needed. English law on evidence is largely compatible with the Act, primarily because the European Court has been reluctant to take a strong line in this area, due to the conflict between giving full protection to a defendant's Convention rights and preventing a defendant from going free where the invasion of their rights does not cast doubt on the safety of the conviction.

The Act incorporates the European Convention on Human Rights, which is only one of many international human rights treaties. In relation to policing, the International Covenant on Civil and Political Rights is another particularly relevant treaty and could be incorporated into domestic law in the same way as the European Convention has been in order to maximise the protection of human rights and civil liberties. There are also further Protocols under the European Convention which have not been ratified and are therefore not incorporated into domestic law by the Act, most significantly Protocol 12 which contains a general prohibition on discrimination. Alternatively, the United Kingdom could create its own Bill of Rights. This would be the best option as it could protect the rights which are most valued in our history and constitution, including the right to a jury trial and rights to freedom of information, in a way that was most compatible with other principles of the constitution.

Notes

1 We would like to thank Rachel Taylor, who has also assisted in researching and writing this chapter.
2 *Chahal* v. *United Kingdom* (1996) 23 EHRR 76.
3 *Malone* v. *Metropolitan Police Commissioner* [1979] Ch 344.
4 *Malone* v. *United Kingdom* (1984) 7 EHRR 14.
5 *Halford* v. *United Kingdom* (1997) 24 EHRR 523.
6 *Esbester* v. *United Kingdom* (1993) 18 EHRR CD 72.
7 [2000] Crim LR 684.
8 Police Act 1997, ss.97(2)(a) and (b).
9 Police Act 1997, ss.93 and 97(3).
10 *Redmond-Bate* v. *DPP* (1999) 7 BHRC 375.
11 *R* v. *Howell (Errol)* [1982] QB 416.
12 *McBean* v. *Parker* [1983] Crim LR 399.
13 *Lewis* v. *Chief Constable of Greater Manchester, The Times,* 22 October 1991.

14 *Beatty* v. *Gillbanks* (1882) 9 QBD 308.
15 *R* v. *Morpeth Justices, ex p Ward* (1992) 95 Cr App R 215.
16 *O'Kelly* v. *Harvey* (1883) 15 Cox CC 435.
17 *Nicol* v. *DPP* (1995) 160 JP 155.
18 Public Order Act 1986, ss 1–5.
19 Section 5(1)(a) and (b).
20 Section 6(4) and *DPP* v. *Clarke* (1991) 94 Cr App R 359.
21 *Re Atkinson* [1987] 8 NIJB 6.
22 Section 137 Highways Act 1980.
23 *Rassemblement Juraissien Unité Jurassienne* v. *Switzerland* (1979) 17 DR 93, EComm HR.
24 *Christians Against Racism and Fascism* v. *United Kingdom* (1980) 21 DR 138, Ecomm HR; *Ezelin* v. *France* (1991) 14 EHRR 362.
25 *S* v. *Austria*, Application 13812/88, 13 December 1990.
26 *Friedl* v. *Austria*, Application 15225/89, 30 November 1992.
27 *Christians Against Racism and Fascism* v. *United Kingdom* (1980) 21 DR 138, Ecomm HR.
28 *Kent* v. *Metropolitan Police Commissioner, The Times*, 15 May 1981. See also Clayton and Tomlinson (2000: 1181).
29 *Platform 'Ärzte für das Leben'* v. *Austria* (1988) 13 EHRR 204.
30 *Platform 'Ärzte für das Leben'* v. *Austria* (1988) 13 EHRR 204.
31 *Hojemeister* v. *Germany* 6 July 1981; unreported.
32 *X* v. *Austria* (1979) 18 DR 154.
33 Prevention of Terrorism (Temporary Provisions) Act 1989, s.13A and s.13B, and Terrorism Act 2000, s.44. See the recent challenge in the High Court to the use of these powers in the context of protest, *The Guardian*, 1 November 2003.
34 [1985] 1 All ER 577.
35 (1999) 27 EHRR 493.
36 Court of Appeal, 3 March 1999, unreported.
37 *Rice* v. *Connolly* [1966] 2 QB 414.
38 Race Relations Act 1976, s.1(1)(a).
39 Race Relations Act 1976, s.1.(1)(b).
40 Race Relations (Amendment) Act 2000, s.2.
41 Home Office March 2002, Police and Criminal Evidence Act 1984 – Code A, *Code of Practice for the Exercise by Police Officers of Statutory Powers of Stop and Search and Recording of Police/Public Encounters*, Consultation Draft, Section 4.
42 *Brogan and Others* v. *United Kingdom* (1988) 11 EHRR 117.
43 Police and Criminal Evidence Act 1984, s.29, and PACE Code C – *Code of Practice for the Detention, Treatment and Questioning of Persons by Police Officers*, para. 3.15.
44 *De Wilde, Ooms and Versyp* v. *Belgium* (1979–80), 1 EHRR 373.
45 (1988) 11 EHRR 117.
46 PACE Code C – *Code of Practice for the Detention, Treatment and Questioning of Persons by Police Officers*, para. 16.

47 *Ireland* v. *United Kingdom* (1978) 2 EHRR 25.

48 *Scheisser* v. *Switzerland* (1979–80) 2 EHRR 417.

49 *Brogan and Others* v. *United Kingdom* (1988) 11 EHRR 117.

50 Sections 41–46.

51 *Brogan and Others* v. *United Kingdom* (1988) 11 EHRR 117.

52 Section 41 and Schedule 8.

53 See the Schedule to the Human Rights Act 1998 (Designated Derogation) Order 2001.

54 Part IV of the Anti-Terrorism, Crime and Security Act 2001.

55 That is where the country to which they would be deported may torture them: *Chahal* v. *United Kingdom* (1996) 23 EHRR 413.

56 See further the section on 'Evidence', below.

57 Sections 58 and 59.

58 *R* v. *Vernon* (1988) Crim LR 445.

59 Section 58.

60 *Murray* v. *United Kingdom* (1996) 22 EHRR 29.

61 *Jordan* v. *United Kingdom* (2000) EHRR and *R (Amin)* v. *the Secretary of State for the Home Department*, House of Lords, 16 October 2003.

62 *Edwards* v. *United Kingdom* (2002) 35 EHRR 19.

63 *Khan* v. *United Kingdom* [2000] Crim LR 684.

64 *R* v. *Sang* [1980] AC 402; *R* v. *Sultan Khan* [1997] AC 558.

65 *Austria* v. *Italy* (1963) 6 YB 740 at 748.

66 *Selmouni* v. *France* (2000) 29 EHRR 403 at para. 99.

67 *Schenk* v. *Switzerland* (1991) 13 EHRR 242; *Khan* v. *United Kingdom* [2000] Crim LR 684.

68 *Khan* v. *United Kingdom* [2000] Crim LR 684.

69 *Clingham* v. *Kensington & Chelsea London Borough Council* [2002] UKHL 39.

70 *International Transport* v. *Roth* [2002] EWCA Civ 158.

71 *Edwards* v. *United Kingdom* (2002) 35 EHRR 19.

Chapter 15

Human rights v. community rights: the case of the Anti-Social Behaviour Order

Roger Hopkins Burke and Ruth Morrill

Introduction

There were increasing concerns during the mid-1990s about anti-social behaviour, disorder and its damaging effects on communities. Between 1995 and 1998, calls to the police for such offences increased by 19 per cent (Home Office, 2000a) and these activities came to be widely acknowledged as having a devastating impact on the lives of a large number of ordinary, law-abiding people: a reality that became increasingly recognised by the 'New' Labour Party while in opposition and latterly in government. Their legislative response, the Crime and Disorder Act 1998 (hereinafter, CDA 1998) introduced a number of measures with the intention of protecting the most vulnerable people in predominantly deprived working-class communities from the intimidating behaviour of the few in their midst (*Crime Prevention News*, 1998). Section 1 of the Act makes provision for Anti-Social Behaviour Orders (hereinafter, ASBOs), a community-based civil response to any individual over the age of 10 who acts in any way that causes 'harassment, alarm or distress'. Prohibitions considered necessary to protect the community from further behaviour of the same kind are contained in the orders. Activities that can lead to the obtaining and enforcement of an ASBO may not necessarily amount to 'criminal' behaviour but significantly – and highly contentiously – it is a criminal offence to breach the order and this can result in a maximum jail term of five years.

It had become widely acknowledged as part of the influential communitarian socio-political agenda that emerged in the 1980s in the

USA that while individuals have rights in the traditional liberal sense they also have social responsibilities to the whole community for which they should be held accountable (see Etzioni, 1993; Hopkins Burke, 1998c). ASBOs were introduced by a 'New' Labour government strongly influenced by the communitarian agenda (see Giddens, 1998, 2001) and its dominant theme that autonomous selves do not live in isolation but are shaped by the values and culture of communities. From this perspective it has been deemed necessary to take measures to protect and enhance the community against the interests of anti-social individuals and groups. The question considered in this chapter is whether that communitarian protectionism has been sought at the expense of individual human rights.

Anti-social behaviour

Anti-social behaviour is difficult to define. Behaviour that one person finds anti-social may to another appear commonplace and tolerable. Moreover, the types of behaviour that the public cite worthy of intervention range from the criminal (e.g. prostitution or damage to property) to sub-criminal (e.g. verbal abuse or noise) (Home Office, 2000b). Research has found that police forces do not have a formal definition of anti-social behaviour, but at a local level, it has been described as, 'whatever "minor" problems intrude on the daily life of the communities and leads to calls for police service' (Bland and Read, 2000). The CDA 1998 (s.1(1)(a)) defines anti-social behaviour as acting 'in a manner that caused or was likely to cause harassment, alarm or distress to one or more persons not of the same household as [the defendant]'.

The Policy Action Team (hereinafter, PAT 8) of the Social Exclusion Unit at the Home Office conducted an extensive study of anti-social behaviour throughout the UK and reached the following conclusions. First, the problem is more prevalent in deprived neighbourhoods. Second, if left unchecked such activities can lead to neighbourhood decline. Third, increases in neighbourhood decline greatly heighten the fear of crime. Four, these problems are invariably exacerbated by issues of social exclusion and deprivation (Home Office, 2000b). There is a clear theoretical link here with the influential 'broken windows theory' developed by the US criminologists Wilson and Kelling – and discussed widely elsewhere in this book – who have observed that disorder and crime is usually inextricably linked in local communities (Wilson and Kelling, 1982).

Research evidence, which seeks to establish a causal link between disorder and serious crime, is nevertheless ambiguous. The 1998 British Crime Survey (BCS) established a correlation between areas of high physical disorder and crime victimisation. For example, burglary victimisation was much higher in areas of high disorder than areas of low disorder (Mirlees-Black et al., 1998). Evidence given to PAT 8 suggests a link between anti-social behaviour, neighbourhood decline, disorder and the creation of an environment in which serious crime could thrive (Home Office, 2000a). Skogan (1990b) had found in a study conducted in the USA that, regardless of ethnicity, class or other variables, residents were in general agreement that disorder played a central role in neighbourhood decline and was closely linked with crime. Kelling and Coles (1996) found that when graffiti and the 'homeless' were challenged on the New York subway system there were dramatic reductions in murder in both the subway and the street. Other researchers have found strong links between anti-social behaviour in childhood and involvement in future criminal behaviour (see Farrington, 1997; Elander et al., 2000).

Clear links have been found between disorder, anti-social behaviour and the fear of crime. The 1994 BCS indicated that respondent perceptions of disorder – for example, noisy neighbours, alcohol and drug misuse – were predictive of concerns about more serious crimes such as mugging and burglary and this fear was independent of the actual level of crime (Hough, 1995). The Audit Commission (1999b) also ascertained that fear of crime is greatest in areas of high physical disorder. Kelling and Coles found that police foot patrols can have an effect on disorder and anti-social behaviour and that this can reduce the fear of crime (Kelling and Coles, 1996)

The 'broken windows' philosophy has been closely linked with 'zero tolerance' policing strategies first introduced in New York City in 1993 and various localities in the UK in subsequent years that have targeted 'quality of life' problems such as graffiti and low-level disorder (Hopkins Burke, 1998b). These have been widely criticised, however, for being 'discriminatory initiatives, which target and criminalise economically excluded groups living on the streets' (Crowther, 1998; Hopkins Burke, 1998c, 2000; Wadham, 1998). ASBOs appear to focus on the same target with similar implications: a drift towards further intolerance of a marginal group with harsh crime control methods.

Anti-social behaviour and disorder may be a problem at a local level but in order for us to explain these issues adequately, it is appropriate to situate them within the context of recent socio-economic change. The majority of the population now participates in unprecedented levels of *consumption*, the 'driving force of action' that has replaced industrial discipline as a motivational force (Reiner, 1997). At the other end of the scale, there is a substantial and growing rump – or underclass – that are permanently excluded, a whole class of people 'with quasi-criminal, anti-social, anti-work cultures of welfare dependency, who now threaten the happy security and ordered stability of wider society' (MacDonald, 1997: 2). For some the underclass is simply synonymous with a dangerous population of socially excluded young people invariably concentrated in particular local authority housing estates characterised by high crime rates and lawlessness (Home Office, 1997b; Bottoms and Wiles, 1997; Hopkins Burke, 1999c; Bland and Read, 2000; Home Office, 2000b). This all came to be recognised by the Labour Party in political opposition and their subsequent legislative response when elected was the CDA 1998.

The ethos of the Crime and Disorder Act 1998

The Crime and Disorder Act provides the framework for a radical new empowerment of local people in the fight against crime and disorder. It gives local authorities, the police and a variety of their key partners, specific new responsibilities for the prevention of crime and disorder. (HMIC, 1999)

In response to a perceived public demand throughout the first half of the 1990s for tough action against crime, 'New' Labour felt they needed to steal the mantle of 'law and order' from the Conservatives. The run-up to the General Election of 1997 witnessed the two parties outbidding each other in making commitments to crackdown on crime and social disorder. The Labour Manifesto criticised the Conservative government for forgetting the 'order' in 'law and order' and promised to 'tackle the unacceptable level of anti-social behaviour and crime on our streets' by being 'tough on crime, tough on the causes of crime' (Labour Party, 1997).

Aims and objectives of New Labour criminal justice policy

New Labour criminal justice policy has been fundamentally influenced by left realist criminology which claims to take crime seriously – particularly, predatory street crime – and prioritises crime committed by working-class people against other working-class people (Hopkins Burke, 2001: 217–30). It is recognised that crime is a reality that makes the lives of many people a misery and that this is particularly true of local authority housing developments and the inner cities.

Left realists argue for reduced central state intervention and its replacement by localised multi-agency-based forms of crime prevention and control. Thus the CDA 1998 gives local authorities and the police a statutory duty to work together in partnership to produce a 'community safety strategy' (Crawford, 1998: 62). They are provided with tools to tackle behaviour previously not deemed criminal and not covered by existing legislation but which poses a threat to the stability and order of communities.

New Labour's criminal justice policy has been termed 'managerialist penology' whereby a 'permanently dangerous segment of the population (the underclass of permanently excluded, irredeemably dysfunctional deviants) are *managed*' (Brownlee, 1998a: 324). It can be considered in terms of the concept of 'actuarial justice' that removes notions of individual need, diagnosis and rehabilitation from the analytical equation and replaces them with 'actuarial techniques' of classification, risk assessment and resource management (Feeley and Simon, 1994). The 'underclass' – and in particular the young underclass – are groups identified in this model as being high risk. The Audit Commission report on youth offending was framed in this language and ignored the traditional criminological agenda of locating the causes of offending by seeking to identify risk conditions, for example lack of parental supervision or truancy (Audit Commission, 1996b). These factors have all been incorporated into the provisions contained in the CDA 1998.

Provisions of the Crime and Disorder Act 1998

The CDA 1998 identified young people as being central to the problem of crime and disorder and the thrust of reform was earlier intervention in their lives. A host of non-criminal orders that proactively seek to prevent offending were introduced but which could be enforced by criminal sanction. It was proposed that 'taken together these measures will provide the victims of serious disorder with new, effective weapons to deter those who seem to take delight in making the lives of others a misery' (Home Office, 1998b). They certainly seemed to uphold Labour's promise to put the 'order' back in 'law and order'.

Fionda (1999) observes, however, the ambiguous nature of the legislation and how it reflects a mixture of conflicting aims and ideologies: punishment, welfare, restorative justice, managerialist issues and a 'responsibilisation strategy' (where central control is rigidly maintained while active responsibility is delegated to the local level). Brownlee (1998b) criticises the ethos of the legislation for blaming the problem of 'crime and disorder' on a particular group in society and hoping to reduce that threat merely through management while ignoring the wider social origins of anti-social and criminal behaviour.

The theoretical context of Anti-Social Behaviour Orders

The ASBO is just one of a plethora of powers introduced by the CDA 1998 to help communities blighted by anti-social behaviour. Existing legislation had been seen to be inadequate to the task: the police were hampered by the rules of criminal evidence while the civil courts provided only lengthy and costly procedures for local authorities and housing associations seeking to pursue injunctions. ASBOs, on the other hand, are a civil action available to both police and local authorities requiring only the civil burden of proof 'on a balance of probabilities' (Home Office, 1998c). The emphasis is – in accordance with the concept of actuarialism – on the reduction of risk and hence the prevention of crime, the primary rationale being the protection of the public. Thus the duration of an order is not reflective of the offence committed (proportionality) but a period deemed necessary to protect the community (with a two-year minimum period available). This is again consistent with the actuarial model where the length of sentence given is not dependent on the crime committed but on the extent of the risk posed by the offender and is therefore contrary to the 'just deserts' principle of proportionality (von Hirsch, 1976).

How Anti-Social Behaviour Orders work

The theory

ASBOs are applied for to the magistrates' court, either by the local authority or the police but only after consultation with each other (s.1(2), CDA 1998). They are available against any individual over the age of 10 who has acted in an anti-social manner, that is caused or was likely to cause harassment, alarm or distress to one or more persons not of the household (s.1(1)(a)). Magistrates act in their civil capacity and civil rules of evidence apply: thus the behaviour need only be proved on a balance of probabilities and hearsay evidence is admissible. Where witnesses feel too intimidated to give evidence in court Home Office guidance allows for the use of professional witnesses (Home Office,

1998c: para. 4.9). If the application is successful, the court can make an order prohibiting the defendant from behaving in the way that had led to the application being sought (ibid.: para. 4.9). Requirements in the order must be *negative* and must last for a minimum of two years.

Breach of the order is an arrestable offence (Home Office, 1998b: s.1(10)). The CPS will conduct the prosecution in a criminal court and evidence of the breach must be of the criminal standard, that is beyond a reasonable doubt. Cases are triable either way. If heard on indictment in the Crown Court the maximum penalty available at the discretion of the judge is imprisonment for five years, or a fine, or both (ibid., s.1(10)(b)). The defendant may use the defence of 'reasonable excuse', thus putting the burden of proof on the prosecution.

The practice

In order to discover how ASBOs work in practice a small qualitative study was undertaken in an East Midlands local authority (hereinafter the East Midlands Study) during the autumn of 2000. At that time there were 140 ASBOs in force across the country and the Home Office database was aware of 19 breaches (between 1 April 1999 and 31 June 2000).

While the government had stressed juveniles are not the main targets of the ASBO (Padfield, 1998) it had been readily acknowledged that 'in the case of 12–17 year olds ... applications may be made more routinely' (Home Office, 1998c: para. 5.9). In practice, it would seem that the orders have been mainly used against this group. Between April 1999 and September 2001 466 ASBOs were granted nationally; 74 per cent were in respect of those 21 years of age and under (Campbell, 2002). Essentially, they have been used as a means of bringing misbehaving youngsters before the courts, where previously their conduct would have gone undeterred (Rowan, 1999). Injunctions are only available for persons of 18 years of age and over. The Protection Against Harassment Act 1997 is designed to deal with situations where harassment is directed against an individual or family but not against a community or where the behaviour is less than harassment but anti-social.

It is much quicker and easier to get an injunction – or use other legislation – once a young person reaches the age of 18. There are nevertheless significant limitations to such a strategy. First, it is not a criminal offence and therefore there is no power of enforcement. Second, they are only available for the actual tenant of local authority accommodation who breaches their contract. ASBOs overcome these problems but take longer to implement because of the need to gather evidence from witnesses and information from other agencies. Third, the police have powers under the Criminal Justice and Public Order Act 1994 and the Protection Against Harassment Act 1997, but this criminal legislation invariably offers only short-term solutions and requires a higher standard of proof. ASBOs offer a long-term solution to problems that fall outside the remit of the criminal law.

ASBOs also provide a potential long-term solution to on-street prostitution in residential areas. The East Midlands Team was applying for orders in respect of ten persistent offenders soliciting on the street in the local vice area. Hitherto, prostitution has been an issue solely appropriate to the criminal courts but, problematically, the predominant criminal sanction of a fine is simply regarded as a tax by the women involved. A successfully obtained ASBO can prohibit a woman from working as a prostitute in the whole local authority area and if she breaches the order she can receive a prison sentence. Ironically, the Criminal Justices Act 1982, s.71 had intentionally removed the power of the courts to hand down a custodial sentence for prostitution.

The East Midland Team was aware of human rights legislation issues but did not foresee any substantial difficulties arising because they considered the alternative would be the criminalisation of the person in the first place. ASBOs were not considered a punishment, simply an attempt to improve the situation in a given geographical area while seeking to constrain the behaviour of an individual. They had been introduced with the intention of protecting the rights of communities and this was exactly what the Team sought to do, irrespective of the rights of the individual.

A subsequent study conducted by the Home Office (Campbell, 2002) sought to find out why ASBOs had been used inconsistently throughout the country and found that a number of steps could be taken to minimise both the bureaucracy and delays associated with an application. Tactics such as fast-tracking more severe cases and creating easy-to-follow steps for those unfamiliar with the process were often successful. It was found that many witnesses viewed ASBOs positively, as they felt that something was being done to combat what they had previously thought to be an intractable problem. However, much evidence was found of fear and intimidation resulting in an under-reporting of the behaviour before the ASBO was applied for and an unwillingness to cooperate with the application process. Solutions had included enlisting witnesses from people working rather than living near the problem and using a large number of witnesses to support each other through the process. The study concluded that when used successfully, ASBOs have managed to curb unruly behaviour, help rebuild the quality of life in communities and cement good relationships both between partner agencies and between these agencies and the community but the question remains at what cost to human rights.

A balance of human rights?

The excess in severity may be useful for society, but that alone should not justify the added intrusion into the rights of the person punished. (Von Hirsch, 1976: 70)

Getting the balance right

ASBOs were introduced by a government with a strong commitment to communitarian values and the intention of protecting the rights of communities susceptible to unacceptable behaviour by individuals or groups in their midst. The interests of the community should nonetheless reasonably be balanced with those of the individual: 'People have a right to be protected against aggression, intimidation and incivilities. At the same time, it is necessary to heed the rights and liberties of disadvantaged citizens' (Hopkins Burke, 2000: 43).

Seeking a balance between the rights of the individual and those of the community was a challenge faced in many US cities during the 1980s and 1990s, as communitarianism became an increasingly influential doctrine to the detriment of the more traditional individualism (Kelling and Coles, 1996). Seattle, for example, had long tolerated a population of street people. During the 1980s, however, they came increasingly to be associated by commercial enterprise with falling revenues; citizens refused to shop in areas in which they felt intimidated and compelled to walk in the road to avoid people begging, insulting them and openly urinating. City Attorney Sidran responded by issuing a set of acceptable behaviour guidelines to the street people. For example, sitting or lying on public sidewalks between the hours of 7 am and 9 pm was prohibited. Opposition came from libertarians who categorised the legislation 'anti-homeless'. Sidran explained:

What you get into is some sort of balancing in the hearts and minds of the court about whose sidewalk this is ... If street people congregate on sidewalks what about those trying to cross the street? Deliver products? Furthermore, if citizens ... withdrew from the streets the homeless would then become victims of predators in their midst. (Cited in Kelling and Coles, 1996: 218)

The Seattle courts decided that this example of order maintenance *did* strike a balance between the rights of the individual (the homeless) and the community (the citizens of Seattle). Had they retained the liberal status quo this would have entailed a violation of the rights of the community, and vice versa had the police chosen to take a 'zero tolerance' approach and excluded the homeless altogether.

Whether such a balance has been achieved in the British context with the introduction of ASBOs has been a matter for extensive discussion, in particular since the incorporation of the European Convention on Human Rights (hereinafter, ECHR) into UK domestic law under the Human Rights Act (hereinafter, HRA) 1998. All domestic law would now have to be compatible with the convention. Critics said that the CDA 1998 is not.

The ECHR provides private individuals with no obligation to protect the human rights of another individual but 'the European Court and Commission have chosen to impose the obligation on state authorities to protect individuals from the actions of other individuals' (Starmer, 2000: 194). Under Article 8 of the Convention – the right to respect for private and family life – individuals are guaranteed a right to peaceful enjoyment of their homes. Primarily this implies a negative obligation on the state to refrain from arbitrary interference of this right. The European Court has, however, extrapolated from this a *positive obligation* to take action to ensure that Article 8 rights are effectively protected when the threat is from private individuals. This suggests compatibility with ASBOs, which give local authorities the capacity to protect the rights of communities from the activities of specific individuals. Interpreted in this way, orders positively protect human rights.

Others have argued that this protection has been achieved at the expense of the protections afforded the 'offender'. Lord Goodhart summarises this argument thus:

> Human rights are not just the right to behave well … People have a right to be bloody-minded; they have a right within reason to make a bit of a nuisance of themselves … We want to live in a law-abiding society with a low level of crime … and a low level of vandalism and disorder of all kinds … but, at the same time, we do not want to live in an authoritarian state. (HL Report, 1998)

Von Hirsch et al. (1999) argue that ASBOs abandon basic legal protections for defendants and thus breach their civil rights. This human rights critique is founded on three fundamental issues. First,

ASBOS require only a civil standard of proof to potentially enforce criminal measures. Indeed, Home Office guidance states that 'the orders are intended to deal with criminal or sub-criminal activity, which, for one reason or another, cannot be proven, to the criminal standard, or where criminal proceedings are not appropriate' (Home Office, 1998c: para. 2.6). Cracknell (2000) argues that this clearly indicates the use of civil law for crime control. The order may have a civil rhetoric but the outcome of the procedure, if violated, can be severe criminal penalties. Von Hirsch et al. (1999) thus observe that the crime control nature of civil procedures contradict fundamental due-process protections and Ashworth (1992) observed that individual rights must be assigned some special weight in the balancing processes.

It is arguable whether the rights of the individual receive sufficient consideration by those applying for an ASBO. While opponents argue that the threshold for proof is too low, in practice, this might not be the case. The Crown Court has suggested that the civil standard of proof is flexible (Tain, 2001). Moreover, the rules of evidence state that, 'if an issue in a civil case involves an allegation that a criminal … act has been committed, the standard of proof on that issue must be commensurate with the occasion and proportionate to the subject matter' (Bagshaw, 1996: 34).

There is an argument that the civil rhetoric of ASBOs violates Article 6 of the ECHR – the right to a fair trial – by not affording suspects the criminal safeguards to which they are entitled. Thus any proceedings established as 'criminal' under Article 6(1) would require further safeguards afforded them by Articles 6(2) and 6(3). The case of *Engels* v. *Netherlands* (A22, 1976) established the meaning of 'criminal' and this is dependent on three criteria. The first is whether an offence is classified as a criminal offence under domestic law. If this is not the case then the other two criteria become applicable. The second is the nature of the offence and the third the degree of severity of the penalty.

Once established as criminal under Article 6(1), it is then necessary to turn to Article 6(2) and 6(3). The former concerns the standard of proof, and the ECHR insists that guilt should be proved beyond reasonable doubt (this is not the case with the ASBO).[1] In respect of the latter, those subject to applications for ASBOs are never formally arrested or advised of their rights, they are not required to be in court for the hearing and they are only entitled to legal aid and witness examination on a civil standard.

The Court of Appeal Judges (Civil) have nonetheless held that ASBOs cannot be deduced as 'criminal' under Article 6(1) because the application procedure is separate from the subsequent criminal proceedings that result from a breach and whose criminal safeguards are provided.[2] Plowden (1999: 20) contests the legitimacy of this finding observing the original order to be merely a 'preliminary warning stage in a single process' in which 'further warnings are inappropriate, illustrated by the lack of conditional discharges as a penalty upon breach'.

The second fundamental issue raised by human rights critics of ASBOs was the nature of restrictions on behaviour that can be included in an order. A wide variety of conduct – for example playing music or walking in a city centre – behaviour that is neither a criminal violation, nor a civil wrong in itself, can be proscribed. This is done to protect the public from future risk of harassment. However, these actuarialist principles are in direct confrontation with the values of commensurate deserts principles: thus an order *must* last a minimum of two years, in the hope of reducing risk, regardless of the offence. In Manchester, a 15-year-old schoolboy who 'terrorised a community with threats of murder and fire-bombings' was banned from entering a designated square mile of the city for a period of ten years (*The Times*, 2001). His behaviour as leader of a gang is certainly worthy of concern and a punitive response would seem in order to protect the community. Nonetheless, a ten-year-long ban on a 15-year-old entering a particular area does appear disproportionate.

Thus, the third fundamental issue raised by human rights critics of ASBOs is the excessive and disproportionate penalties available on breach. The maximum penalty for *intentional* harassment under the Criminal Justice and Public Order Act 1994 is just six months imprisonment and that requires criminal proof. In the Committee stage of discussion of the CDA 1998, Lord Thomas observed that 'prison will not make the offender truly and earnestly repent and be in love and charity with his neighbour' (HL Debate, 1998). If the 'offender' behaves in the proscribed way, not only do they potentially face severe penalties but also they carry the stigma 'even if he is a person who has otherwise been of completely good character' (ibid.: col. 599).

These issues principally appear to contradict the 'balance of proportionality' inherent in human rights legislation. Any restriction on the rights of an individual should, by characterisation of the ECHR, be proportionate to the legitimate aim they pursue (Starmer, 2000: 170). It seems that the combination of civil and criminal law available is confusing and inconsistent and defendants are potentially at risk of losing liberties disproportionate to the aim of defending the rights of the community.

In November 2002, the House of Lords reach judgement in *Clingham v. RB Kensington; R v. Manchester Crown Court, ex p McCann* [2002] UKHL 39; (2002) 146 SJLB 239. The appellants had argued that ASBO proceedings are essentially criminal because they impose a penalty in the form of an order preventing them from doing certain specified acts. Lord Steyn confirmed that it had been the intention of Parliament to adopt the civil model of injunction followed by criminal penalty breach, acknowledging that the purpose had been to avoid the rigours of the criminal law which, he noted, plays into the hands of defendants prepared to intimidate witnesses. He said if the Act did not achieve that purpose, it would be unworkable. Parliament had not got things wrong: 'making an ASBO is not a conviction or condemnation that the person is guilty … It results in no penalty … It cannot be entered on the defendant's record … It is also not a recordable offence' (cited in Tain, 2002: 1037).

Lord Steyn cited authorities which demonstrate that even though the consequences of an injunction breach clearly involve criminal sanction, the application for the injunction itself is not a criminal proceeding. He was clear that in domestic law such proceedings were civil and equally sure Convention jurisprudence led to the same conclusion. Convention law took account of the domestic law classification, the nature of the offence and the severity of the penalty. An ASBO involves no penalty.

Lord Hutton dealt with the issue of hearsay and ruled that it is admissible in these proceedings because s.4 of the Civil Evidence Act 1995 sets out considerations which ensure such evidence is fairly weighed and assessed. For example, s.1 provides: 'in estimating the weight (if any) to be given to hearsay in civil proceedings the court shall have regard to … the reliability of the evidence' (cited in ibid.). Lord Hutton emphasised that the rights of an individual can be displaced in certain circumstances by the overriding general interest of the community. Lord Steyn concluded that it is now safe to assume that the popularity of ASBOs as a means of social control will now develop and local authorities and police will use them to address 'a problem the existing law failed to deal with satisfactorily' (cited in ibid.). Legitimate concerns about the use of ASBOs nonetheless remain.

Widening the net and stigmatisation

A more general criticism of the CDA 1998 has been the potential for drawing into the criminal justice system a group of people who previously would have 'avoided' criminalisation. This has been noted as being particularly true in respect of juveniles. Fionda (1999: 45) observes that '[the legislation extends] the concept of "delinquency" to behaviour that falls short of actual criminal offending. Criminal justice authorities are empowered to intervene in these cases of "delinquency", thus widening the youth justice net'.

Moreover, because of the flexible interpretation of 'anti-social behaviour' in the legislation, 'eventually any conduct that displeases neighbours could be deemed "anti-social conduct" ... The result is to embrace not merely repetitively criminal actors, but also those with unconventional lifestyles' (Von Hirsch et al., 1999: 1501).

The crucial significance is that an ASBO can be obtained without a criminal offence having been committed; the behaviour has to be subjectively deemed disruptive and the offender considered *at risk* of their activities developing into something more serious. The outcome is that the range of actions over which local authorities can claim authority is widening and individual freedom – particularly in the case of juveniles – is being reduced.

These observations are resonant with Stanley Cohen's 'discipline thesis' regarding the development of the decarceration movement during the 1980s and the transition to community sanctions where he argues that an apparently liberal process actually leads to 'net extension and strengthening ... Intervention comes earlier, it sweeps in more deviants, is extended to those not yet formally adjudicated and becomes more intensive' (Cohen, 1985: 126–7). ASBOs can certainly be conceptualised in this way.

Cohen considers the role of labelling and stigmatisation in the net-widening process and this is again an important issue with ASBOs. Subject to an order, the individual may well be labelled: drug addict, prostitute or juvenile delinquent, the formation of a label that predominates when describing the individual or the group. It is a process of 'disintegrative shaming' (Braithwaite, 1989) with the outcome that a community is divided into the law-abiding and a group of outcasts stimulated by their alienation into the formation of deviant subcultures. ASBOs can exacerbate the problem because they offer no potential to de-label and reintegrate the individual but, on the contrary, the stigmatising process will push him or her further and further into a criminal self-identity. In short, targeting these groups in an adversarial way will result in certain sections of the community becoming resentful for being blamed for the 'ills of society', interpret this as dismissal from the mainstream and withdraw from the law completely (Muncie, 1999. 60). Thus, while ASBOs are merely a civil mechanism their potential to 'brand' people as anti-social is a major flaw (Tain, 2001).

Conclusion

'New' Labour is a political party clearly aware of the need to steer a middle path – or 'third way' – between competing interest groups in contemporary societies. The guru of this British version of communitarianism – but with substantial international influence – is the Director of the London School of Economics, Anthony Giddens (1998, 2001). The intention is to balance the undoubted energy of capitalism with the need to foster social solidarity and civic values: 'the third way suggests that it is possible to combine social solidarity with a dynamic economy, and this is a goal contemporary social democrats should strive for' (Giddens, 2001: 5). A crucial identified concern that unites many varied and competing interest groups in communal social solidarity is that of crime and disorder. Thus it was in this context that the CDA 1998 was introduced to tackle the 'root cause of crime' and disorder within local communities. ASBOs were intended to protect the rights of citizens whose lives are blighted by others who behave in a way previously beyond the reach of the criminal law but which nonetheless intrude on the daily life of communities.

Kelling and Coles (1996) describe how authorities in various constituencies in the USA have introduced strategies to deal with 'quality of life' issues while invariably being challenged in the courts by civil liberties and libertarian groups. Debates surrounding the introduction and implementation of ASBOs can be seen as a British example of this conflict between civil rights/human rights pressure groups and the 'back to justice lobby' on the one hand and communitarians on the other hand. There have emerged two sets of discourse, each worthy of consideration as both individuals and communities have undoubtedly legitimate rights.

The CDA 1998 communitarian discourse recognises a problem of anti-social behaviour in our communities. Indeed, people have a right to be protected against harassment, alarm, distress and incivilities and it is fair that this behaviour is targeted to ensure protection. From that perspective, the ASBO is a reasonable measure that has filled a prominent gap in the law. They are not a punishment but a deterrent and act to stem behaviour before it reaches a criminal level. ASBOs are, however, fraught with problems regarding the civil liberties of individuals.

This chapter has suggested that the balance may have shifted too much in favour of 'communities' at the expense of individual liberty. Moreover, due-process values have been sacrificed in the increased pursuit of crime control outcomes with a worrying potential to absorb further into a widening net a whole group of relatively non-problematic young people who left pretty much alone would grow out of their anti-social activities and become respectable members of society.

So, what does the future hold for the ASBO? One possibility is to hear applications in a criminal court so that orders continue in their present form but individuals are afforded better safeguards. There are nonetheless two potential problems with this proposal. First, this would amplify the problem of 'net-widening' by 'criminalising' an excluded group who might not be involved in criminal behaviour. Second, there would be considerable resource implications. ASBOs were introduced in their present civil form so that the police do not have to spend considerable time gathering criminal evidence.

There is nevertheless a case for revision. First, ASBOs are most usefully targeted against those at an early stage in their anti-social/criminal career, but with some (albeit limited) criminal convictions. In most of these cases the individuals have received criminal penalties but with little deterrent effect. The ASBO reinforces the element of deterrence and prohibits the individual only from breaking the law. It is not drawing 'otherwise law-abiding' people into the net for they are proven lawbreakers. Perhaps, therefore, specific conditions should apply before an order can be sought.

ASBOs have a legitimate and appropriate future in a communitarian criminal justice policy. It would be a mistake to abandon or seriously curtail their use because measures are needed to tackle a grievous social threat to many communities. It is, however, appropriate to consider and reconsider the issue of civil liberties and human rights in terms of their long-term implementation.

Notes

1 *Barbera, Messgue & Jabardo* v. *Spain* [1989] 11 EHRR 360.
2 *McCann & Others* v. *Manchester Crown Court* [2001] ENCA CIV 218.

Chapter 16

Conclusion: policing contemporary society revisited

Roger Hopkins Burke

Introduction

It was seen in the introduction to this book that there has been an ever accelerating expansion in the extent of police business, particularly during the past half century. While the public police service never had a total monopoly of policing it was the dominant mode of provision when such matters were seen to be – like all public services – unquestionably the responsibility of government. With that increasing extension to policing business two apparently countervailing but in fact complementary developments have arisen. First, there has been a considerable expansion in non-governmental agencies involved in policing matters. Second, often at the behest of government these agencies have actually come closer together in partnership – to use contemporary descriptive discourse – in a multi-agency policing paradigm that encompasses a multitude of strategies and elements of the social world.

The contributions to this book suggest that some of these policing styles – and invariably ones introduced by the public police service which retains a virtual monopoly on the legitimate use of coercion in society – are apparently 'hard' measures; others such as diversionary schemes for young offenders and the work of the probation service appear to incorporate 'softer' styles. A closer examination nonetheless often betrays an ambiguity and confusion as to what can be considered 'hard' or 'soft' with the invariable reality that both are simply part of an 'all-seeing multiple-agency corporate crime industry' that is pervasive throughout society with 'softer' and more subtle measures preferred to more coercive measures as a more insidious and embedded form of social control.

The theoretical perspective that links these contributions is essentially informed by a variation on the Foucauldian notion of carceral surveillance society (see Foucault, 1980; Donzelot, 1980; Cohen, 1985; Garland, 2001) which recognises that particular areas of the social world are colonised and defined by the norms and control strategies devised by a variety of institutions and experts often completely unaware of the totality of the power matrix to which they are contributing. The left-realist variant on that theme proposes that in a complex fragmented dangerous society it is *we* the general public – regardless of class location, gender or ethnic origin – that have a material interest in the development of that surveillance matrix, an argument to which we will return after the following reflections on the contributions to this book.

Contributions to this book revisited

The first part of the book – 'Policing Contemporary Communities' – presented a series of chapters that consider and reflect on both apparently 'hard' and 'soft' styles of policing and reveal the ambiguities that exist between them. In the first of these contributions Andy Karmen considered the apparently definitive 'hard' policing 'zero tolerance' strategy introduced during the mid-1990s in New York City. He noted that the term 'zero tolerance' has subsequently become an extremely attractive buzzword used by politicians to obtain support for 'get-tough' social policies that extend well beyond the relatively limited territory of public sector policing. This sound-bite style politicisation of social policy is unfortunate because the legitimacy and success of the much touted initiatives against quality of life offences in New York remain debatable at a time when the social costs of implementation are becoming increasingly more apparent. It is proposed that new ways of tackling very legitimate criminal concerns and those involved should be found that do not involve interfering with the lives of the innocent who may have the misfortune of finding themselves in targeted areas and sharing characteristics with the stereotypical criminally inclined. A series of research questions are posed to inform a potential investigative agenda with the aim of reducing the eventuality of disorderly public behaviour, tackling the root causes of such delinquency, but also – and perhaps most importantly – finding imaginative, cost-effective and successful alternatives to arrest and prosecution.

Zero tolerance-style 'hard' policing initiatives have nonetheless been successfully exported well beyond the USA and the previously documented UK (see Dennis, 1997; Hopkins Burke, 1998). Alick Whyte observes that while it was necessary in Britain to introduce specific legislation requiring local authorities and the police to produce local crime audits and introduce strategies for dealing with incivilities and disorder this was not the case in Germany where the long-established organisation of public order departments enabled the achievement of very successful public partnerships to tackle these problems. It is observed that the creation of auxiliary police forces within the public order departments of German cities has been widely welcomed by the general populace and the beginnings of similar street warden schemes in Britain are noted, although it is recognised that such initiatives again require specific legislation and the personnel involved – perhaps in keeping with a very different tradition of public sector policing in the two countries – are less likely to enjoy the same considerable powers as their continental colleagues. The question remains as to how long that will remain the case considering the increasing incremental intervention of central government into local policing in Britain discussed elsewhere in this book and the concurrent emergent pressures for coordinated public sector policing.

In the following chapter, Chris Crowther considered the contemporary policing of the socially excluded, the 'underclass', or what in previous times were known as the 'rough' working class, the traditional focus of police business and seen by many commentators as being unfairly on the receiving end of recent 'hard' policing initiatives. It is observed that neo-Marxist and neo-Weberian perspectives on the policing of social exclusion focus their attention on the globalisation of capital and the consequences for national, regional and local economies: the relationship between a mature capitalist system of production and the criminalisation of economically redundant and generally unproductive groups. Foucauldians, on the other hand, have directed their attention towards discursive practices and political rationalities, such as risk analysis, thus rejecting explanations couched in terms of social class. Both perspectives are nonetheless seen as being both overly over-optimistic and over-pessimistic in terms of their discussion of policing as an effective mechanism for care and control. On the one hand, it is noted that the political economic conditions under which the policing of the socially excluded takes place are so uncertain that the notion the police act simply in the interests of an authoritarian state is highly questionable. On the other hand, the government vision of joined-up solutions to interconnected problems –

including tackling crime – is certainly on the right interventionist lines, but the delivery of services is performed by a range of different statutory and voluntary agencies, invariably competing for funding and status with deep-rooted professional cultures that get in the way of attempts to further reduce crime, disorder and social exclusion.

Colin Webster explores the policing of Bradford Asian communities in the aftermath of the public disorders that occurred during the spring and summer of 2001 and is concerned that those events will lead police officers to make unfounded stereotypical generalisations about Asian young people having a predilection to collective violence and – following the recent international demonisation of Islam – an enthusiasm for terrorism and disorder. The outcome of this labelling process is likely to be the creation of a self-fulfilling prophecy with appropriation of particular interpretations of Islamic identity among some young people and the simultaneous adoption of 'masculinist aggressive forms of resolving conflict and dispute' long associated with white working-class areas. At the same time, it is noted that the great majority of Asians living in poor areas – like other socially excluded ethnic minority groups identified elsewhere in this book – are demanding more not less law and order. Thus a change in the policing of British Asian communities is perceived where a bifurcation approach obscures the boundaries between 'hard' and soft' policing strategies involving at one level attempts to manage social integration and 'social cohesion' while at another level there is a visible move towards the disciplining and 'distancing' of a high-risk, invariably young, 'out-group'.

This ambiguity between 'hard and 'soft' policing strategies in the wider generic sense is pursued in the following two chapters. First, Paul Sparrow and David Webb have considered the case of the apparently previously 'soft' policing agency the probation service, observing that only recently have calls been made to evaluate the consequences of an increasingly 'hard' approach to breach, although, as they note, enforcement and the issue of its appropriate application is far from new. Following Garland (1989) they propose that what we have seen in terms of enforcement is a shift from a constructive approach where breach was conceptualised, rightly or wrongly, within a framework of assistance, to a position where enforcement is the defining feature of a punitive 'hard' approach to community supervision. Noting that current research evidence suggests that the present rigid approach to enforcement is unlikely to encourage compliance on the part of offenders, they call for a measured return to former 'soft' policing probation values that promote a little more consideration and a little less coercion.

Second, Mark Button has considered that formerly paradigmatic example of 'hard' policing, private security, in the context of contemporary debates that perceive the ambiguous nature of the contemporary industry. Whereas there remains a legacy of 'hard' policing styles of private security in the USA – with pockets still in existence in varying degrees throughout the world – the general orientation of the industry in the UK and much of the world has been towards the 'soft' end of the continuum. Thus there is a contemporary emphasis on partnership with the public police, particularly in a supportive and junior capacity, and on the reduction of losses for corporate clients with a focus on preventative and risk management techniques underpinned with surveillance. It is indeed these 'soft' image characteristics of the industry that are emphasised and advanced in advertising promotions. Nonetheless, it is recognised that while there is little evidence of a forthcoming return to coercive 'hard' style private security policing, there is a clear potential that this 'softly, softly' contemporary orthodoxy could disguise a more sinister future where social order is built 'on seduction, corporate control systems and consensually based measures', a significant point to which we will return.

The second part of this book – 'Policing Contemporary Offences' – introduced a series of chapters that explore the issue of 'hard' and 'soft' styles of policing in terms of the targeting of particular contemporary offences. In the first of these contributions, Nick Tilley, noting the negative connotations of the highly publicised/politicised usage of the term 'zero tolerance', observed the circumstances in which short-term 'crackdowns' can be used constructively to target particular offences. It is noted that crackdowns could be usefully introduced to target those offences characteristically or frequently committed by the socially integrated middle classes. Drink driving, tax evasion, fraud, pollution, breaches of safety regulations at work, internal theft, much domestic violence, false accounting and traffic violations are all rightly recognised as potentially highly damaging areas of offending. The costs of detection are nonetheless recognised as likely to be high. Whereas such respectable members of society are unlikely to riot, the costs of criminalising large numbers of the 'pillars of society' might well have serious social implications the outcome of which we can only guess. While legitimate notions of social equity advise us that these damaging crimes should be targeted – just ask any criminology student studying 'white-collar' crime – the whole social consensus on which policing in its narrow and indeed wider generic sense is dependent could be seriously threatened by a further considerable widening of the scope of police business.

In the following chapter, Mike Sutton considers the analogous situation of targeting the stolen goods markets. While there is no doubt that supply to these markets is provided by those with a motivation to steal, the demand for the goods is – in at least many cases – stimulated by respectable people prepared to ask few questions particularly if the product comes in its original box and we are able to neutralise our feelings of guilt (see Matza, 1964). Likewise, the offence of handling stolen goods has been previously a low priority for a resource-stretched public police service and the criminal justice system. It is suggested that judges and their advisors should consider the social harm stolen goods markets do in stimulating the incidence and prevalence of theft – and the unintended consequences of providing subsidies for the illicit sex and drugs industries – and that they should be considerably less tolerant of the local 'fence'. The combination of a crackdown on the thieves and the handlers while replacing illicit markets with legitimate opportunities to obtain a bargain is a suggested strategy for dealing with this multi-faceted problem.

The theme of criminal offences previously considered non-problematic but recently deemed worthy of a serious criminal justice intervention – and again with considerable implicit implications for a further expansion in police business – is apparent in the discussion of stalking by Lorna White Sansom. Stalking is noted to be a serious offence with extremely close – invariably inseparable – links with domestic violence and a higher political public profile is proposed with a much more efficient and consistent intervention from the criminal justice system.

The financial services industry is another area of the social world which has traditionally been outside the gaze of the public police service and the criminal justice system with self-regulation and internal policing mechanisms the orthodoxy. Basia Spalek, however, raises some important concerns about the nature of financial regulation in Britain and its impact on investors and the victims of financial crime in the aftermath of major financial scandals in the USA. There seems little doubt that increasing demands for improved – and indeed state – regulation and policing of the financial services industry has occurred at least as a by-product of the politically promoted popular ownership of shares during the past quarter century but perhaps more importantly given the central importance of private pension funds, with the two of course inextricably linked. It is observed that the current regulatory framework is atavistic in that it views investors as being able to freely choose whether or not to invest in a particular product and institution with victims of financial crime seen to lack knowledge of the system and its inherent risk. However, this is considered an unrealistic scenario which fails to consider the reality that many consumers – including this author – are perfectly aware of the risks involved but have little real choice but to buy into these products often as a means of paying back their mortgages. It is thus imperative that the Financial Services Authority reconsiders notions of the relationship between financial crime and its victims in order to give the latter the appropriate support to which they are entitled.

Mandy Shaw considers the role of Dordrecht offender rehabilitation programmes in tackling the long-established but nonetheless extremely popular contemporary offence of burglary that remains a substantial element of police business. It is noted that neither previously attempted 'hard' criminal justice or 'soft' diversionary interventions have been themselves successful in tackling the involvement of young offenders in burglary. Dordrecht programmes thus synthesise both a 'hard' zero tolerance element and a 'softer' emphasis on dealing with the root causes of criminal activity for individual offenders to provide a complementary strategy to tackle the essential causal factors in offending behaviour.

The contributions in the third part of the book – 'Democracy, Accountability and Human Rights' – discuss those very issues which have been signposted by various authors in the previous two parts. Graham Smith returns to the post-Giuliani/Bratton policing offensive in New York City and notes – as others have done in this text and elsewhere (Hopkins Burke, 1998b; Silverman, 1998) – that a necessary feature of a formal 'hard' policing policy is the constant need to secure the support of the electorate. In the USA police commissioners are appointed by the city mayor and are thus expected to pursue the favoured direction of the latter on pain of dismissal, a fate that will in due course befall both if they lose public support. A very different situation has previously existed in England and Wales with constabularies enjoying considerable operational independence from government, but this situation has changed radically in recent years with executive government incrementally gaining increased control of policing – as with other areas of the social world previously the prerogative of local accountability, such as education – in the name of equity and comparability of standards. It is noted that while the doctrine of constabulary independence may be a utopian concept in contemporary society it does nonetheless provide the foundations for a pragmatic and principled depoliticised policing conforming to the principles of proportionality required since the incorporation of the European Convention on Human Rights in the Human Rights Act 1998.

John Wadham and Kavita Modi have examined some of the most pertinent human rights issues affecting policing, for example and significantly observing that the fast increasing use of surveillance in society conflicts with the fundamental right to respect for privacy and that the proliferation of powers to control public demonstrations and marches is probably incompatible with human rights legislation. It is proposed that the best available option to protect the historical rights we hold most dear would undoubtedly be a Bill of Rights.

Roger Hopkins Burke and Ruth Morrill consider this issue of individual human rights juxtaposed against those arguments for communal rights – or the rights of communities – that have theoretically underpinned both the arguments of zero tolerance-style 'hard' policing proponents and contemporary governments – in particular New Labour in the UK – who have been heavily influenced by the communitarian thinking of Amitia Etzioni. It was thus in this context that the aforementioned government introduced the Crime and Disorder Act 1998 to tackle the 'root cause of crime' and disorder within local communities. The Anti-Social Behaviour Order introduced by that legislation is intended to protect the rights of citizens whose lives have been blighted by those who behave in anti-social ways in their communities. It is suggested, however, that the balance may have shifted too much in favour of 'communities' at the expense of individual liberty. Due-process values are seen to have been sacrificed in the increased pursuit of crime control outcomes with in particular a worrying potential to absorb further into a widening net a whole group of relatively non-problematic young people who left pretty much alone would grow out of their anti-social activities and become respectable members of society. The authors nonetheless observe that ASBOs have a legitimate and appropriate future in a communitarian criminal justice policy, observing that it would be inappropriate to abandon or seriously curtail their use because measures are needed to tackle a serious social threat to many communities. At the same time, it is extremely important to place the issue of civil liberties and human rights at the forefront of debates regarding their implementation.

This tension between the rights of both individuals and collectivities or the wider community, and at the same time between minority communities and the wider society, is central to debates about the policing of contemporary fragmented and diverse multicultural post-industrial societies. Debates about differentiation and diversity are themselves the product of a moral certainty or confidence in the economic and cultural dominance of the post-industrial West. Such certainty has been traditionally stronger among those 'in-groups' who are part of the paid

249

employment-based consumption sectors in those societies. 'Out-groups' currently termed the underclass or the socially excluded have – as we have seen in this book – always been treated with suspicion and have been the central focus of police business. However, near universal acceptance of the legitimacy of such social systems has been engendered in no small part by the obvious empirical evidence all around us that shows the real possibility of transition from 'out-group' to 'in-group' status.

The history of the past two hundred years in western societies has shown that many of the material aspirations of the respectable working class have been realised and that many – if not most – of this group would now consider themselves to be middle class. Now, while classical Marxists are nonetheless quite right correct in observing that the traditional social relations of capitalism remain intact and that this new embourgoisement, or civilising process, obscures the reality that the vast majority of people remain fundamentally workers who have nothing to sell in the marketplace other than their labour power – well, legitimately that is – and that the labour market is a fast-changing entity where skills in high demand yesterday may well be superfluous today or perhaps tomorrow, there is no doubt that mature global capitalism does require, and perhaps far more importantly is extremely dependent on, a highly educated workforce. There is a vast literature that recognises that the emergence of welfare states in such societies have been, at least in part, in response to organised working-class demands. More recent developments such as widespread home and share ownership and private pensions are a clear indication of greater rewards expected by an educated, skilled and valuable workforce, with concordant changes to the nature of its political representation. This process is exemplified in Britain by the transition from 'old' Labour via 'popular' conservatism or 'Thatcherism' to New Labour. With such material gains – and the improved education that has brought this about – come improved expectations of 'rights' and civil liberties. Thus we have all come to expect respect, decency and professionalism from public servants with whom we have dealings, and the public sector police service and other branches of the criminal justice system are no exceptions. These expectations are in no doubt part of the increasing civilising process and resultant pressures have contributed to the great increase in police business.

Rights and liberties at one time – while at least theoretically the prerogative of all Englishmen – were in the main matters of concern for a small propertied and relatively affluent percentage of the population. The great majority of us were controlled and disciplined by the demands of long hours of hard physical toil either paid or unpaid. The increasing process of embourgoisement has led to the expansion of civil rights to whole sections of the population not previously considered to warrant them such as English*women* and children. In the case of the former, a husband no longer enjoys the right, nay the duty as was considered legislatively appropriate in the late nineteenth century, to discipline his wife with a stick, as long as the aforesaid instrument was constituted of a thickness no larger than her husband's thumb, but he is now considered by the criminal justice system to be not just a criminal but increasingly a *serious* criminal. At the same time, we have progressively demanded the right to a peaceful and victimless existence. Thus, in a world where criminal opportunities are forever increasing and victimisation is widespread, public support for rigorous indeed 'hard' policing strategies has been popular as long as these are not perceived as getting in the way of our civil liberties. At the same, time a concurrent component of the growth of the 'crime control industry' (Christie, 1993) has been an apparent increase in the number of civil – or more recently human – rights lawyers who have been eager to ensure that those socially excluded members of society who come into more regular contact with the criminal justice system have their rights safeguarded.

Thus we can observe a constant tension between, on the one hand, a demand for human rights – and in many cases this stretches to a requirement for a minimal intervention in our often hedonistic and sometimes (at least technically in the case of recreational drug use) criminal lifestyles – and, on the other hand, a demand for a peaceful and secure existence which we expect governments and their agents to deliver. It is clear that these two demands cannot be easily reconciled. What does become increasingly clear, however, is that the incremental development of pervasive generic policing throughout society – with an oft confused ambiguity between 'hard' and 'soft' multi-agency policing strategies – is part of an expanding insidious form of social control that has come about with at least our implicit agreement and goes well beyond the public police service as the following discussion demonstrates.

Pervasiveness policing and public demand

A good starting point for a discussion of the role of the general public – or more accurately us – in supporting the increasingly pervasive multi-agency policing of society is to return to the financial services industry discussed by Basia Spalek earlier in this book. It was noted earlier that the industry has been traditionally self-policed and in the main rarely considered a matter for the public police service. This was very much the case when serious financial matters were the preserve of a very small element of the population; with the arrival of mass population purchase of financial products this ceased to be so. Widespread general public motivation for increased regulation and the more comprehensive policing of financial services products is indisputable.

At the time of the financial scandals at Enron and WorldCom in the USA in 2002 – to which Basia Spalek refers – the great economist J.K. Galbraith, then aged 93, observed in an interview that large modern corporations – as manipulated by what he terms the 'financial craftsmen' at Enron and elsewhere – have grown so complex that they are almost beyond monitoring and effective control by their owners, the shareholders (Cornwell, 2002). Galbraith (quoted by Cornwell, 2003: 13) considers the notion of internal policing to be absurd:

> The sense of responsibility in the financial community for the community as a whole it is not small. It is nearly nil. To speak out against madness may be to ruin those who have succumbed to it. So the wise on Wall Street are nearly always silent. The foolish have the field to themselves and none rebukes them ... There is still a tradition, a culture of restraint that keeps one from attacking one's colleagues, one's co-workers, no matter how wrong they seem to be.

Noting the sheer scale of the inadequacy of the accountancy profession and some of its prominent members in the aforementioned scandals, Galbraith observes the need for the strongest public and legal pressure to get honest competent accounting as part of a greater corporate regulation and public control of the private sector. He argues that steps must be taken so that boards of directors, supine and silent for so long, are competent to exercise their legal responsibility to their shareholders.

Public motivation for the increased policing of the financial services industry is both apparent and unquestionably understandable. Other policing, surveillance and control intrusions into various parts of the social world – with even more mooted – are more questionable. Taken individually, these may seem both inoffensive and supportable; taken collectively they are part of an impressive matrix of social control that restricts our freedom as the following examples clearly demonstrate.

The freedom of the authorities to access information on our private lives has grown considerably in recent years. Information from a wide range of sources – the Office for National Statistics, the National Health Service, the Inland Revenue, the VAT office, the Benefits Agency, our school reports – can now be collated into a file on a citizen without a court order showing why this should be the case. Legislative proposals in recent years have included phone and e-mail records to be kept for seven years, the extension of child curfews, keeping DNA of those acquitted of crimes and 'ex-suspects', restrictions on travel of those convicted of drug offences, the extension of compulsory fingerprinting for those cautioned of a recordable offence and public authorities authorised to carry out speculative searches of the DNA database (see Wadham and Modi, 2003). The Social Security Fraud Act 2001 allows for the compilation of a financial inventory from our bank accounts, building societies, insurance companies, telecom companies and the Student Loan Company, while every number on our phone bills may be reverse searched for an address. There may be no evidence that we are involved in fraud for us to be investigated, we may merely belong to a demographic group of people that the authorities feel is 'likely' to be involved in fraud.

Widespread public concern about these increasing surveillance intrusions into our lives led to the promise of freedom of information legislation that would provide us – the individual – with increased power in our dealings with the state. The subsequent Freedom of Information Act 2000 can be considered however, little more than a code of practice that requires public bodies to provide citizens with information unless government ministers veto the request. The Information Commissioner may insist that the information be released, but the decision does not have to be obeyed.

The Law Commission has proposed the ending of the long-established legal safeguard of protection from double jeopardy where a defendant acquitted of a crime can be re-prosecuted if new evidence emerges, and this legislation at the time of writing is before Parliament in the Criminal Justice Bill. Numerous cases have been cited where new prosecutions might be successful and it is not difficult to imagine that considerable public support for such a measure would be obtained when considering the following examples. Billy Dunlop, from Billingham on Teesside, was twice tried and on the second occasion acquitted, of murdering a pizza delivery girl, Julie Hogg. Nine years after his two trials in 1991, Dunlop faced a court again, this time on a charge of perjury, confessed to the murder and was jailed for six years. Freddie Foreman was acquitted of the murders of Frank 'Mad Axeman' Mitchell and Tommy 'Ginger' Marks in the 1960s and more recently admitted on television that he had committed the murders at the instigation of the notorious gangsters the Kray twins. Michael Weir was convicted of murdering 79-year-old Leonard Harris in North London. The crucial evidence was blood found on his gloves which when subjected to DNA analysis showed a match with a sample of the accused's blood taken in connection with drugs offences a year earlier. The Court of Appeal ruled that this was a breach of the Police and Criminal Evidence Act 1984 and should have been ruled inadmissible. Weir was cleared. That decision was overturned by the Law Lords but Weir remains free on a technicality (BBC News, 2001a). It was the murder of Stephen Lawrence and the subsequent Macpherson Report[1] which had prompted the government to ask the Law Commission to reconsider the double jeopardy rule. However, even if the law is changed, the three Lawrence suspects who were acquitted of murder[2] can only in accordance with the proposed new legislation face the same charge again if there is fresh, reliable and compelling evidence.

While there would undoubtedly and understandably be widespread public support for further prosecution in such cases, civil liberties and human rights organisations are concerned that this legislation could lead to serious miscarriages of justice and the ongoing harassment of individuals acquitted by a jury. It would be – it is argued – virtually impossible to have a fair trial the second time round: the prosecution could know the entire defence case from the first hearing and the jury would probably be aware that the Court of Appeal had ruled that new and compelling evidence had become available. Liberty (2003) argues that as it is the prosecution who decides when to bring the case and at the same time have 'such awesome investigatory powers at their disposal', it is not reasonable that the defendant face the same charges twice.

Other legislation that undoubtedly enjoys widespread popular support is the Football (Disorder) Act 2000 passed as an almost immediate response to the violence seen during the Euro 2000 football tournament, particularly in the town of Charleroi, Belgium. Matthew Robb (2003) of the civil liberties watchdog Magnacartaplus nonetheless argues that the legislation which allows for the withdrawal of passports from hooligans represents a significant restriction of the civil liberties of all citizens. He argues that it fails to draw an appropriate balance between law and order and civil liberties; it is rushed, reactive legislation that has used blunt legislative tools and failed to consider other, less draconian options and uses the 'demonisation' of a group – that is, football supporters – to justify powers that would not normally be accorded to the State.

Mental health legislation published last year by the government will allow for hundreds of people with dangerous, incurable personality disorders to be locked up indefinitely in secure mental hospitals, without the need for evidence that they have committed a crime. Jacqui Smith, the health minister, said the legislation would remove a loophole that allowed up to 600 people with dangerous and severe personality disorders to avoid treatment by arguing that they received no benefit from it. The legislation would also permit the compulsory treatment of mentally ill people being cared for in the community and under new powers they could be made to take medication. This plan for the detention of psychopaths who have not committed a crime followed public outrage at the murder by Michael Stone of Lin Russell and her six-year-old daughter Megan in Kent in 1996. He had been left free to commit the crime because his severe personality disorder was considered untreatable and he could not be detained under the Mental Health Act. There are said to be between 2,100 and 2,400 people in the UK with severe personality disorders. The vast majority are in prison or a secure mental hospital, but between 300 and 600 live in the community (Hogg, 2002). Critics ranging from opposition political parties to civil liberties groups and libertarians nonetheless – and perhaps not surprisingly – question the human rights implications of incarcerating people who have committed no criminal offence.

On 8 February 2003 the EU Justice and Home Affairs Council reached a provisional agreement allowing investigating authorities to quickly secure evidence and seize assets in other member states. Effectively, a warrant issued in one member state authorising the freezing of property in relation to criminal investigations in respect of any of a list of 32 agreed offences[3] and carrying a maximum custodial sentence of three years or more will be enforceable throughout the EU. Bob Ainsworth (cited by Statewatch, 2002), the UK Home Office minister, noted just how wide-ranging and intrusive these orders may be:

> The Framework Decision, as far as the freezing of evidence is concerned, will not depend on there being any particular suspect; indeed the investigation maybe at an early stage with no particular offence established. Property will be seized and detained by the police, often from third parties, pending the receipt of a formal request for its transmission to the issuing state.

An example of the effect that mandatory recognition of orders from other states can have comes from Sweden where the UN Security

Council (Taliban Sanctions Committee) list of terrorist organisations whose assets are to be frozen included three Swedish citizens. The three men, all of Somali origin, are members of Al Barakaat, a network of organisations providing support to refugees and assisting financial transactions between the residents of Sweden and Somalia. After public reaction to the freezing of their assets, the Swedish authorities demanded evidence from the US government. When the latter finally provided this, the Swedish Security Police stated that there was no substance to the material sent as 'evidence'. Marianne Eriksson, a Swedish MEP, said:

> These men – and even the partner of one of them – have been left without any economic assets. It means they are without a salary or benefits. All this has been done without any legal evidence or preliminary investigation. We want to draw attention to their plight and the whole process under which they have been condemned.

The three individuals have lodged a case against the Council and the Commission with the European Courts, arguing that the EC Regulations implementing the UN Security Council Resolution are a breach of the EC Treaty and amount to a misuse of powers imposing upon them onerous sanctions while simultaneously denying them the 'fundamental legal principle of the right to a fair and equitable hearing' as guaranteed by Article 6, ECHR. It is an example that alerts us to the effect that terrorism has had in facilitating public support for authoritarian 'hard' policing methods.

The left-realist variation on the panoptican/carceral surveillance society thesis that provides the theoretical underpinnings of this text proposes that in a complex contemporary society we all have interests in – or an enthusiasm for – constraints placed on certain activities that restrict the civil liberties or human rights of some individuals or groups. Taken together collectively these many individual restrictions constitute the complex social control matrix that constrains us all. Major military or terrorist assaults on the sovereignty of our particular societies 'and our way' of life, on the other hand, return us to a less complicated more polarised world where moral certainty or, more accurately, competing moral certainties return to the foreground.

The events of 11 September 2001 when the terrorist group al-Qaeda carried out attacks on the World Trade Center in New York and the Pentagon in Washington causing thousands of casualties provided an inevitable widespread public support for what was to be an extensive authoritarian assault on civil liberties and human rights both in the USA and the UK. Further terrorist attacks on the allies of the USA, again involving large numbers of casualties – including those in Bali on 12 October 2002 and in Turkey on 20 November 2003 – and the almost constant warnings by government of failed attempts and successful interventions by the security forces against terrorists invariably living in our midst have undoubtedly strengthened support for measures to protect society from such attacks. At the same time there has been considerable popular opposition to such measures and particularly to the military intervention in both Afghanistan and Iraq during 2002 and 2003. The US and UK governments have nonetheless stood firm in what they have termed the 'war on terrorism' and 'soft' policing measures have tended to fade into the background as an unambiguously 'harder' policing stance has taken precedence with predictable objections from civil liberties and human rights groups. Speaking six months after the attack on the USA in September 2001 US President Bush (BBC News, 2002a) reinforced his commitment to the fight against terrorism:

> Every terrorist must be made to live as an international fugitive with no place to settle or organise, no place to hide, no governments to hide behind, and not even a safe place to sleep ... Against such an enemy there is no immunity, and there can be no neutrality.

Twelve months later Amnesty International in their annual report saw things rather differently suggesting that the 'war on terror' had made the world a more dangerous place and had created divisions which make conflicts more likely, and accused governments of 'trampling over rights in the name of fighting terrorism' (BBC News, 2003c). Amnesty had investigated claims that Iraqi prisoners of war were tortured by US and British troops and found that a 'substantial proportion' they interviewed said they had been maltreated. The UK Ministry of Defence said: 'All of the prisoners held by the British were held under the terms of the Geneva Convention, and they were frequently visited by members of the International Red Cross.' But Amnesty researcher Said Boumedouha said that: 'In one case we are talking about electric shocks being used against a man and in others people are being beaten for the whole night and are still being kicked and their teeth broken. I think you would call that torture' (BBC News, 2003b). The likely truth of these allegations might be considered in the context of other actions by the USA and the UK in the aftermath of 11 September 2001. We shall consider the case of the USA first.

As the entire world now knows terrorist suspects captured in Afghanistan were taken to the US military base at Guantanamo Bay in Cuba which was deemed by the US government to be outside the jurisdiction of US courts. These prisoners were designated 'unlawful combatants' without the right to a trial, causing concern among human rights organisations. At the time of writing no tribunals or trial have been held but concerns at the conditions in which the men are being held are universal. A spokesman for Amnesty International (quoted in BBC News, 2003d) said that they had real concerns about the use of military tribunals:

> If you have been held for over a year in legal limbo and you have been interrogated then you have to worry very much that 'evidence' is going to be brought before the military tribunal that has been extracted out of individuals ... We want no use of material taken from people under those circumstances – we think it should be thrown out.

Colonel Will Gunn, the newly appointed defence counsel, said he would push for trials to be as open as possible, saying that the US would be judged on the fairness of the process, although by this time worldwide opinion was becoming increasingly wary of US 'hard' policing international-style and its attitude towards human rights. It had been previously disclosed that three 'youths' aged between 13 and 15 were being held at Guantanamo and considered enemy combatants. A spokesperson for Amnesty International said at the time: 'That the USA sees nothing wrong with holding children at Guantanamo and interrogating them is a shocking indicator of how cavalier the Bush administration has become about respecting human rights' (BBC News, 2003a).

However, human rights abuse of children has not just been restricted to those who allegedly engage in terrorist activities against the USA. A further Amnesty report has accused the USA of the widespread mistreatment of children who seek asylum in that country, noting that those who arrive unaccompanied are often denied access to attorneys, detained for prolonged periods and even jailed alongside young criminals (BBC News, 2003e). The treatment of indigenous youth offenders in the USA had itself previously caused Amnesty considerable cause for concern. In a report published in September 2002 it was observed that in the previous decade two-thirds of known executions of under-age offenders had been carried out in the USA. It observed that, of the 190 member states of the United Nations, only the

USA and Somalia had failed to ratify the Convention on the Rights of the Child which bans such executions. A spokesperson for the organisation observed that: 'By allowing the execution of child offenders the US undermines its own claims to be a progressive force for human rights. It is time for the US to come in from the cold' (BBC News, 2002b).

In launching Amnesty International's annual report in May 2003 secretary general Irene Khan criticised the UK's Anti-Terrorism, Crime and Security Act 2001 which had allowed eleven foreign nationals to be detained without charge in 'inhuman and degrading conditions'. The report attacks the power of the Home Secretary to detain foreign nationals indefinitely, without charge or trial, if they are deemed to be a risk to national security, claiming that such power is inconsistent with the right to liberty and security guaranteed in the European Convention for the Protection of Human Rights. The Act is accused of effectively creating a shadow criminal justice system devoid of a number of crucial safeguards present in the ordinary system. Ms Khan (quoted in BBC News, 2003c) said:

> In the name of security, politics and profit, human rights were trampled the world over by governments, armed groups and corporate activity ... What would have been unacceptable on September 10, 2001, is now becoming the norm, What would have been an outrage in Western countries during the Cold War – torture, detention without trial, truncated justice – is readily accepted in some countries today for some people.

Kate Allen, the UK director of Amnesty, noted that the 'war on terror' had an overwhelming impact worldwide with a heavy toll on human rights and human lives. She said that the definition of security had to encompass the safety of people as well as states and that meant a commitment to human rights: 'Governments have spent billions to strengthen national security and the "war on terror". Yet for millions of people, the real sources of insecurity are corruption, repression, discrimination, extreme poverty and preventable diseases' (BBC News, 2003c). The report suggests that divisions during the previous year had made people of different faiths and backgrounds more divided, with 'genuine fears' prompted across all sections of society.

A Home Office spokesperson responding to this attack on the UK's anti-terror measures said: 'The powers are a necessary and proportionate response to the threat that we face. We have to strike the right balance between our civil liberties, our privacy and our expectation that the state will protect us and facilitate our freedom' (BBC News, 2003c). Moreover, the Court of Appeal had previously supported the government position in October 2002, ruling that the power to keep a suspect in prison without trial was acceptable providing that the person was a threat to national security. In the face of considerable criticism from civil liberties and human rights groups Lord Woolf, the Lord Chief Justice, observed that British nationals – who cannot be deported – are not in the same position as foreigners who cannot be deported because of the risk of them being killed or otherwise persecuted: 'Such foreign nationals do not have the right to remain in this country but only a right – for the time being – not to be removed for their own safety' (BBC News, 2003f). He added that such differentiation on the basis of nationality was both in accordance with international law and that, in certain national security situations, the government was better able than a court to make decisions about suspects:

> When doing so in the particular context in which this challenge arises, namely a state of public emergency, the court must also recognise that the executive is in a better position than a court to assess both the situation and the action which is necessary to address it.

Lord Justice Brooke (quoted in BBC News, 2003f), in his contribution to the ruling, said that an element of trust had to be placed in the authorities despite occasional mistakes:

> Unless one is willing to adopt a purist approach, saying that it is better that this country should be destroyed, together with the ideals it stands for, than a single suspected terrorist should be detained without due process, it seems to me inevitable that the judiciary must be willing to put an appropriate degree of trust in the willingness and capacity of ministers and Parliament.

Indeed, it might well be the case that the government could find itself in a situation where even tougher 'hard policing' measures are necessary to deal with serious threats to our society and as a consequence these will lead to further and even greater unambiguous restrictions on our personal freedoms and human rights in the interests of the larger community. There is certainly a potential, and increasingly probable, threat to our society – indeed the whole planet – that is substantially greater than that posed by international terrorism, and that is global warming. In July 2001 – two months before the al-Qaeda terrorist attacks on the

USA – the New Economics Foundation (NEF), a UK-based campaign group, produced a not widely noticed report which argued that the government was failing to warn people what tackling climate change would really mean, noting that the country could become ungovernable when ordinary citizens realised what would have to be done. The author of the report Andrew Simms (BBC News, 2001b) observed:

> The UK and the industrialised world have run up a huge ecological debt to the global community. To balance our books we need to learn from times in our history when we have successfully cut domestic consumption of natural resources in ways that created unexpected human benefits.

The report observes that it is the experience of the Second World War that clearly demonstrates how dramatic cuts in the use of resources could be achieved while at the same time producing positive un-expected consequences. It was observed that the current UK govern-ment is not facing the challenge in the same way and noted that even mild changes to fuel prices and availability of fuel the previous years had brought fuel protestors into the streets and Britain had been brought to the edge of anarchy. The report observes (BBC News, 2001b) that while the government knows that much larger changes will be necessary: 'It is failing to prepare public opinion for the inevitable … Its timidity means that introducing non-negotiable policies will be like playing climate roulette with public reactions'.

Examples are cited of UK success during the 1940s in reducing consumption. First, between 1938 and 1944 there was a 95 per cent reduction in the use of motor vehicles while public transport use increased by 13 per cent. Second, consumption of goods and services declined by 16 per cent and domestic use of coal – the main source of heating at the time – fell by 25 per cent. Third, the number of children dying before their first birthday fell from around 58 to 45 per thousand as more frugal living raised health standards.

The possibility that the NEF report is little more than a moral panic stimulated by moral entrepreneurs (see Becker, 1963) with a material interest in gaining wide support for their political agenda is given short-shrift by support from two unimpeachable sources, the United Nations Environment Programme and the Oxford Commission on Sustainable Development which have both suggested that resource use may have to decrease by as much as 90 per cent. Andrew Simms (BBC News, 2001b) observes that:

> Unless the government prepares public opinion for the changes in lifestyle that will be needed to achieve up to 90 per cent emissions cuts in the coming century, trying to implement the policies necessary will make the country ungovernable ... Rather than focusing on a single term of office, the government needs plans for 30, 50 or even a hundred years ahead.

The political possibilities of such a radical political programme being introduced in contemporary UK-style political democracies where governments need – as we have observed above – to put together complex electoral coalitions to remain in power seems at this juncture incredibly unlikely, indeed probably impossible. It is pertinent to note that the Second World War was fought in the UK by a National Coalition government of all the major political parties and involved the introduction of far-ranging emergency measures to severely restrict individual civil liberties and human rights in the common interest. It would seem that the introduction of any such radical programme as that envisaged by the NEF will require some similar form of government and a range of generic policing measures that extend across the full spectrum between 'hard' and 'soft', with an undoubted emphasis probably on the former. It could well be a major terrorist atrocity – or a series of atrocities or setbacks in the 'war against terrorism' – that provides the crisis situation to instigate the preconditions for such a scenario. Hopefully, you all might think, this is all implausible conjecture. Unfortunately, from where I am sitting today with my knowledge of recent – and less recent – history, this all seems only too plausible. We will see.

Notes

1 See Chapter 13 in this book by Graham Smith.
2 A private prosecution was brought against the three accused by Stephen Lawrence's parents.
3 The list in full: participation in a criminal organisation; terrorism; trafficking in human beings; sexual exploitation of children and child pornography; illicit trafficking in narcotic drugs and psychotropic substances; illicit trafficking in weapons, munitions and explosives; corruption; fraud; laundering of the proceeds of crime; counterfeiting of the euro; computer-related crime; environmental crime, including illicit trafficking in endangered animal species and in endangered plant species and varieties; facilitation of unauthorised entry and residence; murder; grievous bodily injury; illicit trade in human organs and tissue;

kidnapping, illegal restraint and hostage-taking; racism and xenophobia; organised or armed robbery; illicit trafficking in cultural goods, including antiques and works of art; swindling, racketeering and extortion; counterfeiting and product piracy; forgery of administrative documents and trafficking therein; forgery of means of payment; illicit trafficking in hormonal substances and other growth promoters; illicit trafficking in nuclear or radioactive materials; motor vehicle crime; rape; arson; crimes within the jurisdiction of the International Criminal Tribunal; unlawful seizure of aircraft/ships; sabotage (Article 3.2).

Bibliography

Abu-Boakye, K. (2002) *Private Security and Retail Crime Prevention: An Ethnographic Case Study at Retail Shops in Portsmouth.* Unpublished Dissertation submitted for the MSc in Criminal Justice Studies, University of Portsmouth.

Advisory Council on the Penal System (1977) *The Length of Prison Sentences.* London: HMSO.

Advisory Council on the Penal System (1978) *Sentences of Imprisonment: A Review of Maximum Penalties.* London: HMSO.

Alderson, J. (1973) 'The Principles and Practice of the British Police', in J. Alderson and P.J. Stead (eds), *The Police we Deserve.* London: Trinity Press.

Alderson J. (1998) *Principled Policing: Protecting the Public with Integrity.* Winchester: Waterside Press.

Alexander, C. (2000a) *The Asian Gang: Ethnicity, Identity, Masculinity.* Oxford: Berg.

Alexander, C. (2000b) '(Dis) Entangling the "Asian Gang": Ethnicity, Identity and Masculinity', in B. Hesse, (ed.), *Un/settled Multiculturalisms.* London: Zed Books.

Althusser, L. (1969) *For Marx.* London: Allen Lane.

Amnesty International (1996) *Police Brutality and Excessive Force in the New York Police Department.* New York: Amnesty International.

Anderson, D., Chenery, S. and Pease, K. (1995) *Biting Back: Tackling Repeat Burglary and Car Crime*, Crime Detection and Prevention Series Paper 58. London: Home Office.

Anderson, P. (1968) 'Components of the National Culture', *New Left Review* 161, January–February 1987, reprinted in Anderson P. (1992) *English Questions.* London and New York: Verso.

Anderson, S., Kinsey, R., Loader, I. and Smith, C. (1994) *Cautionary Tales: Young People, Crime and Policing in Edinburgh.* Aldershot: Avebury.

Anwar, M. (1976) *Between Two Cultures: A Study of the Relationships Between Generations in the Asian Community in Britain*. London: Community Relations Council.

Ascoli, D. (1979) *The Queen's Peace*. London: Hamish Hamilton.

Ashworth, A. (1992) *Sentencing and Criminal Justice*. London: Weidenfeld & Nicolson.

Ashworth, A. (1998) *The Criminal Process*, 2nd edn. Oxford: Oxford University Press.

Ashworth, A.J. and Gibson, B. (1994) 'The Criminal Justice Act 1993: Altering the Sentencing Framework', *Criminal Law Review*, 101–9.

Associated Press (2000) 'Police Departments Desperate for Recruits: Low Pay, Even Lower Morale Blamed for Shortage', *Newsday*, 2 June, p. 14.

Audit Commission (1996a) *Tackling Crime Effectively*. London: Audit Commission

Audit Commission (1996b) *Misspent Youth: Young People and Crime*. London: Audit Commission

Audit Commission (1999a) *Annual Report on the Police and Fire Services*. London: Audit Commission.

Audit Commission (1999b) *Life's Work, A: Local Authorities, Economic Development and Regeneration*. London: Audit Commission.

Aye Maung, N. (1995) *Young People, Victimisation and the Police: British Crime Survey Findings on the Experiences and Attitudes of 12–15 Year Olds*, Research Study 140, London: Home Office.

Bagshaw, R. (ed.) (1996) *Cross & Wilkins Outline of the Law of Evidence*, 7th edn. London: Butterworth.

Baker, S. and English, J. (1994) *A Guide to the Police and Magistrates Courts Act 1994*. London: Butterworths.

'Baltimore Police Department Seeks Ticket Option For Some Crimes' (2003), *Law Enforcement News*, 31 August, p. 7.

Bamfield, J. (1998) 'Retail Civil Recovery: Filling a Deficit in the Criminal Justice System?', *International Journal of Risk, Security and Crime Prevention*, 3: 257–67.

Banton, M. (1964) *The Policeman in the Community*. London: Tavistock.

Barker, M. and Bridgeman C. (1994) *Preventing Vandalism. What Works?* Police Research Group Crime Detection and Prevention Series: Paper No 56. London: Home Office.

Barnett, A. (1988) 'Drug Crackdowns and Crime Rates: A Comment on the Kleiman Paper', in M. Chaiken (ed.), *Street-Level Law Enforcement: Examining the Issues*. Washington, DC: National Institute of Justice.

Barry, B. (2001) *Culture & Equality: An Egalitarian Critique of Multiculturalism*. Cambridge: Polity Press.

Barstow, D. (2000) 'View from New York Streets: No Retreat by Police', *New York Times*, 25 June: 1/28.

Baxter, J. and Koffman, L. (eds) (1985) *Police: The Constitution and the Community*. Abingdon: Professional Books.

BBC News (2001a) *Double Jeopardy What it Means*, http://news.bbc.co.uk/1/hi/uk/1204095.stm.

BBC News (2001b) *UK 'Hiding Scale of Climate Threat'*, http://news.bbc.co.uk/1/hi/english/sci/tech/newsid/1204095.stm.

BBC News (2002a) *Bush Urges Renewed Campaign on Terror*, http://news.bbc.co.uk/1/hi/world/americas/1865988.stm.

BBC News (2000b) *US Condemned for Youth Executions*, http://news.bbc.co.uk/1/hi/world/americas/2280250.stm.

BBC News (2003a) *Teens Held in Guantanamo*, http://news.bbc.co.uk/1/hi/world/south_asia/2970279.stm.

BBC News (2003b) *Coalition 'Tortured' Iraqi POWS'*, http://news.bbc.co.uk/1/hi/world/middle_east/3034031.stm.

BBC News (2003c) *Warning over War on Terror*, http://news.bbc.co.uk/1/hi/uk_politics/2943192.stm.

BBC News (2003d) *Bush Approves Terror Suspect Trials*, http://news.bbc.co.uk/1/hi/world/americas/3043332.stm.

BBC News (2003e) *US 'Mistreats' Young Immigrants'*, http://news.bbc.co.uk/1/hi/world/americas/3001588.stm.

BBC News (2003f) *Judges Back Anti-Terror Law*, http://news.bbc.co.uk/1/hi/uk/2360319.stm.

BBC News (2003g) *Domestic Abusers Face Crackdown*, http://news.bbc.co.uk/1/hi/uk_politics/3254466.stm.

BBC News (2003h) *Police Face Race Inquiry*, http://news.bbc.co.uk/1/hi/uk/3228261.stm.

Bean, P. (1976) *Rehabilitation and Deviance*. London: Routledge & Kegan Paul.

Beck, M., Rosenberg, D., Chideya, F., Miller, S., Foole, D., Manly, H. and Katel, P. (1992) 'Murderous Obsession', *Newsweek*, 13 July, pp. 60–2.

Beck, U. (1992) *The Risk Society*. London: Sage.

Bennet, T. and Wright, R. (1984) *Burglars on Burglary*. Aldershot: Gower.

Bennett, T., Holloway, K. and Williams, T. (2001) *Drug Use and Offending: Summary Results From the First Year of the NEW-ADAM Research Programme*, Findings 148. London: Home Office.

Bernstein, S.E. (1993) 'Living Under Siege: Do Stalking Laws Protect Domestic Violence Victims?', *Cardozo Law Review*, 15: 525–57.

Bittner, E. (1970) *The Functions of Police in Modern Society*. Chevy Chase, MD: National Institute of Mental Health.

Blair, I. (2002) 'The Policing Revolution: Back to the Beat', *New Statesman*, 23 September.

Blair, T. (2002) 'Reforming Criminal Justice Speech', *Guardian Unlimited*, http://politics.guardian.co.uk/homeaffairs/story/0,11026,739672,00.html.

Bland, N. and Read, T. (2000) *Policing Anti-Social Behaviour*, Police Research Series Paper 123. London: Home Office.

Blatch, Baroness (1996) HL Deb col. 1824, 28 June.

Blumstein, A. and Wallman, J. (eds) (2000) *The Crime Drop in America*. New York: Cambridge University Press.

Bochel, D. (1976) *Probation and After-Care: Its Development in England and Wales.* Edinburgh: Scottish Academic Press.

Boles, G. (2001) 'Developing a Model Approach to Confronting the Problem of Stalking: Establishing a Threat Management Unit', in J.A. Davis (ed.), *Stalking Crimes and Victim Protection: Prevention, Intervention, Threat Assessment and Case Management.* New York: CRC Press.

Boon, J. and Sheridan, L. (eds) (2002) *Stalking and Psychosexual Obsession.* London: Wiley.

Bottoms, A.E. (2001) 'Compliance and Community Penalties' in A. Bottoms, L. Gelsthorpe and S. Rex, *Community Penalties: Change and Challenges.* Cullompton: Willan Publishing.

Bottoms, A.E. and McWilliam, W. (1979) 'A Non-Treatment Paradigm for Probation Practice', *British Journal of Social Work,* 9(2): 159–202.

Bottoms, A. and Wiles, P. (1997) *Environmental Criminology,* in M. Maguire, R. Morgan and R. Reiner (eds), *Oxford Handbook of Criminology,* 2nd edn. Oxford: Clarendon Press.

Bowden, T. (1978) *Beyond the Limits of the Law.* Harmondsworth: Penguin.

Bowling, B. (1996) 'Cracking Down on Crime in New York City', *Criminal Justice Matters,* 25, Autumn.

Bowling, B. (1998) Review of N. Dennis (ed.) 'Zero Tolerance: Policing a Free Society', *British Journal of Criminology,* 38(2): 318–21.

Bowling, B. (1998) *The Rise and Fall of New York Murder.* Paper presented to the University of Cambridge/Police Research Group Seminar, 'Police and Crime Reduction', 3 March 1998.

Bowling, B. (1999) *Violent Racism: Victimisation, Policing and Social Context.* Oxford: Clarendon Press.

Bowling, B. (1999) 'The Rise and Fall of the New York Murder: Zero Tolerance or Crack's Decline?', *British Journal of Criminology,* 39(4): 531–54.

Bowling, B., and Phillips, C. (2002) *Race, Crime and Criminal Justice.* London: Longman.

Bradburn, W.E. (1992) 'Stalking Statutes', *Ohio Northern University Law Review,* 19.

Bradford Commission Report (1996) *The Bradford Commission Report: The Report of an Inquiry into the Wider Implications of Public Disorders in Bradford which Occurred on 9, 10 and 11 June 1995,* Bradford Congress. London: Home Office.

Braga, A., Kennedy, D. and Piehl, A. (1999) 'Problem-Oriented Policing and Youth Violence: An Evaluation of the Boston Gun Project'. Unpublished Report to the National Institute of Justice, Washington, DC.

Brah, A. (1978) 'South Asian Teenagers in Southall', *New Community,* 6(3): 197–206.

Braithwaite, J. (1989) *Crime, Shame and Reintegration.* Cambridge: Cambridge University.

Brake, M. and Hale, C. (1992) *Public Order and Private Lives: The Politics of Law and Order.* London: Routledge.

Bratton, W.J. (1997) 'Crime is Down in New York City: Blame the Police', in N. Dennis (ed.), *Zero Tolerance: Policing a Free Society*. London: Institute for Economic Affairs.

Bratton, W. (1998) *Turnaround: How America's Top Cop Reversed the Crime Epidemic*. New York: Random House.

Bratton, W.J. and Andrews, W. (1998) 'What We've Learned about Policing', *City Journal*, Spring: 14–27.

Braun, H. and Lee, J. (1971) 'Private Police Forces: Legal Powers and Limitations', *University of Chicago Law Review*, 38: 555–82.

Broadhurst, J. (2002) 'Hard Times A-coming?', *New Law Journal*, 152(7022): 333.

Brogden, M. (1982) *The Police: Autonomy and Consent*. London: Academic Press.

Brown, H. (2000) *Stalking: An Investigator's Guide*. London: HMSO.

Brown, S. (1994a) *Whose Challenge? Youth, Crime and Everyday Life in Middlesbrough*. Middlesbrough: Middlesbrough City Challenge.

Brown, S. (1994b) *Time of Change? Adult Views of Youth and Crime in Middlesbrough*. Middlesbrough: Middlesbrough City Challenge and Safer Cities.

Brown, S. (1995b) 'Crime and Safety in Whose "Community"?: Age, Everyday Life, and Problems for Youth Policy', *Youth & Policy*, 48: 27–48.

Brown, S. (1995a) *Nobody Listens? Problems and Promise for Youth Provision*. Middlesbrough: Middlesbrough City Challenge and Safer Cities.

Brownlee, L. (1998a) 'New Labour – New Penology? Punitive Rhetoric and the Limits of Managerialism in Criminal Justice Policy', *Journal of Law and Society*, 25(3): 313–35.

Brownlee, I. (1998b) *Community Punishment: A Critical Introduction*. London: Longman.

Bucke, T. and Brown, D. (1997) *In Police Custody: Police Powers and Suspects' Rights Under the Revised PACE Codes of Practice*, Home Office Research Study 174. London: Home Office.

Bullock, K, and Tilley, N. (2002) *Shootings, Gangs and Violent Incidents in Manchester: Developing a Crime Reduction Strategy*, Crime Reduction Research Series Paper 13. London: Home Office.

Bunyan, T. (1976) *The Political Police in Britain*. London: Julian Friedmann Publishers.

Burton, D. (1994) *Financial Services and the Consumer*. London: Routledge.

Butler, J. (1997) *Excitable Speech: A Politics of the Performative*. London: Routledge.

Butler, T. (2000) 'Managing the Future: A Chief Constable's View', in F. Leishman, B. Loveday and S. Savage (eds), *Core Issues in Policing*, 2nd edn. Harlow: Longman.

Butterfield, F. (2003) 'Study Finds Hundreds of Thousands of Inmates Mentally Ill', *New York Times*, 22 October: 1/14.

Button, M. (2002) *Private Policing*. Cullompton: Willan Publishing.

Button, M. and John, T. (2002) 'Plural Policing in Action: A Review of the

Policing of Environmental Protests in England and Wales', *Policing and Society*, 12: 111–21.

Cain, M. (1973) *Society and the Policeman's Role*. London: Routledge.

Cairns, D. (2001) 'Guarding by Communication', *SMT*, December: 13.

Campbell, B. (1993) *Goliath: Britain's Dangerous Places*. London: Methuen.

Campbell, S. (2002) *A Review of Anti-social Behaviour Orders*, Home Office Research Study 236. London: Home Office.

Cantle, T. (2002) *Community Cohesion: A Report of the Independent Review Team*. London: Home Office.

Carey, C. (2002) 'Those We Leave Behind: Drug Policy and the Poor', *Harm Reduction Communication*, 13 (Spring): 4–10.

CARF/Southall Rights (1981) *Southall – The Birth of a Black Community*. London: Institute of Race Relations.

Cashmore, E. and McLaughlin, E. (1991) *Out of Order? Policing Black People*. London: Routledge

Celona, L. and Neuman, W. (1999) 'NYPD to Bare "Stop and Frisk" Data', *New York Post*, 12 April: 19.

Chan, J. (1997) *Changing Police Culture: Policing in a Multicultural Society*. Cambridge: Cambridge University Press.

Cheney, D., Dickson, L., Fitzpatrick, J. and Uglow, S. (1999) *Criminal Justice and the Human Rights Act 1998*. Bristol: Jordans.

Chevigny, P. (1969) *Police Power*. Toronto: Vintage Books.

Chevigny, P. (1995) *Edge of the Knife: Police Violence in the Americas*. New York: New Press.

Choongh, S. (1997) *Policing as Social Discipline*. Oxford: Oxford University Press.

Christie, N. (1986) 'The Ideal Victim', in E. Fattah (ed.), *From Crime Policy to Victim Policy*. London: Macmillan: 1–17.

Christie, N. (1993) *Crime Control as Industry: Towards Gulags, Western Style?* London: Routledge.

Clark, A. (2001) *Burnley Task Force*. Burnley: Burnley Borough Council.

Clarke, J. and Newman, J. (1997) *The Managerial State: Power, Politics and Ideology in the Remaking of Social Welfare*. London: Sage.

Clarke, M. (1986) *Regulating the City: Competition, Scandal and Reform*. Milton Keynes: Open University Press.

Clarke, M. (1990) *Business Crime: Its Nature and Control*. Cambridge: Polity Press.

Clarke, R.V. (1977) 'Introduction', in R.V. Clarke (ed.), *Situational Crime Prevention Successful Case Studies*, 2nd edn. Guilderland, NY: Harrow & Heston.

Clarke, R.V. (1992) *Situational Crime Prevention; Successful Case Studies*, 3rd edn. Albany, NY: Harrow & Heston.

Clarke, R.V. (1999) *Hot Products: Understanding, Anticipating and Reducing Demand for Stolen Goods*, Police Research Series Paper 112, Policing and Reducing Crime Unit, Research Development and Statistics Directorate. London: Home Office.

Clayton, R. and Tomlinson, H. (2000) *The Law of Human Rights*. Oxford: Oxford University Press.

Clear, T. and Cordner, G. (1999) 'Does "Zero Tolerance" Really Reduce Crime? A Look at New York's Experience', *Community Corrections Report on Law and Corrections Practice*, 6(4): 53–4.

Cohen, L.E. and Felson, M. (1979) 'Social Inequality and Predatory Criminal Victimization: An Exposition and Test of a Formal Theory', *American Sociological Review*, 44: 588–608.

Cohen, P. (1979) *Policing the Working Class City'*, in B. Fine, R. Kinsey, J. Lea, S. Picciotto and J. Young (eds), *Capitalism and the Rule of Law*. London: Hutchinson.

Cohen, S. (1985) *Visions of Social Control*. Cambridge: Polity Press.

Coid, J., Kittler, Z., Healey, A. and Henderson, J. (2000a) *The Impact of Methadone Treatment on Drug Misuse and Crime*, Research Findings No. 120. London: Home Office.

Colb, S. (2000) *Deconstructing Diallo*. Findlaw: <http:// writ.corporate.findlaw.com.

Coleman, F.L. (1997) 'Stalking Behavior and the Cycle of Domestic Violence', *Journal of Interpersonal Violence*, 12(3): 420–32.

Colquhoun, P. (a Magistrate) (1796) A Treatise on the Police of the Metropolis; Containing a detail of the various crimes and Misdemeanours by which Public and Private Security are, at present, injured and endangered: and suggesting Remedies for their prevention, 3rd edn, Poultry. London: C. Dilly.

Cornwell, R. (2002) 'Shocked and Angry: The Prophet Whose Warnings Over Wall Street Were Ignored', *The Independent*, 1 July.

Couch, S.R. (1987) 'Selling and Reclaiming State Sovereignty: The Case of Coal and Iron Police', *The Insurgent Sociologist*, 4: 85–91.

Cracknell, S. (2000) 'Anti-Social Behaviour Orders', *Journal of Social Welfare and Family Law*, 22(1): 108–15.

Crawford, A. (1997) *The Local Governance of Crime*. Oxford: Oxford University Press.

Crawford, A. (1998) *Crime Prevention & Community Safety: Politics, Policies & Practices*. London: Longman.

Crawford, A., Jones, T., Woodhouse, T. and Young, J. (1990) *The Second Islington Crime Survey*. Middlesex: Middlesex Polytechnic Centre for Criminology.

Crime Prevention News (1998) 'Flagship Bill Unveiled', Jan.–Mar.

Critchley, T.A. (1978) *A History of Police in England and Wales*, 2nd edn. London: Constable.

Croall, H. (1992) *White Collar Crime*. Buckingham: Open University Press.

Croft, J. (1978) *Research in Criminal Justice*, Home Office Research Study No. 44. London: Home Office.

Crowther, C. (1998) 'Policing the Excluded Society', in R. Hopkins Burke (ed.), *Zero Tolerance Policing*. Leicester: Perpetuity Press.

Crowther, C. (2000a) *Policing Urban Poverty*. Basingstoke: Macmillan.

Crowther, C. (2000b) 'Thinking About the "Underclass": Towards a Political Economy of Policing', *Theoretical Criminology*, 4(2): 149–67.

Crowther, C. (2002) 'The Politics and Economics of Disciplining an Inclusive and Exclusive Society', in R. Sykes, C. Bochel and N. Ellison (eds), *Social Policy Review 14*. Bristol: Policy Press, pp. 199–224.

Cunneen, C. (1999) 'Zero-tolerance Policing and the Experience of New York City', *Current Issues in Criminal Justice*, 10(3): 299–313.

Cunningham, W.C., Strauchs, J. and Van Meter, C.W. (1990) *Private Security Trends 1970–2000*, Hallcrest Report II. Stoneham, MA: Butterworth-Heinemann.

Currie, E. (1997) *Confronting Crime: An American Challenge*. New York: Pantheon.

Davies, H. (1998) 'Why is Financial Regulation Necessary?' Speech by the Chairman of the Financial Services Authority Henry Thornton Lecture London

Davies, H., Nutley, S. and Smith, P. (eds) (2000) *What Works? Evidence-Based Policy and Practice in Public Services*. Bristol: Policy Press.

Davis, J.A. (ed) (2001) *Stalking Crimes and Victim Protection: Prevention, Intervention, Threat Assessment and Case Management*. New York: CRC Press.

Davis, M. (1990) *The City of Quartz: Evacuating the Future in Los Angeles*. London: Verso.

Dean, M. (1999) *Governmentality: Power and Rule in Modern Society*. London: Sage.

DeLillo, D. (1997) *Underworld*. New York: Scribner.

Denham, J. (2002) *Building Cohesive Communities: A Report of the Ministerial Group on Public Order and Community Cohesion*. London: Home Office.

Dennis, N. (ed.) (1997) *Zero Tolerance: Policing a Free Society*. London: Institute of Economic Affairs.

Dennis, N. and Mallon, R. (1997) 'Confident Policing in Hartlepool', in N. Dennis (ed.), *Zero Tolerance: Policing a Free Society*. London: Institute of Economic Affairs.

Department of Social Security (2001) *Households Below Average Income*. London: HMSO.

Desai, P. (1999) *Spaces of Identity, Cultures of Conflict: The Development of New British Asian Masculinities*. PhD thesis, Goldsmiths College, University of London.

Dickinson, D. (2002) 'Our Mission? To Support the Police', *Security Direct* 2002–2003: 2.

Dixon, B. and Smith, G. (1998) 'Laying Down the Law: the Police, the Courts and Legal Accountability', *International Journal of the Sociology of Law*, 26(4): 419–35.

Dixon, D. (1997) *Law in Policing: Legal Regulation and Police Practices*. Oxford: Clarendon Press.

Dixon, D. (1998) 'Broken Windows, Zero tolerance, and the New York Miracle', *Current Issues in Criminal Justice*, 10(1): 96–106.

Dixon, D. (1999) 'Reform, Regression and the Royal Commission into the NSW Police Service', in D. Dixon (ed.), *A Culture of Corruption: Changing an Australian Police Service*. Sydney: Hawkins Press.

Donzelot, J. (1980) *The Policing of Families: Welfare versus the State*. London: Hutchinson University Library.

Drakeford, M. (1993) 'The Probation Service, Breach and the Criminal Justice Act 1991', *Howard Journal of Criminal Justice*, 32(4): 291–303.

Draper, H. (1978) *Private Police*. Sussex: Harvester Press.

Dwyer, J. (1999) 'Stats Don't Justify Frisks', *New York Daily News*, 20 April, p. 10.

Editors, Baltimore Sun (2002) 'Collateral Damage', *Baltimore Sun*, 28 April, p. 28.

Edozien, F. (2002) 'Crime Fell a Stunning 62% During Rudy Years', *New York Post*, 1 January, p. 4.

Ekblom, P. (1997) 'Gearing up against Crime: A Dynamic Framework to Help Designers Keep Up With the Adaptive Criminal in a Changing World', *International Journal of Risk, Security and Crime Prevention*, 2(4): 249–65.

Ekblom, P. and Tilley, N. (2000) 'Going Equipped: Criminology, Situational Crime Prevention and the Resourceful Offender', *British Journal of Criminology*, 40(3): 375–98.

Elander, J., Rutter, M., Sminoff, E. and Pickles, A. (2000) 'Explanations for Apparent Late Onset Criminality in a High-Risk sample of Children Followed Up in Adult Life', *British Journal of Criminology*, 40(3): 497–509.

Elias, N. (1978) *The Civilising Process, Vol. 1: The History of Manners*. Oxford: Blackwell.

Elias, N. (1982) *The Civilising Process, Vol. 2: State-Formation and Civilisation*. Oxford: Blackwell.

Ellis, T. (2000) 'Enforcement Policy and Practice: Evidence-Based or Rhetoric-Based?', *Criminal Justice Matters*, 39 (Spring): 6–7.

Ellis, T., Hedderman, C. and Mortimer, E. (1996) *Enforcing Community Sentences: Supervisors' Perspectives on Ensuring Compliance and Dealing with Breach*, Home Office Research Study, No. 158. London: Home Office.

Emery, R. (1999) 'Op-ed: Dazzling Crime Statistics Come at a Price', *New York Times*, 20 February, p. 24.

Emmerson, B. and Ashworth, A. (2001) *Human Rights and Criminal Justice*. London: Sweet & Maxwell.

Emsley, C. (1996) *The English Police: A Political and Social History*. Harlow: Longman.

Emsley, C. (2001) 'The Origins and Development of the Police', in E. McLaughlin and J. Muncie (eds), *Controlling Crime*. London: Sage with the Open University.

Ericson, R. and Haggerty, K. (1997) *Policing the Risk Society*. Oxford: Oxford University Press.

Everson, S. and Pease, K. (2001) 'Crime Against the Same Person and Place: Detection Opportunity and Offender Targeting', in G. Farrell and K. Pease (eds), *Repeat Victimisation*, Crime Prevention Studies Volume 12. New York: Criminal Justice Press.

Ewald, F. (1991) 'Insurance and Risk', in G. Burchell, C. Gordon and P. Miller (eds), *The Foucault Effect: Studies in Governmentality*. London: Harvester Wheatsheaf, pp. 197–210.

Farnham, F.R., James, D.V. and Cantrell, P. (2000) 'Association between Violence, Psychosis, and Relationship to Victims in Stalkers', *Lancet*, 355: 199.

Farrell, G. (1995) 'Preventing Repeat Victimisation', in M. Tonry and D.P. Farrington (eds), *Building a Safer Society: Strategic Approaches to Crime Prevention*, Crime and Justice 19. Chicago: University of Chicago Press.

Farrell, G. and Bouloukos, A. (2001) 'International Overview: A Cross-National Comparison of Rates of Repeat Victimisation', in Farrell, G. and Pease, K. (eds), *Repeat Victimisation*, Crime Prevention Studies Volume 12. New York: Criminal Justice Press.

Farrell, G. and Pease, K. (2001) 'Why Repeat Victimisation Matters', in G. Farrell and K. Pease (eds), *Repeat Victimisation*, Crime Prevention Studies Volume 12. New York: Criminal Justice Press, pp. 1–4.

Farrell, G., Chenery, S. and Pease, K. (2000) *Consolidating Police Crackdowns: Findings from an Anti-Burglary Project*, Police Research Series Paper 113. London: Home Office.

Farrall, S. (2002) 'Long-Term Absences from Probation: Officers' and Probationers' Accounts', *Howard Journal of Criminal Justice*, 41(3): 263–78.

Farrington, D.P. (1997) 'Human Development and Criminal Careers', in M. Maguire, R. Morgan and R. Reiner (eds), *Oxford Handbook of Criminology*, 2nd edn. Oxford: Clarendon Press, pp. 361–408.

Faulkner, D. (2000) 'Policy and Practice in Modern Britain: Influences, Outcomes and Civil Society', in P. Green and A. Rutherford (eds), *Criminal Policy in Transition*. Oxford: Hart.

Feeley, M. and Simon, J. (1994) 'Actuarial Justice: The Emerging New Criminal Law', in D. Nelken (ed.), *The Futures of Criminology*. London: Sage.

Felson, M. (1998) *Crime and Everyday Life*, 2nd edn. Thousand Oaks, CA: Pine Forge Press/Sage.

Felson, M. (2002) *Crime and Everyday Life*, 3rd edn. Thousand Oaks, CA: Pine Forge Press/Sage.

Felson, M. and Clarke, R.V. (1997) 'The Ethics of Situational Crime Prevention', in G. Newman, R.V. Clarke and S. Gloria Shoham (eds), *Rational Choice and Situational Crime Prevention*. Aldershot: Dartmouth.

Ferguson, G. and Wadham, J. (2003) 'Privacy and Surveillance: A Review of the Regulation of Investigatory Powers Act 2000', *European Human Rights Law Review*, Privacy. London: Sweet & Maxwell.

Field, S. (1990) *Trends in Crime and Their Interpretation: A Study of Recorded Crime in Post-War England and Wales*, Home Office Research Study 119. London: Home Office.

Fielding, N. (1988) *Joining Forces*. London: Routledge.

Financial Services Authority (2001/02) *Annual Report*, http://www.fsa.gov.uk/pubs/annual/ar01-02/.

Financial Services Authority (2002) http://www.fsa.gov.uk/consumer-education/.

Finch, E. (2001) *The Criminalisation of Stalking: Constructing the Problem and Evaluating the Solution*. London: Cavendish.

Fine, B. and Millar, R. (eds) (1985) *Policing the Miners Strike*. London: Lawrence & Wishart.

Fionda, J. (1999) 'New Labour, Old Hat: Youth Justice and the Crime and Disorder Act 1998', *Criminal Law Review*: 36–47.

Fionda, J. (2000) 'New Managerialism, Credibility and the Sanitisation of Criminal Justice', in P. Green and A. Rutherford (eds), *Criminal Policy in Transition*. Oxford: Hart, pp. 109–27.

Fisher, B.S., Cullen, F.T. and Turner, M.G. (2002) 'Being Pursued: Stalking Victimization in a National Study of College Women, *Criminology and Public Policy*, 1(2): 257–308.

Fitzgerald, M. (2001) 'Ethnic Minorities and Community Safety', in R. Matthews and J. Pitts (eds), *Crime, Disorder and Community Safety*. New York: Routledge.

FitzGerald, M. and Hale, C. (1996) *Ethnic Minorities: Victimisation and Racial Harassment: Findings from the 1988 and 1992 British Crime Surveys*, Home Office Research Study 154. London: Home Office.

FitzGerald, M. and Sibbitt, R. (1997) *Ethnic Monitoring in Police Forces: A Beginning*, Home Office Research Study 173. London: Home Office.

Fletcher, D. (2002) 'Going Private? It's Plain Common Sense', *Security Direct 2002–2003*: 65.

Flynn, K. (2000a) 'Shooting Raises Scrutiny of Police Antidrug Tactics', *New York Times*, 25 March, p. 1/4.

Flynn, K. (2000b) 'Police Feel Scorn on Beat and Pressure From Above', *New York Times*, 26 December, p. 1/6.

Flynn, K. (2001) 'After Criticism of Street Frisk Records, Police Expand Report Form', *New York Times*, 5 January, p. 6.

Flynn, K. (2002) 'City's Deficit Forces Police to Study Cuts in Overtime', *New York Times*, 15 March, p. 1/4.

Forrester, D., Frenz, S., O'Connell, M. and Pease, K. (1988) *The Kirkholt Burglary Prevention Project, Rochdale*, Crime Prevention Unit Paper 13. London: Home Office.

Foucault, M. (1971) *Madness and Civilisation: A History of Insanity in the Age of Reason*. London: Tavistock.

Foucault, M. (1976) *The History of Sexuality*. London: Allen Lane.

Foucault, M. (1977) *Discipline and Punish – the Birth of the Prison*. London: Allen Lane.

Foucault, M. (1980) *Power/Knowledge: Selected Interviews and Other Writings 1972–77*, ed. C. Gordon. Brighton: Harvester Press.

Foundation 2000 (1995) *Bradford Riots*. Bradford.

Garland, D. (1989) 'Critical Reflections on "Punishment, Custody and the Community"', in H. Rees and H. Williams (eds), *Punishment, Custody and the Community: Reflections and Comments on the Green Paper*, papers presented at the Second International Criminal Justice Seminar April 1989 at the London School of Economics.

Garland, D. (1994) 'Of Crimes and Criminals: The Development of Criminology in Britain', in M. Maguire, R. Morgan and R. Reiner (eds), *The Oxford Handbook of Criminology*. Oxford: Clarendon Press, pp. 17–68.

Garland, D. (2001) *The Culture of Control: Crime and Social Order in Contemporary Society*. Oxford: Oxford University Press.

Gaskell, G. and Smith, P. (1985), 'Young Blacks' Hostility to the Police: An Investigation into its Causes', *New Community*, 12(1): 66–74.

Gatrell, V. (1980) 'The Decline of Theft and Violence in Victorian and Edwardian England', in V. Gatrell, B. Lenman and G. Parker (eds), *Crime and the Law: The Social History of Crime in Europe Since 1500*. London: Europa.

Giddens, A. (1990) *The Consequences of Modernity*. Oxford: Polity Press.

Giddens, A. (1998) *The Third Way: The Renewal of Social Democracy*. Oxford: Polity Press.

Giddens, A. (2001) *The Third Way and Its Critics*. Oxford: Polity Press.

Gill, M. and Hart, J. (1997) 'Exploring Investigative Policing', *British Journal of Criminology*, 37: 549–67.

Gilroy, P. and Sim, J. (1987) 'Law, Order and the State of the Left', in P. Scraton (ed.), *Law, Order and the Authoritarian State: Readings in Critical Criminology*. Buckingham: Open University Press, pp. 71–106.

Giuliani, R. (1997) 'How New York is Becoming the Safest Big City in America', *USA Today Magazine*, 125(2620): 28–32.

Giuliani, R. (2001) 'Farewell Address', *Federal News Service*, 27 December.

Glaberson, W. (2003) 'Suit Accuses Police in Brooklyn of Strip Searches in Minor Cases', *New York Times*, 30 October, p. 2/3.

Goldstein, H. (1990) *Problem-Oriented Policing*. New York: McGraw-Hill.

Goldthorpe, J.H. (1989–9) *The Affluent Worker in The Class Structure*, 3 vols. Cambridge: Cambridge University Press.

Gondolf, G.W. (1985) 'Anger and Oppression in Men who Batter: Empiricist and Feminist Perspectives and their Implications for Research, *International Journal of Victimology*, 10.

Goode, M. (1995) 'Stalking: Crime of the Nineties?' *Criminal Law Journal*, 19 (Winter): 21–31.

Gootman, E. (2000) 'A Police Dept's Growing Allure: Crime Fighters from Around World Visit for Tips', *New York Times*, 24 October, p. 1/10.

Gordon, P. (1983) *White Law*. London: Pluto Press.

Gowland, D. (1990) *The Regulation of Financial Markets in the 1990's*. Aldershot: Edward Elgar.

Graef, R. (1989) *Talking Blues: The Police in Their Own Words*. London: Collins Harvill.

Graham, J. and Bowling, B. (1995) *Young People and Crime*. London: Home Office.

Gramsci, A. (1977, 1978) *Selections from the Political Writings*. London: Lawrence & Wishart.

Greater Manchester Police (2000) *Racist Incidents Monitoring Report 1999–2000*. Manchester: Greater Manchester Police.

Greene, J. (1999) 'Zero Tolerance: A Case Study of Police Policies and Practices in New York City', *Crime and Delinquency*, 45(2): 171–87.

Gross, J. (2001) 'Looking for a Line the Police Shouldn't Cross', *New York Times*, 2 January, p. 32.

Hall, C. (2002) *Civilising Subjects: Metropole and Colony in the English Imagination 1830–1867*. Cambridge: Polity Press.

Hall, J. (1952) *Theft, Law and Society*, 2nd edn. Indianapolis, IN: Bobbs-Merrill.

Hall, S., Critcher, C., Jefferson, T., Clarke, J. and Roberts, B. (1978) *Policing in Crisis: Mugging the State and Law and Order*. London: Macmillan.

Hanmer, J. and Griffiths, S. (2000) *Reducing Domestic Violence ...What Works? Policing Domestic Violence*. London: Home Office (Policing and Reducing Crime).

Harris, J. (2000) *An Evaluation of the Uses and Effectiveness of the Protection from Harassment Act 1997*. London: Home Office.

Hart, J. (1978) 'Police', in W. Cornish (ed.), *Crime and Law*. Dublin: Irish University Press.

Hartless, J.M., Ditton, J., Nair, G. and Phillips, S. (1995) 'More Sinned Against than Sinning: A Study of Young Teenagers' Experience of Crime', *British Journal of Criminology*, 35(1): 114–33.

Haxby, D. (1978) *Probation: A Changing Service*. London: Constable.

Hay, C. (1999) *The Political Economy of New Labour: Labouring Under False Pretences?* Manchester: Manchester University Press.

Hebenton, B. and Thomas, T. (1996) 'Sexual Offenders in the Community: Reflections on Problems of Law, Community and Risk Management in the USA, England and Wales', *International Journal of the Sociology of Law*, 24: 427–43.

Hedderman, C. (1999) *The ACOP Enforcement Audit – Stage One*. London: Association of Chief Officers of Probation.

Hedderman, C. and Hearnden, J. (2000) *Improving Enforcement – The Second ACOP Audit*. London: Association of Chief Officers of Probation.

Hedderman, C. and Hearnden, J. (2001) *Setting New Standards for Enforcement – The Third ACOP Audit*. London: Association of Chief Officers of Probation.

Henry, S. (1976) 'Fencing with Accounts: The Language of Moral Bridging', *British Journal of Law and Society*, 3: 91–100.

Hill, C. (1996) *Liberty Against the Law*. London: Penguin.

HMIC (1999) *Keeping the Peace: Policing Disorder*. London: HMSO.

Hogg, C. (2002) 'Examining the Mental Health Bill', BBC News, http://news.bbc.co.uk/1/hi/health/2191648.stm.

Holdaway, S. (1983) *Inside the British Police: A Force at Work*. Oxford: Blackwell.

Holland, B. (2001) *Oldham: Context and Challenges*. Submission to the Oldham Independent Review.

Home Affairs Committee (1995) *The Private Security Industry*, Vols I and II, HC 17 I and II. London: HMSO.

Home Office (1936) *Report of the Departmental Committee on the Social Services in the Courts of Summary Jurisdiction*, Cmnd. 5122. London: HMSO.

Home Office (1962) *Report of the Departmental Committee on the Probation Service*, Cmnd. 1650. London: HMSO.

Home Office (1977) *A Review of Criminal Justice Policy 1976*. London: HMSO.

Home Office (1984) *Probation Service in England and Wales: Statement of National Objectives and Priorities*. London: HMSO.

Home Office (1988) *Punishment, Custody and the Community*, Cmnd. 424. London: HMSO.

Home Office (1990a) *Supervision and Punishment in the Community: A Framework for Action*, Cmnd. 966. London: HMSO.

Home Office (1990b) *Crime, Justice and Protecting the Public*, Cmnd. 965. London: HMSO.

Home Office (1991a) *Organising Supervision and Punishment in the Community: A Decision Document*. London: HMSO.

Home Office (1991b) *Safer Communities: The Local Delivery of Crime Prevention Through the Partnership Approach* (Morgan Report). London: Home Office.

Home Office (1992) *National Standards for the Supervision of Offenders in the Community*. London: Home Office.

Home Office (1993) *Monitoring of the Criminal Justice Act 1991: Data from a Special Data Collection Exercise*, Home Office Statistical Bulletin 25/93. London: Home Office.

Home Office (1995a) *Strengthening Punishment in the Community: A Consultation Document*, Cmnd. 2780. London: HMSO.

Home Office (1995b) *National Standards for the Supervision of Offenders in the Community*. London: Home Office.

Home Office (1996) *Protecting the Public*, Cmnd. 3190. London: HMSO.

Home Office (1997a) *Select Committee on Home Affairs Third Report*, http://www.parliament.thestationaryoffice.co.uk//pa/cm199798/cmselect/cmhaff/486/486ap38htm.

Home Office (1997b) *Community Safety Order: A Consultation Paper*. London: Home Office.

Home Office (1998a) *Crime and Disorder Act 1998*. London: Home Office.

Home Office (1998b) *The 1998 British Crime Survey*. London: Home Office.

Home Office (1998c) *The Crime and Disorder Act: Community Safety and the Reduction and Prevention of Crime – A Conceptual Framework for Training and the Development of a Professional Discipline*. London: Home Office.

Home Office (2000a) *Crime Reduction Toolkits: Anti-Social Behaviour*, http//www.crimereduction.gov.uk/toolkits.

Home Office (2000b) *Social Exclusion Unit: National Strategy For Neighbourhood Renewal – Report of Policy Action Team 8: Anti-Social Behaviour*, http://www.cabinet-office.gov.uk/seu/2000/pat8.

Home Office (2000c) *Prison Statistics England and Wales 1999*, Cm 4805. London: Home Office.

Home Office (2000d) *Statistics on Race and the Criminal Justice System 2000*. London: Home Office.

Home Office (2000e) *A Guide to the Criminal Justice System in England and Wales*. London: Home Office.

Home Office (2000f) *National Standards for the Supervision of Offenders in the Community*. London: Home Office.

Home Office (2001a) *Stephen Lawrence Inquiry, Home Secretary's 2nd Annual Report on Progress*. London: Home Office.

Home Office (2001b) *Policing a New Century: A Blueprint for Reform*, Cm 5326. London: HMSO.

Home Office (2001c) *Probation Statistics England and Wales 1999*. London: Home Office.

Home Office (2002a) *Stop and Search Statistics 2001/2002*. London: Home Office.

Home Office (2002b) *Race and the Criminal Justice System 2000/2001*. London: Home Office.

Home Office (2002c) *Tackling Discrimination in the Criminal Justice System*, Press Release 292/2002.

Home Office (2002d) *When the Carrot Meets the Stick*, http://www.crimereduction.gov.uk/workingoffenders27.htm

Home Office (2002e) *The National Policing Plan 2003–2006*. London: HMSO.

Home Office (2002f) *Probation Statistics England and Wales 2000*. London: Home Office.

Home Office (2003) *Crime in England and Wales Quarterly Update to June 2003*, Crime Statistical Bulletin 13/03. London: Home Office.

Homel, R. (1995) 'Can Police Prevent Crime?', in K. Bryett and C. Lewis (eds), *Contemporary Policing: Unpeeling Tradition*. Sydney: Macmillan.

Hope, T. (2001) 'Crime Victimisation and Inequality in Risk Society', in R. Matthews and J. Pitts (eds), *Crime, Disorder and Community Safety*. New York: Routledge.

Hopkins Burke, R. (ed.) (1998a) *Zero Tolerance Policing*. Leicester: Perpetuity Press.

Hopkins Burke, R. (1998b) 'A Contextualisation of Zero Tolerance Policing Strategies', in R. Hopkins Burke (ed.), *Zero Tolerance Policing*. Leicester: Perpetuity Press.

Hopkins Burke, R. (1998c) 'Begging, Vagrancy and Disorder', in R. Hopkins Burke (ed.), *Zero Tolerance Policing*. Leicester: Perpetuity Press.

Hopkins Burke, R. (1999a) 'Tolerance or Intolerance: The Policing of Begging in Contemporary Society', in H. Dean (ed.), *Begging and Street Level Economic Activity*. Bristol: Social Policy Press.

Hopkins Burke, R. (1999b) 'The Socio-Political Context of Zero Tolerance Policing Strategies', *Policing: An International Journal of Police Strategies & Management*, 21(4): 666–682.

Hopkins Burke, R. (1999c) *Young Offending and the Fragmentation of Modernity: Models of Youth Justice*. Leicester: Scarman Centre.

Hopkins Burke, R. (2000) 'The Regulation of Begging and Vagrancy: A Critical Discussion', *Crime Prevention and Community Safety: An International Journal*, 2(2): 43–52.

Hopkins Burke, R. (2001) *An Introduction to Criminological Theory*. Cullompton: Willan Publishing.

Hopkins Burke, R. (2002) 'Zero Tolerance Policing: New Authoritarianism or New Liberalism?' *Nottingham Law Journal*, 11(1): 20–35.

Hough, M. (1995) *Anxiety About Crime: Findings from the 1994 British Crime Survey*, Home Office Research Study No 147. London: HMSO.

Huggins, M.K. (2000) 'Urban Violence and Police Privatisation in Brazil: Blended Invisibility', *Social Justice*, 27: 113–34.

Hughes, G. (2002) 'The Shifting Sands of Crime Prevention and Community Safety', in G. Hughes, E. McLaughlin and J. Muncie (eds), *Crime Prevention and Community Safety: New Directions*. London: Sage, pp. 1–10.

Human Rights Watch (1998) *Shielded from Justice: Police Brutality and Accountability in the United States*. New York: Human Rights Watch.

Hunt Saboteurs Association (1994) *Public Order, Private Armies*. Nottingham: Hunt Saboteurs Association.

Hutton, W. (1996) *The State We're In: Revised Edition*. London: Vintage.

Independent Black Collective (1986) *Bradford Black*, July/August.

Initial Security (undated) *Security Officers Handbook*. Initial Security.

Innenministerium des Landes Nordrhein-Westfalen (1998). *Sicherheit in Städten und Gemeinden* (Safety in Towns and Communities). Neuss: Fortbildungsinstitut.

Innenministerium des Landes Nordrhein-Westfalen (1999) *Mehr Sicherheit in Städten und Gemeinden* (Further Safety in Towns and Communities). Köln: Otto-Häuser-KG.

Innes, M. (1999) 'An Iron Fist in an Iron Glove? The Zero Tolerance Policing Debate', *The Howard Journal*, 38(4): 397–410.

Jacobson, M. (2001) 'Trends in Criminal Justice Spending, Employment, and Workloads in New York City Since the Late 1970s', in A. Karmen (ed.), *Crime and Justice in New York City*, Vol. 2. Mason, OH: Thomson Learning Custom Publishing.

James, L. (1997) *Raj: The Making of British India*. London: Abacus.

Jefferson, T. and Grimshaw, R. (1984) *Controlling the Constable*. London: Muller.

Jefferson, T. and Walker, M.A. (1992) 'Ethnic Minorities in the Criminal Justice System', in B. Hudson (ed.), *Race, Crime and Justice*. Aldershot: Ashgate.

Jessop, B. (2000) 'From the KWNS to the SWPR', in G. Lewis, S. Gerwitz and J. Clarke (eds), *Rethinking Social Policy*. London: Sage, pp. 171–84.

Jessop, B. and Stones, R. (1992) 'Old City and New Times: Economic and

Political Aspects of Deregulation', in L. Budd and S. Ehimster (eds), *Global Finance and Urban Living: A Study of Metropolitan Change*. London: Routledge, pp. 171–94.

Johnson, L., MacDonald, R., Mason, P., Ridley, L. and Webster, C. (2000) *Snakes and Ladders: Young People, Transitions and Social Exclusion*. Bristol: Policy Press.

Johnson, L. and Shearing, C. (2003) *Governing Security*. London and New York: Routledge.

Johnston, L. (2000) *Policing Britain: Risk, Security and Governance*. London: Longman.

Jones, T. (1993) *Britain's Ethnic Minorities*. London: Policy Studies Institute.

Jones, T. and Newburn, T. (1997) *Policing After the Act*. London: Policy Studies Institute.

Jones, T. and Newburn, T. (1998) *Private Security and Public Policing*. Oxford: Clarendon Press.

Jones, T., Maclean, B. and Young, J. (1986) *The Islington Crime Survey: Crime, Victimisation and Policing in Inner-City London*. Aldershot: Gower.

Jordan, P. (1998) 'Effective Policing Strategies for Reducing Crime', in P. Goldblatt and C. Lewis (eds), *Reducing Offending: an Assessment of Research Evidence on Ways of Dealing With Offending Behaviour*, Home Office Research Study 187. London: Home Office, pp. 63–81.

Jordan, T. (1995) 'The Efficacy of Californian Stalking Law: Surveying its Evolution, Extracting Insights from Domestic Violence', *Hastings Women's Law Journal*, 6(2): 362–83.

Kakalik, J. and Wildhorn, S. (1971a) *Private Police in the United States, Findings and Recommendations*, Vol. 1. Washington, DC: Government Printing Office.

Kakalik, J. and Wildhorn, S. (1971b) *The Private Police Industry: Its Nature and Extent*, Vol. 2. Washington, DC: Government Printing Office.

Kakalik, J. and Wildhorn, S. (1971c) *Current Regulation of Private Police: Regulatory Agency Experience and Views*, Vol. 3. Washington, DC: Government Printing Office.

Kakalik, J. and Wildhorn, S. (1971d) *The Law and Private Police*, Vol. 4. Washington, DC: Government Printing Office.

Kakalik, J. and Wildhorn, S. (1971e) *Special Purpose Public Police*, Vol. 5. Washington, DC: Government Printing Office.

Kalunta-Crumpton, A. (1999) *Race and Drug Trials: The Social Construction of Guilt and Innocence*. Aldershot: Ashgate.

Kant, M. and Pütter, N. (1998). 'Sicherheit und Ordnung in den Städten' ('Urban Safety and Order'), in *Bürgerrechte & Polizei/CILIP 57 (2/97)*, www.cilip.de/ausgabe/57/krimi.htm.

Karmen, A. (2000) *New York Murder Mystery: The True Story Behind the Crime Crash of the 1990s*. New York: NYU Press.

Keith, M. (1993) *Race, Riots and Policing*. London: UCL Press.

Keith, M. (1995a) 'Making the Street Visible: Placing Racial Violence in Context', *New Community*, 21(4): 551–65.

Keith, M. (1995b) 'Shouts of the Street: Identity and the Spaces of Authenticity', *Social Identities*, 1(2): 297–315.

Keith-Lucas, B. (1960) 'The Independence of Chief Constables', *Public Administration*, 38(3): 2–15.

Kelling, G.L. (2002) 'A Policing Strategy New Yorkers Like', *New York Times*, 3 January, p. 23.

Kelling G.L. and Coles C.M. (1996) *Fixing Broken Windows*. New York: Free Press.

Kelly, L. (1999) *Domestic Violence Matters: An Evaluation of a Development Project*. London: Home Office.

Kennedy, D. (1997) 'Pulling Levers: Chronic Offenders, High Crime Settings, and a Theory of Prevention', *Valparaiso University Law Review*, 31(2): 449–84.

Kershaw, C., Chivitie-Matthews, N., Thomas, C. and Aust, R. (2001) *The 2001 British Crime Survey*, Home Office Statistical Bulletin, 18/01. London: Home Office.

Kershaw, C., Budd, T., Kinshott, G., Mattinson, J., Mayhew, P. and Myhill, A. (2000) *The 2000 British Crime Survey*. London: Home Office.

Kienlen, K. (1998) 'Developmental and Social Antecedents of Stalking', in J. Reid Meloy (ed.), *The Psychology of Stalking*. London: Academic Press.

King, M. (1981) *The Framework of Criminal Justice*. London: Croom Helm.

Kleiman, M. (1988) 'Crackdowns: The Effects of Intensive Enforcement on Retail Heroin Dealing', in M. Chaiken (ed.), *Street-Level Law Enforcement: Examining the Issues*. Washington, DC: National Institute of Justice.

Klockars, C. (1974) *The Professional Fence*. New York: Free Press.

Klug, F., Starmer K. and Weir S. (1996) *The Three Pillars of Liberty: Political Rights and Freedoms in the United Kingdom*. London: Routledge.

Knapp Commission (1972) *The Knapp Commission Report on Police Corruption*. New York: George Braziller.

Knights, B. (1998) '"The Slide to Ashes": An Antidote to Zero Tolerance', in R. Hopkins Burke (ed.), *Zero Tolerance Policing*. Leicester: Perpetuity Press.

Knutsson, J. (1984) *Operation Identification: A Way to Prevent Burglaries?*, Report No. 14. Stockholm: National Council for Crime Prevention, Research Division.

Kocieniewski, D. (1999) 'Success of Elite Police Unit Exacts a Toll on the Streets', *New York Times*, 15 February, p. 1/5.

Krauss, K. (1995) 'The Commissioner vs. The Criminologists', *New York Times*, 19 November, p. 43.

Kropp, P.R., Hart, S., Lyon, D. and LePard, D. (2002) 'Managing Stalkers: Coordinating Treatment and Supervision', in J. Boon and L. Sheridan (eds), *Stalking and Psychosexual Obsession*. London: Wiley.

Kurt, J.L. (1995) 'Stalking as Variant of Domestic Violence', *Bulletin of the Academy of Psychiatry and the Law*, 23(2): 219–31.

Labour Party (1997) *Labour Party Manifesto*. London: Labour Party.

Landau, S.F. and Nathan, G. (1983) 'Selecting Delinquents for Cautioning in the London Metropolitan Area', *British Journal of Criminology*, 23(2): 128–49.

Langworthy, R. and Lebau, I. (1992) 'The Spatial Evolution of Sting Clientele', *Journal of Criminal Justice*, 20(2), 135–45.

Lea, J. (2002) *Crime & Modernity*. London: Sage.

Lea, J. and Young, J. (1984) *What Is to be Done about Law and Order?* Harmondsworth: Penguin.

Lefkowitz, M. (2001) 'Kerik Orders Community Meetings', *Newsday*, 16 January, p. 8.

Leigh, A., Read, T. and Tilley, N. (1996) *Problem-Oriented Policing: Brit Pop*, Crime Detection and Prevention Series Paper 75. London: Home Office.

Leigh, A., Read, T. and Tilley, N. (1998) *Brit Pop II: Problem-Oriented Policing in Practice*, Police Research Series Paper 93. London: Home Office.

Leigh-Pemberton, R. (1992) 'Man Bites Watchdog', *Bank of England Quarterly Bulletin*, 32 (May): 210–13.

LeMesurier, L. (1935) *A Handbook of Probation*. London: National Association of Probation Officers.

Levi, M. and Pithouse, A. (1992) 'The Victims of Fraud', in D. Downes (ed.), *Unravelling Criminal Justice*. London: Macmillan Press, pp. 229–46.

Levitas, R. (1998) *The Inclusive Society? Social Exclusion and New Labour*. Basingstoke: Macmillan.

Liberty (1995) 'Memorandum of Evidence', in House of Commons Home Affairs Committee, 'The Private Security Industry', Volume II. London: HMSO.

Liberty (2002) *Extension of Power under Regulation of Investigatory Powers Act 2000 – the RIP (Communications Data: Additional Public Authorities) Order 2002 – Liberty Response*. London: Liberty.

Liberty (2003) *Criminal Justice: Double Jeopardy*, http://www.liberty-human-rights.org.uk/issues/criminal-justice-double-jeopardy.shtml.

Livingstone, K. (2000) *Manifesto for London*, www.london.gov.uk.

Lloyd, C. (1986) *Response to SNOP*. Cambridge: Institute of Criminology.

Loader, I. (1996) *Youth, Policing and Democracy*. London: Macmillan.

Lombardi, F. and Weir, F. (2001) 'Cops Like New Rules on Frisks', *New York Daily News*, 2 January, p. 8.

Loveday, B. (1998) 'The Impact of Performance Culture on Criminal Justice Agencies in England and Wales', *International Journal of Sociology of Law*, 27(4): 351–77

Loveday, B. and Read, A. (2003) *Going Local: Who Should Run Britain's Police?* London: Policy Exchange.

Lueck, T. (2001) 'City Council Speaker to Seek Legislation Requiring More Accountability by the Police', *New York Times*, 16 January, p. 5.

Lustgarten, L. (1986) *The Governance of the Police*. London: Sweet & Maxwell.

Lyotard, J.-F. (1984) *The Postmodern Condition: A Report on Knowledge*. Manchester: Manchester University Press.

McAnaney, K.G., Curliss, L.A. and Abeyta-Price, C.E. (1993) 'From Impudence to Crime: Anti-stalking Laws', *Notre Dame Law Review*, 68: 174–184.

Macauley, S. (1986) 'Private Government', in L. Lipson and S. Wheeler (eds), *Law and the Social Sciences*. New York: Russell Sage Foundation.

McBarnet, D.J. (1981) *Conviction*. London: Macmillan.

McConville, M., Sanders, A. and Leng, R. (1991) *The Case for the Prosecution*. London: Routledge.

MacDonald, R. (ed.) (1997) *Youth, the 'Underclass' and Social Exclusion*. London: Routledge.

MacFarquhar, N. (1999) 'Police Get Good Ratings from Most, But Not All, New Yorkers', *New York Times*, 3 June, p. 3.

McLaughlin, E. (2001) 'Key Issues in Policework', in E. McLaughlin and J. Muncie (eds), *Controlling Crime*. London: Sage in Association with the Open University.

McLaughlin, E. and Murji, K. (2001) 'Lost Connections and New Directions: Neo-liberalism, New Public Management and the "Modernization" of the British Police', in K. Stenson and R.A. Sullivan (eds), *Crime, Risk and Justice: the Politics of Crime Control in Liberal Democracies*. Cullompton: Willan Publishing, pp. 104–22.

McPhee, M. (2002) 'They're Menace to Quality of Life', *New York Daily News*, 8 July, pp. 4–5.

Macpherson, W. (1999) *The Stephen Lawrence Inquiry: Report of an Inquiry by Sir William Macpherson of Cluny*, Cm 4262. London: HMSO.

McQuillan, A. (1997) 'Mayor, Bratton Agree: No Like', *New York Daily News*, 2 September, p. 16.

MacVean, A. (2001) 'Risk, Policing and the Management of Sex Offenders', *Crime Prevention and Community Safety: An International Journal*, 4(2): 7–18.

McWilliams, W. (1981) 'The Probation Officer at Court: From Friend to Acquaintance', *The Howard Journal*, 20: 97–116.

McWilliams, W. (1985) 'The Mission Transformed – Professionalisation of Probation Between the Wars', *Howard Journal*, 24: 257–74.

McWilliams, W. (1986) 'The English Probation System and the Diagnostic Ideal', *Howard Journal*, 25: 241–60.

McWilliams, W. (1987) 'Probation, Pragmatism and Policy', *Howard Journal*, 26: 97–121.

McWilliams, W. and Pease, K. (1990) 'Probation Practice and an End to Punishment', *The Howard Journal of Criminal Justice*, 29(1): 14–24.

Mahoney, M.R. (1991) 'Legal Images of Battered Women: Redefining the Issue of Separation', *Michigan Law Review*, 90: 1–94.

Mair, G. (1997) 'Community Penalties and the Probation Service', in M. Maguire, R. Morgan and R. Reiner (eds), *The Oxford Handbook of Criminology*, 2nd edn. Oxford: Clarendon Press.

Maple, J. (1999) *The Crime Fighter: Putting the Bad Guys Out of Business*. New York: Doubleday.

Mark, R. (1978) *In the Office of Constable*. London: Collins.

Marshall, G. (1965) *Police and Government*. London: Methuen.

Marshall, G. (1978) 'Police Accountability Revisited', in D. Butler and A.H. Halsey (eds), *Policy and Politics*. Macmillan: London.

Martin, D. (1996) *Battered Wives*, 3rd edn. London: Pocket Books.

Martin, D. (2003) 'The Politics of Policing, Managerialism, Modernisation and Performance', in R. Matthews and J. Young (eds), *The New Politics of Crime and Punishment*. Cullompton: Willan Publishing.

Marzulli, J. and Cauvin, H. (1999) 'Nice NYPD On Way', *New York Daily News*, 7 April, p. 4.

Matthews, R. and Young, J. (eds) (1986) *Confronting Crime*. London: Sage.

Matza, D.M. (1964) *Delinquency and Drift*. New York: Wiley.

Mawby, B.I. and Batta, I.D. (1980) *Asians and Crime: The Bradford Experience*. Middlesex: Scope Communication.

Maxey, W. (2001) 'Stalking the Stalker: Law Enforcement Investigation and Intervention', in J.A. Davis (ed.), *Stalking Crimes and Victim Protection: Prevention, Intervention, Threat Assessment and Case Management*. New York: CRC Press.

May, T. (1991) *Probation: Politics, Policy and Practice*. Milton Keynes: Open University Press.

May, T., Edmunds, M., Hough, M. with the assistance of Claire Harvey (1999) *Street Business: The Links Between Sex and Drugs Markets*, Police Research Series Paper 118. London: Home Office, Policing and Reducing Crime Unit.

May, T., Harocopos, A., Turnbull, P. and Hough, M. (2000) *Serving Up: The Impact of Low-Level Police Enforcement on Drug Markets*, Police Research Series Paper 133. London: Home Office.

Mayhew, P., Aye Maung, N. and Mirless-Black, C. (1993) *The 1992 British Crime Survey*, Home Office Research Study 132. London: Home Office.

Mayhew, P., Elliot, D. and Dowds, L. (1989) *The 1988 British Crime Survey*, Home Office Research Study 111. London: Home Office.

Mechanic, M.B., Weaver, T.L. and Resick, P.A. (2000) 'Intimate Partner Violence and Stalking Behavior: Exploration of Patterns and Correlates in a Sample of Acutely Battered Women', *Violence and Victims*, 15(1): 55–72.

Meloy, J.R. (1998) *The Psychology of Stalking*. London: Academic Press.

Meloy, J.R. (1999) 'Stalking: An Old Behaviour, A New Crime', *Psychiatric Clinics of North America*, 22(1): 85–99.

Meloy, J.R. (2002) 'Stalking and Violence', in J. Boon and L. Sheridan (eds), *Stalking and Psychosexual Obsession*. London: Wiley.

Meyer, J. (1998) 'Cultural Factors in Erotomania and Obsessional Following', in J. Reid Meloy (ed.), *The Psychology of Stalking*. London: Academic Press.

Miers, D. (2001). *An International Review of Restorative Justice*, Crime Reduction Series Paper 10. London: Home Office.

Miles, R. and Brown, M. (2003) *Racism*. London: Routledge.

Miller, D. (2001) 'Poking Holes in the Theory of "Broken Windows"', *Chronicle of Higher Education*, 157(22): 14–16.

Miller, N. (2001) 'Stalking Investigation, Law, Public Policy, and Criminal

Prosecution as a Problem Solver', in J.A. Davis (ed.), *Stalking Crimes and Victim Protection: Prevention, Intervention, Threat Assessment and Case Management*. New York: CRC Press.

Miller, W. (1999) *Cops and Bobbies,* 2nd edn. Columbus, OH: Ohio State University Press.

Mirlees-Black, C., Mayhew, P. and Percy, A. (1998) *The 1998 British Crime Survey*. London: Home Office, Research and Statistics Directorate.

Modood, T. (1992) *Not Easy Being British*. Stoke-on-Trent: Trentham Books.

Modood, T. and Berthoud, R. with the assistance of Lakey, J., Nazroo, J., Smith, J., Virdee, S. and Beistion, S. (1997) *Ethnic Minorities in Britain: Diversity and Disadvantage*. London: Policy Studies Institute.

Mollen Commission (1994) *Report of the Commission to Investigate Allegations of Police Corruption and the Anti-Corruption Procedures of the Police Department.* City of New York: Mollen Commission.

Molotsky, I. (1988) 'Capital's Homicide is at a Record', *New York Times*, 30 October, Eastern edn.

Moore, E. and Mills, M. (1990) 'The Neglected Victims and Unexamined Costs of White-Collar Crime', *Crime & Delinquency*, 36(3): 408–18.

Morgan, R. (1997) 'Swept Along by Zero Option', *The Guardian*, 22 January.

Morgan, R. and Newburn, T. (1997) *The Future of Policing*. Oxford: Clarendon Press.

Morn, F. (1982) *The Eye that Never Sleeps.* Bloomington, IN: Indiana University Press.

Morris, S., Anderson, S. and Murray, L. (2002) *Stalking and Harassment in Scotland*. Edinburgh: Scottish Executive Social Research.

Mullen, P.E. and Pathé, M. (1994) 'Stalking and the Pathologies of Love', *Australian and New Zealand Journal of Psychiatry*, 28: 469–77.

Mullen, P.E., Pathé, M. and Purcell, R. (2000) *Stalkers and their Victims*. Cambridge: Cambridge University Press.

Muncie, J. (1999) *Youth and Crime: A Critical Introduction*. London: Sage.

Murray, G. (1993) *Enemies of the State*. London: Simon & Schuster.

Mustaine, E.E. and Tewksbury, R. (1999) 'A Routine Activity Theory Explanation for Women's Stalking Victimizations', *Violence Against Women*, 5(1): 43–62.

National Advisory Commission On Civil Disorders (Kerner Commission) (1986) *Report*. Washington, DC: US Government Printing Office.

National Advisory Committee on Criminal Standards and Goals (1976) *Private Security. Report of the Task Force on Private Security.* Washington, DC: Government Printing Office.

Nelken, D. (1994) *The Futures of Criminology*. London: Sage.

Nellis, M. (2001) 'Community Penalties in Historical Perspective', in A. Bottoms, L. Gelsthorpe and S. Rex (eds), *Community Penalties: Change and Challenges*. Cullompton: Willan Publishing.

Newburn, T. (2002) 'Community Safety and Policing: Some Implications of the Crime and Disorder Act 1998', in G. Hughes, E. McLaughlin and J. Muncie (eds), *Crime Prevention and Community Safety*. London: Open University Press/Sage, pp. 102–22.

Newman, A. (2002) '127 at Airports Face Charges of Hiding Past', *New York Times*, 20 November, p. 1/6.

New York Civil Liberties Union (2002) *City Settles Lawsuit Brought on Behalf of NYPD Officer Fired for Revealing Racial Profiling by Street Crime Unit After Diallo Shooting*, www.nyclu.org/y_walton111102.html.

Neyroud, P. and Beckley, A. (2001) *Policing, Ethics and Human Rights*. Cullompton: Willan Publishing.

Nifong, C. (1997) 'One Man's Theory is Cutting Crime in Urban Streets', *Christian Science Monitor*, 18 February, p. 1/10–11.

Noel, P. (2000) 'Portraits in Racial Profiling: When Clothes Make the Suspect', *Village Voice*, 24 March, pp. 47–51.

Oldfield, M. (2002*) From Welfare to Risk: Discourse, Power and Politics in the Probation Service*. London: NAPO.

Oldham Metropolitan Borough Council and Greater Manchester Police (2001) *Building a Shared Future for Oldham: Interim Report to the Home Secretary*. Oldham: Oldham Partnership Board.

Oldham Metropolitan Borough Council and Greater Manchester Police (2002) *Response to the Oldham Independent Review Report*. Oldham: Oldham Borough Council.

Oliver, I. (1997) *Police, Government and Accountability*, 2nd edn. Macmillan: Basingstoke.

O'Malley, P. (1992) 'Risk, Power and Crime Prevention', *Economy and Society*, 21(3): 253–75.

O'Malley, P. (1997) 'Policing, Politics and Post-modernity', *Social and Legal Studies*, 6(3): 363–81.

Ouseley, H. (2001) *Community Pride Not Prejudice: Making Diversity Work in Bradford*. Bradford: Bradford Vision.

Packer, H. (1968) *The Limits of the Criminal Sanction*. Stanford, CA: Stanford University Press.

Padfield, N. (1998) *A Guide to the Crime and Disorder Act 1998*. London: Butterworths.

Page, M. (1992) *Crimefighters of London: A History of the Origins and Development of the London Probation Service 1876–196*. London: Inner London Probation Service.

Pagelow, M.D. (1992) 'Adult Victims of Domestic Violence', *Journal of Interpersonal Violence*, 7: 87–120.

Pain, R. (2003) 'Youth, Age and the Representation of Fear', *Capital & Class*, 80, (Summer).

Painter, K. (1989) *The Hammersmith and Fulham Crime and Policing Survey, 1988 Final Report*. London: Middlesex Polytechnic.

Pathé, M. and Mullen, P.E. (1997) 'The Impact of Stalkers on their Victims', *British Journal of Psychiatry*, 170: 12–17.

Pawson, R. and Tilley, N. (1997) *Realistic Evaluation*. London: Sage.

Pearson, G. (1976) '"Paki Bashing" in a North-East Lancashire Cotton Town: A Case Study and its History', in G. Mungham and G. Pearson (eds), *Working Class Youth Culture*. London: Routledge.

Pease, K. (1998) *Repeat Victimisation: Taking Stock*, Crime Detection and Prevention Series Paper 90. London: Home Office

Pease, K. and Laycock, G. (1996) *Reducing the Heat on Hot Victims*. Washington, DC: Bureau of Justice Statistics.

Percy, A. (1998) *Ethnicity and Victimisation: Findings from the 1996 British Crime Survey*, Home Office Statistical Bulletin 6(98), 3 April. London: Home Office.

Percy-Smith, J. (ed.) (2000) *Policy Responses to Social Exclusion: Towards Inclusion?* Buckingham: Open University Press.

Phillips, C. and Bowling, B. (2002) 'Racism, Ethnicity, Crime and Criminal Justice', in M. Maguire, R. Morgan and R. Reiner (eds), *The Oxford Handbook of Criminology*, 3rd edn. Oxford: Clarendon Press.

Phillips, C. and Brown, D. (1998) *Entry into the Criminal Justice System: A Survey of Police Arrests and Their Outcomes*, Home Office Research Study 185. London: Home Office.

Philips, D. and Storch, R. (1999) *Policing Provincial England, 1829–1856*. Leicester: Leicester University Press.

Pinkerton (2002) *A World Leader in Security*, http://www.pinkertons.com/value/index.asp.

Plews, G. (2001) 'A Guard's Right to Bear Arms', *SMT*, October: 17.

Plowden (1999) 'Love Thy Neighbour', *New Law Journal*, 479(6993): 520.

Police Complaints Authority (2002) *Police Complaints Authority Annual Report 2001–2002*, HC 1008. London: PCA.

Policy and Partnerships Division Policy (2001a) *Socio-demographic Profile of Oldham*. Oldham: Performance and Regeneration Department, Oldham Metropolitan Borough Council.

Policy and Partnerships Division (2001b) *Social Inclusion Audit*. Oldham: Oldham Metropolitan Borough Council.

Policy and Research Unit (1999) *Population Estimates and Forecasts*. Bradford: Bradford Metropolitan District Council.

Policy Unit (1999) *Crime and Disorder Audit*. Oldham: Oldham Metropolitan Borough Council.

Pollard, C. (1997) Zero-Tolerance: Short-Term Fix, Long-Term Liability', in N. Dennis (ed.), *Zero Tolerance: Policing a Free Society*. London: Institute of Economic Affairs.

Pooley, E. (1996) 'One Good Apple', *Time*, 15 January, pp. 55–6.

Port, B. and Zambito, T. (2002) 'Nursing Home No. 1 in Felons: Drug Dealers, Hookers Find Work in E. Harlem', *New York Daily News*, 16 September, p. 4.

Purpura, P. (2001) *Police and Community: Concepts and Cases*. Needham Heights, MA: Allyn & Bacon.

Race Today Collective (1986) *The Struggles of Asian Workers in Britain*. London: Race Today.

Radford, J. and Stanko, B. (1991) 'Violence Against Women and Children: The Contradictions of Crime Control under Patriarchy', in K. Stenson and D. Cowell (eds), *The Politics of Crime Control*. London: Sage.

Radzinowicz, L. (ed.) (1958) *The Results of Probation*, a Report of the Cambridge Department of Criminal Science. London: Macmillan.

Radzinowicz, L. (1968) *A History of English Criminal Law, Vol IV: Grappling for Control*. London: Stevens & Sons.

Rahman, M., Palmer, G. and Kenway, P. (2001) *Monitoring Poverty and Social Exclusion 2001*, York: Joseph Rowntree Foundation.

Rahman, M., Palmer, G., Kenway, P. and Howarth, C. (2000) *Monitoring Poverty and Social Exclusion 2000*. York: Joseph Rowntree Foundation.

Rashbaum, W. (2000) 'Legal Setbacks Against Police Policies Mount, But City Officials See No Pattern', *New York Times*, 14 December, p. 3.

Rashbaum, W. (2001a) 'Broad Plan Aims to Improve Police Rapport With the Public', *New York Times*, 15 January, p. 5.

Rashbaum, W. (2001b) 'U.S. Says City Has Failed to Release Data on Frisks', *New York Times*, 31 January, p. 4.

Rashbaum, W. (2001c) 'Officials Move to Increase Police Recruits', *New York Times*, 14 April, p. 1/4.

Rawlings, P. (2002) *Policing: A Short History*. Cullompton: Willan Publishing.

Raynor, P (1988) *Probation as an Alternative to Custody*. Aldershot: Avebury.

Raynor, P. (2000) 'Community Penalties – Probation, Punishment, and "What Works"', in M. Maguire, R. Morgan and R. Reiner (eds), *The Oxford Handbook of Criminology*. Oxford: Oxford University Press, pp. 1168–205.

Raynor, P. and Vanstone, M. (2002) *Understanding Community Penalties: Probation, Policy and Social Change*. Milton Keynes: Open University Press.

Read, S. (1997) 'Below Zero', *Police Review*, 17 January.

Read, T. and Tilley, N. (2000) *Not Rocket Science? Problem-Solving and Crime Reduction*, Crime Reduction Research Series Paper 6. London: Home Office.

Reiner, R. (1993) 'Police Accountability: Principles, Patterns and Practices', in R. Reiner and S. Spencer (eds), *Accountable Policing*. London: Institute for Public Policy Research.

Reiner, R. (1997) 'Policing and the Police', in M. Maguire, R. Morgan and R. Reiner (eds), *Oxford Handbook of Criminology*, 2nd edn. Oxford: Clarendon Press, pp. 1051–93.

Reiner, R. (2000a) *The Politics of the Police*, 3rd edn. Oxford: Oxford University Press.

Reiner, R. (2000b) 'Crime and Control in Britain', *Sociology*, 34(1): 71–94.

Reith, C. (1956) *A New Study of Police History*. London: Oliver & Boyd.

Rennison, C.M. and Welchans, S. (2000) *Intimate Partner Violence*. Washington, DC: Bureau of Justice Statistics, US Department of Justice.

Reuter, P., Haaga, J., Murphy, P. and Praskac, A. (1988) *Drug Use and Drug Programs in the Washington Metropolitan Area.* Santa Monica, CA: Rand.

Rider, B. (1987) 'Change in the Stock Exchange and Regulation in the City', *Bank of England Quarterly Bulletin,* Autumn: 54–65.

Ritchie, D. (2001) *Oldham Independent Review: Panel Report.* Oldham: Oldham Metropolitan Borough Council and Greater Manchester Police.

Roane, K. (1999) 'Spitzer Threatens Subpoena for Police Data on Frisking', *New York Times,* 16 May, p. 39.

Robb, M. (2003) *Football (Disorder) Act 2000 – Summary and Commentary.* London: Magnacartaplus.

Rohde, D. (1999) 'Crackdown on Minor Offenses Swamps New York City Courts', *New York Times,* 2 February, p. 1/7.

Romeanes, T. (1998) 'A Question of Confidence: Zero Tolerance and Problem-Oriented Policing', in Hopkins R. Burke (ed.), *Zero Tolerance Policing.* Leicester: Perpetuity Press.

Rose, D. (1996) *In the Name of the Law.* London: Jonathan Cape.

Rosenthal, A. (1993) 'Problem-oriented Policing: Now and Then: Reprint of a 1977 Article', *Law Enforcement News,* 31 March, p. 1/10.

Ross, H. (1973) 'Law, Science and Accidents: The British Road Safety Act of 1967', *Journal of Legal Studies,* (2): 1–78.

Ross, H. (1981) *Deterring the Drink Driver: Legal and Social Control.* Lexington, MA: Heath.

Ross, H., Campbell, D. and Glass, G. (1970) 'Determining the Social Effects of a Legal Reform: The British "Breathalyser" Crackdown of 1967', *American Behavioral Scientist,* 13: 493–509.

Roth, J.A. (1994) *Psychoactive Substances and Violence.* Washington, DC: National Institute of Justice.

Rowan, M. (1999) 'Anti-social Behaviour Orders – Further Comment', *Justice of the Peace,* 163(40): 794.

Royal Commission on Criminal Procedure (1981) *Report of the Royal Commission on Criminal Procedure,* Cmnd. 8092. London: HMSO.

Royal Commission on Police Powers and Procedure (1929) *Report of the Royal Commission on Police Powers and Procedure,* Cmnd. 3297. Parliamentary Papers 1928–1929, vol. 9, p. 127.

Royal Commission on the Police (1962) *Final Report of the Royal Commission on the Police,* Cmnd. 1782. London: HMSO.

Safir, H. (1997) 'Goal Oriented Community Policing: The NYPD Approach', *The Police Chief,* 56(58): 31–9.

Said, E. (1991) *Orientalism.* London: Penguin

Said, E. (1993) *Culture and Imperialism.* London: Vintage.

Salame, L. (1993) 'A National Survey of Stalking Laws: A Legislative Trend Comes to the Aid of Domestic Violence Victims and Others', *Suffolk University Law Review,* 27: 67–111.

Sanders, A. and Young, R. (2000) *Criminal Justice,* 2nd edn. London: Butterworths.

Saulny, S. (2003) 'Lawyers' Fees to Defend Poor Will Increase', *New York Times*, 13 November, p. 1/7.

Savage, S. (2002) 'Forces of Independence', *Police Review*, 11 May: 20.

Scarman, Lord (1981) *Report on the Brixton Disorders of 10–12 April 1981*, Cmnd 8427. London: HMSO.

Scarman, Lord (1982) *The Scarman Report: The Brixton Disorders, 10–12 April 1981*. Harmondsworth: Penguin Books.

Schwartz, A. (1996) ' "Just Take Away Their Guns": The Hidden Racism of *Terry v. Ohio*', *Fordham Urban Law Journal*, 23(2): 317–74.

Schwartz, B. (2002) *Memories of Empire*. London: Verso.

Scott, C. (2000) 'Accountability in the Regulatory State', *Journal of Law and Society*, 27(1): 38–60.

Scott, T.M. and McPherson, M. (1971) 'The Development of the Private Sector of the Criminal Justice System', *University of Chicago Law Review*, 6: 267–88.

Scraton, P. (1985) *The State of the Police*. London: Pluto.

Scraton, P. and Chadwick, K. (1996, originally 1992) 'The Theoretical Priorities of Critical Criminology', in J. Muncie, E. McLaughlin and M. Langan (eds), *Criminological Perspectives: A Reader*. London: Sage.

Sebok, A.J. (2001) *New York City's $50million Strip-Search Suit Settlement: How a Fourth Amendment Violation Became a Mass Tort Lawsuit*. Findlaw: http://writ.corporate.findlaw.com.

Select Committee on the Police of the Metropolis (1828) 'Report of the Select Committee on the Police of the Metropolis', *Parliamentary Papers*, Vol. VI, 1–33.

Sentencing Advisory Panel (2001). Available online at: http://www.sentencing-advisory-panel.gov.uk/c_and_a/advice/stolen_goods/stolen_goods.pdf.

Shapiro, B. (2000) 'NYPD – Out of Control', *The Nation*, 270(15): 5.

Shapiro, S. (1987) 'The Social Control of Impersonal Trust', *American Journal of Sociology*, 3: 623–58.

Shapiro, S. (1990) 'Collaring the Crime, Not the Criminal: Reconsidering the Concept of White-Collar Crime', *American Sociological Review*, 55: 346–65.

Shaw, J. (1994) 'Detecting Guns Through Trial and Error'. Unpublished manuscript circulated at a conference, cited in A. Schwartz (1996) ' "Just Take Away Their Guns": The Hidden Racism of *Terry v. Ohio*', *Fordham Urban Law Journal*, 23(2): 317–74.

Shaw, M. and Pease, K. (2000) *Research on Repeat Victimisation in Scotland*. Edinburgh: Scottish Executive.

Shearing, C.D. (1992) 'The Relation Between Public and Private Policing', in M. Tonry and N. Morris (eds), *Modern Policing*, Vol. 15. Chicago: University of Chicago Press.

Shearing, C.D. and Stenning, P.C. (1985) 'From the Panopticon to Disney World: the Development of Discipline', in A. Doob and E. Greenspan (eds), *Perspectives in Criminal Law*. Ontario: Canada Law Books.

Sheehy, P. (1993) *Report of the Inquiry into Police Responsibilities and Rewards*, Cm. 2280. HMSO: London.

Sheptycki, J.W.E. (1991) 'Using the State to Change Society: The Example of Domestic Violence', *Journal of Human Justice*, 3(1): 44–66.

Sheridan, L. and Boon, J. (2002) 'Stalker Typologies: Implications for Law Enforcement', in J. Boon and L. Sheridan (eds), *Stalking and Psychosexual Obsession*. London: Wiley.

Sheridan, L. and Davies, G.M. (2001) 'Stalking: The Elusive Crime', *Legal and Criminological Psychology*, 6: 133–47.

Sheridan, L., Davies, G.M. and Boon, J. (2001) 'The Course and Nature of Stalking: A Victim Perspective', *Howard Journal of Criminal Justice*, 40: 215–34.

Sherman, L. (1990) 'Police Crackdowns: Initial and Residual Deterrence', in M. Tonry and N. Morris (eds), *Crime and Justice: A Review of Research*, Vol 12. Chicago: University of Chicago Press.

Sherman, L., Shaw, J. and Rogan, D. (1995) *The Kansas City Gun Experiment*, Research in Brief. Washington, DC: National Institute of Justice.

Shover, N., Fox, G. and Mills, M. (1994) 'Long-term Consequences of Victimisation by White-Collar Crime', *Justice Quarterly*, 11: 213–40

Sibbitt, R. (1997) *The Perpetrators of Racial Harassment and Violence*, Research Study 176. London: Home Office.

Silverman, E. (1998) 'Below Zero Tolerance: The New York Experience', in R. Hopkins Burke (ed.), *Zero Tolerance Policing*. Leicester: Perpetuity Press.

Silverman, E. (1999) *NYPD Battles Crime. Innovative Strategies in Policing*. Boston: Northeastern University Press.

Silverman, E. (2000) 'The New York Policing Revolution and Old Tensions: A View from Abroad', in A. Marlow and B. Loveday (eds), *After Macpherson: Policing after the Stephen Lawrence Inquiry*. Lyme Regis: Russell House.

Simon, J. (1988) 'The Ideological Effects of Actuarial Practices', *Law & Society Review*, 22(4): 771–800.

Sims, L. and Myhill, A. (2001) *Policing and the Public: Findings from the 2000 British Crime Survey*, Home Office Research Findings No. 136. London: Home Office.

Skogan, W. (1990a) *The Police and Public in England and Wales: A British Crime Survey Report*. London: HMSO.

Skogan, W. (1990b) *Disorder and Decline: Crime and the Spiral Decay in American Neighbourhoods*. New York: The Free Press.

Skolnick, J.K. (1966) *Justice Without Trial*. New York: John Wiley.

Skolnick, J.K. and Fyfe, J.J. (1993) *Above the Law: Police and the Excessive Use of Force*. New York: Free Press.

Slaughter, P. (2003) 'Of Crowds, Crimes and Carnivals', in R. Matthews and J. Young (eds), *The New Politics of Crime and Punishment*. Cullompton: Willan Publishing.

Smith, D.J. (1991) 'The Origins of Black Hostility to the Police', *Policing and Society*, 2: 1–15.

Smith, D.J. (1997) 'Ethnicity, Crime, and Criminal justice', in M. Maguire, R. Morgan and R, Reiner (eds), *The Oxford Handbook of Criminology*. Oxford: Clarendon Press.

Smith, D.J. (1997) 'Case Construction and the Goals of Criminal Process', *British Journal of Criminology*, 37(3): 319–46.

Smith, D.J. and Gray, J. (1983) *Police and People in London, IV: The Police in Action*. London: Policy Studies Institute.

Smith, D.J. and Gray, J. (1985) *Police and People in London: The PSI Report*. London: Gower.

Smith, G. (2001) 'Police Complaints and Criminal Prosecutions', *Modern Law Review*, 64(3): 372–92.

Smith, M., Clarke, R. and Pease, K. (2002) 'Anticipatory Benefits in Crime Prevention', in N. Tilley (ed.), *Analysis for Crime Prevention*. Crime Prevention Studies Vol. 13. Cullompton: Willan Publishing.

Smith, S., Steadman, G. and Minton, T. (1999) *Criminal Victimization and Perceptions of Community Safety in 12 Cities, 1998*. Bureau of Justice Statistics Report. Washington, DC: US Department of Justice.

Southgate, P. and Crisp, D. (1992) *Public Satisfaction with Police Services*, Home Office Research and Planning Paper 73. London: Home Office.

Southgate, P. and Ekblom, P. (1984) *Contact between Police and Public: Findings from the British Crime Survey*. London: Home Office.

Spalek, B. (1999) 'Exploring White Collar Victimisation: A Study Looking at the Impact of the Maxwell Scandal Upon the Maxwell Pensioners', *International Review of Victimology*, 6(3): 213–30.

Spalek, B. (2001a) 'White Collar Crime and Secondary Victimisation: An Analysis of the Effects of the Closure of BCCI upon Former Employees', *Howard Journal of Criminal Justice*, 40(2): 64–75.

Spalek, B. (2001b) 'Policing the UK Financial System: The Creation of the New FSA and its Approach to Regulation', *International Journal of the Sociology of Law*, 29: 75–87.

Spalek, B. (2002) *White Collar Crime and the Issue of Trust*. Paper presented to the British Criminology Conference, Keele University.

Sparrow, P., Brooks, G. and Webb, D (2002), 'National Standards for the Probation Service: Managing Post-Fordist Penality', *Howard Journal of Criminal Justice*, 41(1): 27–40.

Spitzer, E. (1999) *The New York City Police Department's 'Stop & Frisk' Policies: A Report to the People of the State of New York from the Office of the Attorney General*. Albany, NY: Civil Rights Bureau, Office of the Attorney General.

Spitzer, S. and Scull, A.T. (1977) 'Privatisation and the Capitalist Development of the Police', *Social Problems*, 25: 18–29.

Stanko, B. (1992) *Plenary Address. Violence Against Women Conference*. Manchester Metropolitan University, May.

Stanley, C. (1992) 'Serious Money: Legitimation of Deviancy in the Financial Markets', *International Journal of the Sociology of Law*, 20: 43–60.

Starmer, K. (2000) *European Human Rights Law*. London: Legal Action Group.

Starmer, K., Strange, M., Jennings A. QC and Owen, T. QC (2001) *Criminal Justice, Police Powers & Human Rights*. London: Blackstone Press.

Statewatch (2002) 'EU to Adopt Arbitrary Powers to Freeze Assets and Seize Evidence', http://www.statewatch.org/news/2002/may/01freezing.htm.

Steedman, C. (1984) *Policing the Victorian Community*. London: Routledge & Kegan Paul.

Steffensmeier, D. (1986) *The Fence: In the Shadow of Two Worlds*. Trenton, NJ: Rowman & Littlefield.

Stenson, K. (2000a) 'Some Day Our Prince Will Come: Zero-tolerance Policing and Liberal Government', in T. Hope and R. Sparks (eds), *Crime, Risk and Insecurity*. London: Routledge.

Stenson, K. (2000b) 'Crime Control, Social Policy and Liberalism', in G. Lewis, S. Gerwitz and J. Clarke (eds), *Rethinking Social Policy*. London: Sage, pp. 229–44.

Stenson, K. and Edwards, A. (2001) 'Crime Control and Liberal Government: the "Third Way" and the Return to the Local', in K. Stenson and R.A. Sullivan (eds), *Crime, Risk and Justice: The Politics of Crime Control in Liberal Democracies*. Cullompton: Willan Publishing, pp. 117–44.

Stephen, J.F. (1883) *A History of the Criminal Law of England: Vol I*. London: Macmillan & Co.

Stevens, P. and Willis, C.F. (1979) *Race, Crime and Arrests*. Home Office Research Study 58. London: Home Office.

Storch, R. (1975) 'The Plague of the Blue Locusts: Police Reform and Popular Resistance in Northern England 1840–57', *International Review of Social History*, 20: 61–90.

Storch, R. (1989) 'Policing Rural Southern England before the Police: Opinion and Practice 1830–1856', in D. Hay and F. Snyder (eds), *Policing and Prosecution*. Oxford: Clarendon Press.

Suttles, G. (1967) *The Social Construction of Communities*. Chicago: University of Chicago Press.

Suttles, G. (1968) *The Social Order of the Slum: Ethnicity and Territory in the Inner City*. Chicago: University of Chicago Press.

Sutton, M. (1993) *From Receiving to Thieving: The Market for Stolen Goods and the Incidence of Theft*, Home Office Research Bulletin, No 34. London: Home Office.

Sutton, M. (1995) 'Supply by Theft: Does the Market for Second-hand Goods Play a Role in Keeping Crime Figures High?', *British Journal of Criminology*, 38(3): 352–65.

Sutton, M. (1998) *Handling Stolen Goods and Theft: A Market Reduction Approach*, Home Office Research Study 178. London: Home Office.

Sutton, M. (2002) 'Fencing', in D. Levinson (ed.), *Encyclopaedia of Crime and Punishment*, Vol. 2. Thousand Oakes, CA: Sage.

Sutton, M., Schneider, J. and Hetherington, S. (2001) *Tackling Theft with the Market Reduction Approach*, Home Office Crime Reduction Research Series Paper 8. London: Home Office.

Tain, P. (2001) 'Anti-social Behaviour Orders', *Solicitors Journal*, 145(2): 36.

Tain, P. (2002) 'Civil or Criminal', *Solicitors Journal*, 146(43): 1037.

Task Force on The Police, President's Commission on Law Enforcement and The Administration of Justice (1967) *The Police*. Washington, DC: US Government Printing Office.

Taylor, D. (1997) *The New Police in Nineteenth-Century England: Crime, Conflict and Control*. Manchester: Manchester University Press.

Taylor, I. (1994) 'The Political Economy of Crime', in M. Maguire, R. Morgan and R. Reiner (eds), *The Oxford Handbook of Criminology*. Oxford: Clarendon Press.

Taylor, R. (2001) *Breaking Away From Broken Windows: Baltimore Neighborhoods and the Nationwide Fight Against Crime, Grime, Fear, and Decline*. Boulder, CO: Westview.

Teather, D. (2002) 'Guilty Verdict Forces Andersen to Give Up Clients', *The Guardian*, 17 June.

Teather, D. (2002) 'Enron Paid Out $681m to Top Executives', *The Guardian*, 18 June.

Thompson, E.P. (1975) *Whigs and Hunters*. London: Penguin.

Tilley, N. (1993) *Understanding Car Parks, Crime and CCTV: Evaluation Lessons from Safer Cities*, Police Research Group, Crime Prevention Unit Series Paper No. 42. London. Home Office Police Department.

Tilley, N. and Webb, J. (1994) *Burglary Reduction: Findings from Safer Cities Schemes*, Crime Prevention Unit Series Paper 51. London: Home Office.

Timms, N. (1966) *Social Casework: Principles and Practice*. London: Routledge.

Titus, R., Heinzelmann, F. and Boyle, J. (1995) 'Victimisation of Persons by Fraud', *Crime & Delinquency*, 41(1): 54–72.

Times, The (2001) 'Boy, 15 is Exiled after Reign of Terror', 24 April, p. 5.

Tran, M. (2002) 'Share and Share Alike?' *The Guardian*, 18 January.

Turk, A.T. (1969) *Criminality and the Social Order*. Chicago: Rand-McNally.

Tversky, A. and Kahnemen, D. (1974) 'Judgement Under Uncertainty: Heuristics and Biases', *Science*, 185: 1124–31.

United States Committee on Education and Labour (1971) *Private Police Systems*. New York: Arno Press and the New York Times.

Vanstone, M. (2000) 'Cognitive-Behavioural Work with Offenders in the UK: A History of Influential Endeavour', *Howard Journal of Criminal Justice*, 39(2): 171–83.

Vidal, J. (1997) *McLibel Burger Culture on Trial*. London: Macmillan.

Volkov, V. (2000) 'Between Economy and the State: Private Security and Rule Enforcement in Russia', *Politics and Society*, 28: 483–501.

Von Heussen, E. (2000) 'The Law and Social Problems: The Case of Britain's Protection From Harassment Act 1997', *Web Journal of Current Legal Issues*, 1.

Von Hirsch, A. (1976) *Doing Justice: The Choice of Punishments*. New York: Hill & Wang.

Von Hirsch, A., Ashworth, A., Wasik, M., Smith, A.T.H., Morgan, R. and Gardner, J. (1995) 'Overtaking on the Right', *New Law Journal*: 1501.

Waddington, P.A.J. (1994) *Liberty and Order: Public Order Policing in the Capital*. London: UCL Press.

Waddington, P.A.J. (1999) 'Finding the Right Motives', *Police Review*, 23 April, p. 13.

Waddington, P.A.J. and Braddock, Q. (1991) ' "Guardians or "Bullies"? Perceptions of the Police Among Adolescent Black, White and Asian Boys', *Policing and Society*, 2: 1.

Wadham, J. (1998) 'Zero Tolerance Policing: Striking the Balance, Rights and Liberties', in R. Hopkins Burke (ed.), *Zero Tolerance Policing*. Leicester: Perpetuity Press.

Wadham, J. and Modi, K. (2003) 'National Security and Open Government in the United Kingdom', in *National Security and Open Government: Striking the Right Balance*. Syracuse University, NY: Campbell Public Affairs Institute.

Waine, B. (1992) 'Workers as Owners: The Ideology and Practice of Personal Pensions', *Economy and Society*, 21(1): 27–44.

Walker, L.E. (1979) *The Battered Woman*. London: Harper & Row.

Walker, L.E. (1989) *Terrifying Love: Why Battered Women Kill and How Society Responds*. New York: Harper & Row.

Walker, L.E. and Meloy, J.R. (1998) 'Stalking and Domestic Violence', in J. Reid Meloy (ed.), *The Psychology of Stalking*. London: Academic Press.

Walklate, S. (1989) *Victimology: The Victim and the Criminal Justice Process*. London: Unwin Hyman.

Walklate, S. (2001) *Gender, Crime and Criminal Justice*. Cullompton: Willan Publishing.

Wardak, A. (2000) *Social Control and Deviance: A South Asian Community in Scotland*. Aldershot: Ashgate.

Way, R. (1994) 'The Criminalization of Stalking: An Exercise in Media Manipulation and Political Opportunism', *McGill Law Journal*, 39.

Webster, C. (1995) *Youth Crime, Victimisation and Racial Harassment: The Keighley Crime Survey*. Bradford: Bradford & Ilkley College Corporation, Centre for Research in Applied Community Studies.

Webster, C. (1996) 'Local Heroes: Violent Racism, Spacism and Localism Among White and Asian Young People', *Youth and Policy*, 53: 15–27; reprinted in N. South (ed.) (1999) *Youth Crime, Deviance and Delinquency*, International Library of Criminology, Criminal Justice and Penology, Vol. II. Aldershot: Ashgate.

Webster, C. (1997) 'The Construction of British "Asian" Criminality', *International Journal of the Sociology of Law*, 25: 65–86.

Webster, C. (2003) 'Race, Space and Fear: Imagined Geographies of Racism, Crime, Violence and Disorder in Northern England', *Capital and Class*, 80, Summer.

Weiss, R. (1978) 'The Emergence and Transformation of Private Detective and Industrial Policing in the United States, 1850–1940', *Crime and Social Justice*, 1: 35–48.

Westley, W. (1970) *Violence and the Police: A Sociological Study of Law Custom and Morality*. Cambridge, MA: MIT Press.

Whitehead, P. and Gray, P. (1998) *Pulling the Plug on Computer Theft*, Police Research Series Paper 101. London: Home Office.

Wiles, P. and McClintock, F. (eds) (1972) *The Security Industry in the United Kingdom*. Cambridge: Institute of Criminology, University of Cambridge.

Wilgoren, J. and Cooper, M. (1999) 'New York Police Lags in Diversity', *New York Times*, March, p. 1.

Williams, G. (1985) 'Handling, Theft and the Purchaser Who Takes a Chance', *Criminal Law Review*: 432–39.

Wilson, D., Ashton, J. and Sharp, D. (2002) *What Everyone in Britain Should Know About the Police*. London: Blackstone Press.

Wilson, J.Q. (1994) 'Just Take Away Their Guns', *New York Times Sunday Magazine*, 20 March, pp. 46–9.

Wilson, J.Q. and Kelling, G.L. (1982) 'Broken Windows', *Atlantic Monthly*, March: 29–38.

Worrall, A. (1997) *Punishment in the Community: The Future of Criminal Justice*. London: Addison-Wesley-Longman.

Wright, A. (1994) 'Short-Term Crackdowns and Long-Term Objectives', *Policing*, 10(4): 253–9.

Wynn, J. (2001) 'Can Zero Tolerance Last? Views from Inside the Precinct', in A. Cardle and T. Erzen (eds), *Zero Tolerance: Quality of Life and the New Police Brutality in New York City*. New York: New York University Press.

Young, J. (1997) 'Left Realist Criminology: Radical in its Analysis: Realist in its Policy', in M. Maguire, R. Morgan and R. Reiner (eds), *The Oxford Handbook of Criminology*, 2nd edn. Oxford: Clarendon Press.

Young, J. (1999) *The Exclusive Society*. London: Sage.

Young, M. (1991) *An Inside Job: Policing and Police Culture in Britain*. Oxford: Oxford University Press.

Young, M. (1993) *In the Sticks*. Oxford: Oxford University Press

Zedner, L. (1994) 'Victims', in M. Maguire, R. Morgan and R. Reiner (eds), *The Oxford Handbook of Criminology*. Oxford: Oxford University Press.

Zimmer, L. (1986) 'Proactive Policing in New York and the Disruption of Street-Level Drug Trade'. Unpublished manuscript, State University of New York at Geneseo, Department of Sociology.

Zona, M.A., Palarea, R.E. and Lane, J.C. (1998) 'Psychiatric Diagnosis and the Offender–Victim Typology of Stalking', in J. Reid Meloy (ed.), *The Psychology of Stalking*. London: Academic Press.

Index

accountancy profession, inadequacy of 252

actuarial models, risk measurement 66

actuarialism
  criminal justice policy 65, 230
  Financial Services Authority 165–7, 173

adaptation/innovation, crackdowns 122

African/Caribbeans
  perception of being over-policed 72
  police treatment 71

agent-principle relationships, financial system 166

aggravated trespass 213

Aktion Sicherheitsnetz 43

Allen, Kate 259

Amnesty International 257, 258–9

anti-social behaviour 227–9
  Crime and Disorder Act 229–31
  New Labour obsession with 200, 226

Anti-Social Behaviour Orders 226, 227, 249
  future for 241
  human rights issues 234–8
  net widening and stigmatisation 238–9
  in practice 232–4
  theoretical context 231–2

Anti-Social Behaviour White Paper 199

Anti-Terrorism, Crime and Security Act (2001) 222, 259

anticipatory deterrence 119

arrests
  British Asians 72
  human rights issues 217–18
  zero tolerance policing 27–8

ASBOs *see* Anti-Social Behaviour Orders

Asians *see* British Asians

assembly, right of 212, 214

assets, seizure of 255–6

association, right of 212

attitudes
  of police to stalking 154
  towards police 71–2

Audit Commission
  clear-up rate, England and Wales 6
  youth offending 230

audits, local crime and disorder 60

Aufenthaltsverbot 50